Conviction & Credence

Conviction & Credence

US Policymaking
in the Middle East

Melvin A. Friedlander

Lynne Rienner Publishers ▪ Boulder & London

Two sections of Chapter 3 were originally published in *Southeastern Political Review Special Symposium Issue on the Carter Presidency,* vol 16 no 1, Spring 1988, Atlanta, Georgia: Georgia Political Science Association and the Department of Political Science, West Georgia College; and in *American-Arab Affairs* 25, Summer 1988, Washington, D.C.: American-Arab Affairs Council.

Published in the United States of America in 1991 by
Lynne Rienner Publishers, Inc.
1800 30th Street, Boulder, Colorado 80301

and in the United Kingdom by
Lynne Rienner Publishers, Inc.
3 Henrietta Street, Covent Garden, London WC2E 8LU

Library of Congress Cataloging-in-Publication Data
Friedlander, Melvin A.
   Conviction and credence: US policymaking in the Middle
East / Melvin A. Friedlander.
      p. cm.
   Includes bibliographical references and index.
   ISBN 1-55587-177-1
      1. Middle East—Foreign relations—United States. 2. United
States—Foreign relations—Middle East. 3. United States—Foreign
relations—1945–   I. Title.
DS63.1.U6F75 1991
327.73056—dc20   91-20190
                                                                    CIP

British Cataloguing in Publication Data
A Cataloguing in Publication record for this book
is available from the British Library.

Printed and bound in the United States of America

The paper used in this publication meets the requirements
of the American National Standard for Permanence of
Paper for Printed Library Materials Z39.48.

To Sandy,
whose devotion and love
made this project possible

Contents

Acknowledgments

This book has been long in the making, as with many such efforts, and many people have helped along the way. First, for the generous encouragement they have given me, I wish to thank my colleagues—Adeed Dawisha, John Paden, Mark Katz, and Richard Stillman—in the Public Affairs Department at George Mason University. Second, both material support and the solitude required for study and contemplation were generously provided by the George Mason University Summer Stipend program, the university's Fenwick Library fellowship, grants from the Lucius Littauer Foundation, the Truman Institute of the Hebrew University of Jerusalem, and the Rockefeller Foundation's Summer Residency program at Bellagio, Italy. To the administrators and managers of these programs—Charles Rowley, Charlene Hurt, Bill Frost, Harold Schiffren, Susan Garfield, and the late Roberto Celli—much gratitude is offered.

I have many fond remembrances of discussions into the late evening hours with friends, experts, and professionals in the field of US and Middle East policy. A debt of gratitude, therefore, must be paid to Joseph Sisco, Bill Quandt, Hal Saunders, Roy Atherton, Thomas Pickering, Samuel Lewis, and Jimmy Carter, here in the United States; to Osama el Baz, Mohammed Wahby, Tahseen Basheer, Ahmed Baha Eldine, Mohammed Heikel, Sayid Yassin, Ali Dessouki, and Said Ibrahaim in Egypt; to Hanna Sinora, Ziad Abu Zayyad, Gabi Baramki, and Emile Sahliyeh in the West Bank; and to Abba Eban, Ariel Sharon, Yossi Ben Aharon, Roni Milo, Elihau Ben Elissar, Shlomo Avineri, Raymond Cohen, Simcha Dinitz, Mordecai Gazit, Menachem Milson, Yiehel Kadishai, Harry Hurvitz, Rivka Yadlin, Aharon Kleiman, Itamar Rabinovich, Gaby Sheffer, Emanuel Sivan, Shimon Shamir, Avner Yaniv, Moshe Maoz, Gadi Gilbar, Mark Heller, Hannoch Smith, Gabi Ben Dor, Martin Kramer, Dan Meridor, Meir Buber, Yossi Kostiner, Nimrod Novik, and Amitzai Baram in Israel.

Acknowledgment and thanks go to Ginny McCaslin, Carole Poland, and Mary Blackwell and her group of extraordinary typists at George Mason University—especially Anne Bonanno—for their technical support and assistance. I am now convinced that a modern word processor is superior to my twenty-year-old portable typewriter. Pam Ferdinand is due a particular thanks for her patience, skill, and good cheer in making this work more literate.

A special word must go to my dear mother and father, without whom this project could hardly have been conceived, never mind completed. Their faith and steadfastness will always be treasured. And special thanks go to my wife, Sandy, and children, Ellen, Marcy, Sharon, and Danny, whose confidence and love have been a source of great comfort during the bleakest moments of this enterprise. Sandy, in particular, has been the necessary element in a marriage of thirty-one years that has brought great joy to this struggling author. It is to her and the special way she brings happiness to our life that I dedicate this book.

M. A. F.

Conviction & Credence

Introduction

US officials have worked since 1945 to limit the growth of Soviet influence in the major regions of the world. After the extraordinary turn in East-West relations touched off by unexpected East European democracy, German reunification, and Soviet government reform, the United States may now be ready to modify the focus of its regional policy. In the Middle East this could mean starting new alliances without reference to the conflicts of the Cold War while closer attention is paid to a regional ethos.

THE CONVENTIONAL WISDOM

But even as the Middle East responded to Saddam Hussein's march into Kuwait, the US record there was seen locally as a matter of self-interest. US officials, nonetheless, look at their Middle East policies from the perspective of the conventional wisdom that speaks most forcefully for arranging stable conditions on behalf of all parties, for strengthening moderate states in the region, for protecting ties to the West, for preserving US access to oil, and for assuring the survival of Israel as a democracy.[1] How to achieve these objectives in tandem has been the task of creative diplomacy. And US administrations have struggled, oftentimes in vain, to bring coherence to what otherwise was viewed as a set of contradictory goals.

When direct US presidential involvement in the affairs of the Middle East was minimal or altogether absent, especially during Reagan's first term of office, the bureaucracy ensured that it could vie for a place in setting policy. The Departments of State and Defense, the Central Intelligence Agency, and the National Security Council each brought a view about how best to resolve the matters at issue. Whether policymakers explained a disputed decision on grounds of globalism or regionalism depended on the state of East-West tensions, how reluctant the bureaucrat was to commit force, what level of confidence there was in diplomacy, and whether the source of conflict rested in a local or international arena.[2] As Islamic reform movements grew and contributed to the development of a renewed religious dynamic in the Middle East, maintaining (or reaching) stability became a much more delicate task.

1

Holding Israel to its pre-1967 borders (with minor territorial adjustments) and inducing Arab states to adhere to a well-defined peace plan—the land-for-peace formula—was seen as essential to any scheme for achieving regional stability. For a variety of reasons, most Arabs (particularly Egyptians, Palestinians, and Jordanians) regarded bargaining directly with Israel as impossible. The United States, believing that flexibility could be gained from a steady flow of arms, financial arrangements, and technical assistance, offered material incentives to shore up shaky governments and stave off efforts by neighbors recalcitrant enough to block the peace process.[3]

Meanwhile, in keeping with the politics of the Cold War, US leaders saw Soviet policy in the Middle East as provocative. Angry and frustrated indigenous elements that sponsored violence were being rewarded by loyalty and support.[4] The US government responded by talking tough, and on at least two occasions used military force—first in a failed effort to rescue US hostages from the clutches of Iranian fundamentalists[5] and then successfully as punishment for Soviet-backed Libya's assistance for terrorists.[6] US disapproval of Syria deepened after that country was implicated in the bombing of Pan Am flight 103.[7]

Conventional wisdom, though, led to discomfort when the United States sided with Iraq during the final phase of the Iran-Iraq war. But neither the brutality Saddam Hussein visited on his own citizens, nor the threat posed to neighbors by Iraqi possession of destructive weapons (chemical and biological agents as well as long-range missiles) seemed to deter Washington. The United States convinced itself that a larger and more immediate regional destabilization threat loomed in Iranian fundamentalism.[8] The US tilt toward Iraq, supplying Saddam with sophisticated military intelligence data and waiving restrictions on sale of armaments components,[9] coincided with Washington's offer of naval protection to Kuwaiti vessels threatened with Iranian speedboat attack in the Gulf.[10]

Arab states such as Saudi Arabia and Jordan also urged US support for their Iraqi ally,[11] and these moderate Arab regimes were playing a crucial role in the revival of a solution to the conflict with Israel.

Europeans, Israelis, and US citizens, meanwhile, were being warned by Tehran that they could become targets as a consequence of their governments' opposition to Iran.[12]

Thoughts of US personnel bound and tortured during the 1979 embassy takeover in Iran, as well as more recent hostage snatching by Lebanese groups in alliance with Tehran, haunted Washington officials. As if to cap these offenses against decency and international norms of behavior, Ayatollah Khomeini called for the death of author Salman Rushdie, accused of defaming the Prophet Muhammad in his novel, *Satanic Verses*.[13]

US backing for Saddam Hussein may have revolved mostly around how Washington measured citizen satisfaction in the region. The United States, reacting against Iran's fundamentalist revolution, welcomed almost any sign of governmental economic growth and the promotion of a secularist life pattern in any Middle Eastern nation. Any upsurge in religious orthodoxy, conversely, was seen as a sure path to radicalism and instability. Iraq's eight-year conflict with Iran had nearly wrecked Baghdad's economy, but the war's end gave promise that a program of recovery could be managed. Oil derivatives were expected to generate sufficient foreign exchange earnings to begin rebuilding industry and recapturing the agricultural base—intelligible and sympathetic goals to US policymakers.[14]

Presidents Assad and Saddam devoted much energy and national resources to bring about healthy economic infrastructures in Syria and Iraq during the 1970s. And in the 1980s Lebanon's capital, Beirut—once the "Paris of the East"—retained its reputation as a center for commercial activity despite civil war. All three states embraced secularism, yet in all three some of the bloodiest and most inhumane acts were perpetrated by leaders in the name of a stable order. Assad arranged the slaughter of more than 10,000 Syrians to curb an internal rebellion;[15] Saddam Hussein gassed untold numbers of Kurds (an Iraqi minority group);[16] and Lebanese Christian Phalangists mourning the death of their assassinated sectarian leader massacred women and children in several Muslim encampments.[17]

Violence in the Arab states coincided with a shift in the terms of conflict in disputed territory in the Holy Land. It was becoming a competition for daily survival between Arabs and Jews, but US mediators—in whose custody peace temporarily resided—did not fully realize the new dimensions of the problem. In the aftermath of the October 1973 war, US officials still saw a region caught up in historical controversy—disputes about ownership of land, the demarcation of borders, the location of armies, the conditions under which force could be used, and how to specify nation-state status. A brief overview of the positions and philosophies of some major US players in Mideast policymaking provides some insight into the successes and failures of peace negotiations.

Henry Kissinger's system for negotiating disengagement agreements between Israel, Egypt, and Syria following the October 1973 war dispensed with justifications of law and morality. Instead, he focused on determining how each side saw the other, whether they defined the problem similarly, what the proper context to the negotiation was, and when conditions would ripen for the taking of small steps to promote overall confidence in the peace process. He eschewed any move toward substance as long as there existed differences in perception and an unwillingness to overcome obstacles. Devising new situations and creating new mindsets, he believed, would promote greater flexibility and a broadened framework in which to elicit concessions leading to agreements.[18] Discussions were tedious and progress tortuously slow, but the method recognized the limits inherent in national abilities to perform during multilateral negotiation.

Kissinger was also sensitive to the domestic implications of bargaining: he was acutely aware that states were often subject to the vicissitudes of a rapidly changing environment, which itself may be influenced by elite preferences marginally in support of scheduled talks.[19] An incremental approach to negotiating therefore permitted those constrained by an unresponsive or recalcitrant public to dispel misgivings through a succession of discrete moves.[20] Kissinger's design for peace envisaged segregating issues, employing constructive ambiguity and secret talks, offering material support as incentive, and guaranteeing compliance with each step leading to full resolution of the problem. Each bargaining lever would in time enhance his ability to control the entire peace agenda.[21]

Kissinger's study of nineteenth-century European diplomacy was a sufficient reminder that creative leadership was lodged not in manipulation, but in readiness to overcome obstacles, to contemplate the veritable "abyss." He was quite sure that bureaucracy slowed, if it did not jettison, statesmanlike efforts at diplomacy, whereas inspired, intuitive behavior was a more certain guide to achievement in a less than perfect universe.[22] "Shuttle diplomacy" had its origins in the decision to rescue a negotiation torn by conflicting purposes as well as separate perceptions of reality. Even the appearance of momentum challenged a hardening of positions and allowed some flexibility to creep into the bargaining process. Pacing the discussions permitted sequenced accords when the parties were ready to consider alternative solutions.[23]

The creative statesman, in fact, was motivated, as Kissinger would demonstrate, to conduct therapy in order to induce a capacity for change. Kissinger's sessions with Sadat, Assad, King Faisal, and Golda Meir are legendary and were carried out to produce new insights regarding the character of each leader's national decisionmaking process. These very different but similarly rough-edged heads of government were at first educated toward, then persuaded by, the necessity for compromise as a basis for reaching even limited understandings.[24] The Arab custom of conducting business as an adjunct to social exchange fitted Kissinger's academic habit of philosophical nuance, but Israel's Hobbesian outlook, its obsession with security, contrasted sharply with the more deliberate sociological pattern displayed by Kissinger's new Arab constituency. Nevertheless, Arabs and Israelis both were now made aware of what issues shaped each other's investment in Middle East peace.[25]

Jimmy Carter's eagerness to promote a comprehensive peace strategy was based in part on regional conditions but sought as well to allay misgivings resulting from Kissinger's bargaining during 1974–1975. The step-by-step method was believed to have run its course.[26] Moreover, Kissinger's approach had failed to address fundamental questions of equity and human rights that had been touted throughout the 1976 election campaign as a crucial aspect of Carter's foreign policy.[27]

Carter was convinced that justice for Arab and Jew could be meted out only within the broad context of a Geneva-style meeting, and preferably by the end of his first year in office. His perception that Arabs and Israelis were incapable of directly communicating argued for convening a conference in which all obstacles to peace could be confronted and removed.[28] But experience had taught Jimmy Carter that before the leaders of Mideast states would be ready to share in his aspirations, they must be persuaded that the United States properly assessed the regional situation. His one-on-one meetings with area statesmen at the White House and in Europe during the early months of 1977, therefore, were in the nature of educating each side to the other's dilemma.

Carter, wishing to avoid his predecessor's example of incrementally moving the parties toward peace—and even with Secretary of State Cyrus Vance reporting on the depth of Arab-Israeli suspicions—was incautious over the techniques of how, decisively, to end the historic conflict.[29] As a born-again Christian, he could hardly squelch the habit of considering each individual as the equal of another. Carter's own strong sense of purpose, combined with a serious reading of biblical history, enabled him to view sympathetically the struggle engaged in by "peoples of the book";[30] he would therefore ensure equitable standards. The Aswan Formula, worked out with Anwar Sadat in January 1978 and sustained at Camp David months later, was intended to protect what Carter perceived as the legitimate rights of the Palestinian people while securing their participation in the determination of their future.[31]

Jimmy Carter respected and admired the founders of the State of Israel. When his grand strategy to produce an agreement at Geneva floundered on Sadat's and Begin's desire for return of territory in exchange for peace, Carter turned to transitional arrangements. The Camp David meetings, as well as sessions held in the Middle East during March 1979, resulted in Carter's discarding the concept of a comprehensive peace settlement. Carter's State Department had come away from earlier bargaining encounters convinced that a single, conclusive conference was not possible.[32] Direct discussions between Sadat and Begin had only poisoned the atmosphere, leading to much controversy and general confusion.[33] Jimmy Carter's performance as mediator became more appealing to the parties when he offered a set of interim arrangements.[34] Carter's tactical achievements had relied on his search for mutual tolerance, a zest for encouraging both gentility and respect among the negotiators, and the desire for worthiness. Peace in the Middle East was unquestionably approached by Carter from the vantage of full participant instead of idle spectator.[35]

The end of the decade, coming on the heels of Camp David and signature of a peace treaty between Egypt and Israel, gave evidence of a transformation in the contest from one between states to one of peoples. But Ronald Reagan left Middle East peace unattended to until Anwar Sadat's assassination, nine months into the Reagan administration's first term, caustically reminded US officials that regional events were not likely to wait for US calendars to be swept free. Israelis turned the Sinai over to Egypt without serious incident on April 25, 1982, but Reagan had not improved on Carter's record of bettering Palestinian life in the West Bank. Months of meetings at Israeli and Egyptian locations had failed to elicit significant movement on the issues of land, water, security, or self-government in the territories. The Israeli invasion of Lebanon on June 6 only added to the anguish of a US government caught between attempting to deal with matters that had sparked the attack and seeking to limit a more general conflict growing from active engagement between Jews and Arabs.

Reagan's decision neither to resurrect Kissinger's step-by-step approach nor to continue Carter's pursuit of a Geneva conference solution showed sensitivity and compassion for the parties who had found previous US peace options unsound as well as biased toward one or another of the players. The virtue of Reagan's September 1, 1982, West Bank plan—its egalitarian standards—was, however, unappealing to the parties. Their priorities and their principles—even Israel's—were less devoted to a US value system. Their concerns were not connected to equality as much as to ensuring commitment to, and support for, claims of national identity and historical inevitability.[36] In that sense they were closer to Kissinger than to Carter or Reagan regarding the course that peace was likely to follow.

It is a small wonder that when Israel, the Palestinians, and Jordan refused to support the Reagan plan, and King Hussein was unable to persuade Yasir Arafat to accept delegations for future negotiations,[37] the White House withdrew from active engagement.[38] Ronald Reagan would not be seen betraying his principles of offering equal rights to each party, under duress. And neither could he have expected that states or entities that had warred with one another for decades could be made to surrender their suspicions and hatreds easily while embracing a value system that was foreign to their experiences.

THE INTERACTION OF RELIGION AND POLITICS

Although most students of the Middle East are quite familiar with the record of regional peace efforts by the United States, few have been exposed to the link between religion and politics in the lives and perceptions of ordinary Middle Eastern citizens. A new wisdom, therefore, might have to be devised if US policymakers are to be better equipped to deal with a region increasingly populist and fundamentalist in its worldview. The meaning and influence that such an ethical foundation could have on how the United States goes about managing its Middle East role can be gauged by tracing religion's unique function in the US political system. How has the United States understood religion within the broad context of national and international society? Has there been an agreed set of legitimating beliefs that characterize a US perspective on religion, without at the same time doing harm to its principle of avoiding an establishment of religion?

US citizens have been thought of as a distinctively secular people, and their country as a place in which avarice, greed, and self-indulgence have thrived. This overly negative portrait was boosted by public disclosures of Wall Street insider-trading schemes, Pentagon contractor fraud, and scandals among televangelists. Nevertheless, the regular churchgoing public remained at more than 60 percent of the population while the number of those who disbelieve in God declined.[39] Moreover, the struggle to bring religion into governance—what some refer to as a "spiritual politics"[40]—has been joined because of, rather than in spite of, moral abnegation by a segment of US society. The widespread development of cults, an increase in the breakup of families, spiraling crime rates, pervasive use of drugs, and general public disappointment in institutions of government as well as in those who officiate have strengthened the bonds of religion among a majority wishing to defeat these ills.[41] In particular, puritanical themes such as school prayer and the rights of an unborn fetus have won strong and passionate approval from a significant portion of the voting public.

Although the US people have traditionally grouped around political philosophies that supported the nation's special circumstances, eschatological premises were often dependent on the nature of selection. The battle for national identity, as a result, floated between the essence of classical republicanism and liberal constitutionalism. Then, as now, tensions emanating from these unresolved choices provided the structural basis for fixing religion within society.[42]

The conservative agenda featured many of the substantive declarations that had given rise to a fusing of religion and politics. Political conservatives favored implementation of classical republican themes enshrined in the Declaration of Independence and illustrated by stands taken by the evangelical movement. The divinity, according to these views, had a close alliance with the nation and was an inspiration for its founding and subsequent growth. Critically, the commanding presence of God appeared in the language of the Pledge of Allegiance, numerous presidential inaugural addresses, and a host of congressional statements. The fate of the nation seemed inextricably bound to the religious devotion of its leaders, when placed under the banner of republicanism.[43]

US liberalism, though, drew its political strength from the Constitution and was conditioned on the state's ability to guarantee individual rights, including the freedoms to decide how, when, or whether to practice an attachment to God. The intrinsic self-worth and dignity of each human being took precedence over any exigency connected to divine worship. Liberals pressed the virtue of asserting equalities within a broad range of categories, from food supply and ecological advantage to peace, justice, and some rein on the manufacture as well as flow of armaments. They envisioned faith as a healer for those who in the first instance were unwilling to grant relief for inequities regularly befalling men and women. They also regarded ethical norms as a necessary concomitant of US acceptance of the burden of assuring human rights, international security, and economic fairness. But liberals offered a distinction between imposing a moral judgment on the actions of others and the requisites of a state-driven theology or theological system.[44]

The much-divided response to what constitutes an establishment of religion, moreover, has been accentuated as a direct consequence of the perceived US decline in the world. Those who see a downward slope in the global reputation of the United States have tended to cite the growth of relativism as a major contributing factor.[45] Undoubtedly, an explosion of information, the high degree of technological advancement, and stunning scientific achievement have accelerated a value-free environment, particularly among the nation's youth. But the energy and binding that drove the United States to reach an unrivaled world position in the first place may now help it regain its cultural address. In any case, how the United States chooses to respond—whether it sweeps away past contradictions and advances a single but appealing explanation for the link between religion and politics—could well affect the nature of fundamentalist impulses in the Middle East.

Reconciling republican and liberal themes will surely test the creative talents of US leaders as they move toward a vital relationship of faith to power, and the soundness of this uncommon approach may turn on how each side speaks to the other about its minimum demands. Republicans, for example, have to be convincing about an improvident United States resulting from the absence of God in society, whereas liberals must spell out why liberties have been essential to the body politic, both in antecedent terms and as a constituent element for the nation's belief system. Meanwhile, in the workings of civil religion, the United States has invested in a historically proven method for achieving intimacy between the practices of freedom and of faith.[46]

Civil religionists strive for a noncoercive societal order based on agreed norms, beliefs, symbols, dogmas, traditions, rituals, and practices that have some foundation in the meaning and character of transcendence. Religion in such a context has no official standing and is unestablished, but receives general community acceptance as a result of organized opposition to the profane, corruptible, and disruptive. Society, in these terms, is given a cultural permanence and legitimacy from the common thread of law and theology, and sacredness itself is expected to preserve unity and set limits, as well as to define boundaries for an otherwise vulnerable public.[47]

Civil religion, though, has its share of critics. Theologians question whether civil religion can be truly regarded as transcendental. Social theorists wonder how claims could be made for a complete moral order or meaning system when the modern state is disunited by the demands of a secularized society. Moreover, whereas civil religion in a Durkheimean sense gives symbolic expression to social unity, Jean-Jacques Rousseau in his *Social Contract* spoke of the concept as providing an engine for political virtue.[48]

Where civil religion can be expected to develop, it is structured and functions in ways that duplicate traditional religion. For example, both religious orders link their ethos to a worldview that allows for beliefs and behavior patterns as well as sentiments that offer inspiration. Both seek to legitimate and integrate audience myths, rituals, stories, ceremonies, and histories. But civil religion's focus is the civic and political institutions of the community. Although the concept of divinity is invoked in civil religion, God is not the primary concern of civil religion. Social and historical experience, especially as performed politically, remain the ultimate personality of civil religion. Politically conscious individuals as well as their leaders, therefore, are the standard bearers of civil religion instead of the ecclesiastical community. Civil religion in this sense exists solely because the sociopolitical order has a need to sanctify and legitimate the moral order. Civil religion thereby also differs from a political order and nation that does not wish to state the meaning of a society's institutions in transcendental terms.[49]

Because civil religion expects to make meaningful judgments about the sociopolitical order alone, its scope is narrow. Traditional religion embraces the totality of human existence and life concerns; civil religion treats only the part of an individual that is public. The strength of civil religion, therefore, is in integrating people and groups with a diversity of beliefs and other meaning systems. Civil religion's weakness is its inability to displace alternative meaning systems as well as anchor core beliefs in a pervasive worldview that promises either social or personal fulfillment. Civil religion, as a consequence, usually establishes a working arrangement with traditional religion instead of seeing it replaced in society. Although those who lose their moral way may be thought of as having the least chance to generate a civil religion, and the best opportunity belongs to the religiously homogenous, societies looking to be righteous have often contested with equally meritorious visions of how to fulfill state responsibility.[50]

Therefore, although concern for public welfare and protection of "democratic" standards (free enterprise, egalitarianism) have been central to the ideals and standards that characterize the "American way of life," founding fathers such as Franklin, Adams, and Madison as well as foreign observers such as French civil servant Alexis de Tocqueville subscribed to an affinity between the cause of religion and the republic. But none wished to tear down the "wall of separation" that Jefferson intended in the first Bill of Rights amendment to the US Constitution.[51]

Tocqueville, in fact, attributed the harmony and exceptional moral behavior exhibited by the United States to its religious "feeling."[52] John Adams regarded the Christian ethic as indispensable to a free and stable society,[53] and Benjamin Franklin lauded Christianity as the most virtuous, humane, and equitable religion yet founded.[54] James Madison described Christian beliefs as better and purer than any other,[55] and a venerable judge of the same period, Justice Joseph Story, called Christianity the religion of liberty.[56]

Thomas Jefferson was unconvinced that religion would be forever the handmaiden of liberty. He remained unalterably committed to the perpetuation of all personal freedoms, including the right to choose how and where to worship. He saw Christian doctrine as both utilitarian and universal, but he worried most about tyranny. Having individuals answer to a preselected form of religious devotion struck him as despotism.[57]

Jefferson's dissent from Tocqueville's later judgment of the salutariness of joining religion to freedom derived from their separate historical experiences. By the middle of the nineteenth century, Tocqueville had lived through a frightful epoch of national struggle for libertarian and communitarian principles in France. He had also inherited a past secured by a republican-led bloodbath and terrorism to drive empire-thirsty monarchs from office.[58] Jefferson's heritage, by contrast, was drawn from Puritanism with its special emphasis on religious toleration.[59] The prerevolutionary colonies had been shaped by a mood of independence, freeing the colonists from the control of secular or ecclesiastical authority.

John Locke, England's premier seventeenth-century political philosopher, built a wall between religion and politics by offering up a god of reason, not of scripture, to his colonial cousins. He questioned whether the business of governing ought to be fair inquiry for the church, because clerical usurpation of civil authority was a dreaded consequence.[60] Locke's ideas penetrated the intellectual climate in the British colonies and united with a puritan spirit that rejoiced in voluntarism based on freedom of conscience.[61]

Religious pluralism in the colonies owed much of its fervor, however, to a proliferating church doctrine that portrayed spiritual rejuvenation in many different constellations of light. But it was puritan trust in the individual, his place in a moral society, and the bond to civil, not ecclesiastical, authority that stimulated Madison's and Jefferson's disposition to impose a church-state separation on the new United States.[62]

Jefferson and Madison ushered in an era removed from the unrestrained religiopolitical relationship that preceded it, but neither intended an ungodly nation to result. Each saw the folly of making government and religion adversaries. They wished instead to guarantee, by their act of segregation, a firmer, freer role for religion in republican society. Both statesmen believed that religion could be useful in the teaching of public morality.[63] Jefferson, for example, anticipated that nonsectarian instruction would be a sounder base for proving the existence of God and His true moral intention. He therefore instituted a professoriat of ethics at the University of Virginia but hoped that a slew of seminaries—representing various denominations—could as well become a fixture on the state campus at Charlottesville. Servicing a multiplicity of religious sects would prevent domination by any single member of the group.[64] Meanwhile, Madison presumed that government unburdened by religious obligation could take responsibility for managing how to encourage citizen virtue. The task would be helped enormously by the family, church, and school, all contributing to a promotion of freedom and stability.[65]

In any case, the framers of the US Constitution had achieved a separation of church and state that was consistent with the spirit of democracy. The doctrine mostly provided for citizens already steeped in religious observance and instructional faith, but the concept probed for the power of choice as to when, how, and under what conditions the faithful would exercise the privilege of prayer. Because inferences were frequently drawn that freedom of religion meant an exclusive right to avoid practicing faith altogether, US citizens bridled at the suggestion that they would be remembered principally as a people unbecoming to virtue and indifferent to morality and justice. Civil religion, then, became a way of collapsing republican and liberalist differences, as well as pointing toward standards that even those in more difficult circumstances might find satisfying. Fundamentalists throughout the Middle East have a compelling need to see equity, populism, and spiritualism prosper. They could be expected, therefore, to welcome a US civil religion, but the US role in the Middle East has suffered by comparison to its position there a decade ago because of the distance separating the perceived value system of the United States from that of ordinary Middle Eastern citizens.

THE US CREED AND MIDDLE EAST PRACTICE

The ideals making up the US creed—liberty, equality, democracy, and individualism—have combined to restrict both the power and institutions of government. The framers of the peculiar governance of the United States lodged sovereignty in the people rather than in a single, centralized authority.[66] European practice—the *raison d'état*—was a discredited idea, replaced by the US traditions of liberalism, constitutionalism, and natural rights—even into the present century, when government's role in society has markedly increased.[67] Neither the religious nor the radicalists opposed to the state have sought to remedy their quarrels by resorting to calls for a stronger government.[68]

The uncommon opposition to authority in the United States, meanwhile, has kept faith with a Hobbesian view of human nature,[69] and, although the founding fathers initially saw the individual as a benevolent and perfectible figure, fears that the powerful would be tempted toward egoism and sin encouraged the establishment of weak institutions.[70] Eventually, those who conceptualized mankind as more generous by nature came also to insist that government ought to be enfeebled because the well-intentioned and essentially good person has no need of strong government in order to achieve either self-control or true direction.[71]

The agony of US politics has been how to reconcile legitimate government—that is, the drawing down of power—with a life made more bearable for the weakest members of society.[72] The United States was spared having to deal with feudalism or traditionalism, constituents of the history of Europe and the societies that grew out of colonialism in Asia, Africa, and the Middle East.[73] The United States also enjoyed a long period free of worry about the sanctity of its borders, until World War II. Immunity from those anxieties allowed the country a significant period in which to ensure that cherished values survived the political exigencies of the moment.[74]

The critical discontinuity in US life, then, results not from strengthened rule, but as an outcome of the necessity that restraint be placed on authority. The US creed established criteria upon which to inquire and resist rather than to obey.[75] In the US value system, there is little room for the idea that superior wisdom, deserving of unquestioning fealty, endows leaders. The US creed—itself composed of contradictory elements—could therefore be a less than appropriate device with which to approach dilemmas bound by traditions held sacred by Middle Eastern policymakers.

Individualism, democracy, liberty, and equality have geographical as well as definitional boundaries. A large segment of the globe, particularly the nations of the Middle East, feels little attraction to the individualist. Arabs of the Middle East owe their loyalties to the group: They subordinate their rights as individuals and remain confident that personal reward follows group cooperation. The Islamic Middle Easterner chooses a pattern of shifting attachments, maintaining membership in a vast array of interlocking and overlapping organizations. The web of personal associations thus built up includes family, friends, and school chums, in addition to professional, recreational, and political contacts.[76]

Israelis, for their part, belong to a culture that also has historically given lower priority to individualism. The Jewish state developed from a history of statism, elitism, and government by agreement with a dominant party.[77] The political party process has since fragmented, but transition to two-party rule, including tolerance for new elements and those more at the fringe as contestants in the electoral competition, has not altered the essentially centralized and hierarchical framework in which authority tends to be exercised.[78]

Whether any form of democracy finds a receptive audience among the states of the Middle East, meanwhile, has depended upon how the concept equips Arab leaders to use their power—otherwise practiced according to custom—and upon which set of conditions—substantive or procedural—meets Israel's need to cope with rising demands from its citizens.[79] Leadership, in the Arab sense, has followed a patrimonalist pattern. Policy ideas and strategies for implementation emanate from the ruler, and a retinue of personal advisers, ministers, military commanders, secretaries, and confidants carry out instructions. These courtiers are, in turn, leaders of various groups of officials at lower levels. The sovereign prudently ensures that no one seeks to challenge his rule, whereas the subordinates remain locked in constant struggle. The division and rivalry that result from such competition have been typical features of Arab politics and have shaped the state system during many centuries of tribal tension.[80] Authority, moreover, has been nurtured within a religious fabric that calls for imitation of the characteristics managed to near-perfection in the life of Muhammad. Islam is strengthened by Muhammad's use of personal relationships, charisma, military prowess, nearness to direction, informal politics, balanced conflict, and the unbreakable links between policy and theology.[81]

When Arab leaders have chosen to expand political participation in their communities, energies and frustrations stored up by the populace have been unleashed, endangering stability and order. Resultant crackdowns by the government have often led to a cycle of further violence and repression with unpredictable consequences. Therefore, modern-day leaders are at ease solely with a modest lifting of restraint on the public appetite. They may offer a more open press, the broadening of parliamentary representation, greater competition in the party system, a slightly increased tolerance for secularism, or release of political prisoners. Each reform is weighed carefully in order to mute or altogether avoid arguments of government illegitimacy. Taken together, however, the introduction of such measured improvements still falls far short of even procedural democracy.[82]

Rulers in the Arab world strengthen their claim to legitimacy when they give evidence of meeting citizens' needs, and public demand for equal rights as well as social justice have coincided with, and been given formal expression by, a resurgent Islam.[83] Arab leaders tend to look to religion as a purveyor of authenticity; thus, when the downtrodden are inspired by themes of piety and equality, Arab heads of government welcome the implications for governing. But when equality as an idea strikes at the roots of Muslim faith, those in command regard liberty as a concomitant to disorder.[84]

Arab leaders fear that if their regimes were assigned a major role in protecting individual liberties, chaos would result. They see stability as a ritualistic element in governance, and, when instability arises and becomes a persistent challenge to governing, the ensuing struggle is often perceived as leading to the state's disintegration and the leader's fall. Resource advantages notwithstanding, the economy plunges into ruin. The desire for order has meant that the Arab world operates on a hierarchy of values.[85]

Muslim leaders who show significant interest in their public's desire for equal rights and social justice are conforming to a standard established in the revealed thought of Muhammad and confirmed in Islamic law and practice. Equality and fairness are important concepts in the teachings of Islam, and the life of Muhammad exhibits a special sensitivity to issues of discrimination, sexism, slavery, infanticide, and imbalance.[86] Islamicists such as the famed fourteenth-century Tunisian Ibn Khaldun were particularly preoccupied with unjust behavior and its resultant undermining of the ruler. He, like others in the Middle Ages, was devoted to ensuring that illicit, corrupt conduct would not be practiced in a community sometimes subject to capricious leadership.[87]

Whereas the process of democracy may be too costly a departure for an orthodoxy arising out of the Arab state system, Israeli leaders have taken comfort in their nation's reputation for openness and fairness for its citizens.[88] But the Jewish state's purposes have been attacked as a result of the most recent military confrontation with the Palestinian minority in its midst. The intifada,[89] however, has been merely the latest in a chain of events that could totally circumscribe the democratic spirit in Israel.[90] Israelis have long been at odds with the founding values of their society. Ethnic and religious cleavages that reached epic proportions in the aftermath of the 1967 war are paralleled by an even deeper schism between Jews and Arabs over the basic right to be heard, as well as claims of cultural authenticity in the land they share.

Leaving aside territorial questions, Jewish behavior toward Arabs under occupation severely challenges Israel's claim to be a democracy.[91] Respect for minority views, the public's active involvement in government, and a tolerant attitude on the part of most citizens are no longer key features of Israel's civic culture.[92] Instead, the majority of Jews perceive West Bank and Gaza Arabs as a threatening element and demand security and protection from the army.[93] Moreover, the desire for a military devoted to assuring internal order, the need for effective leadership, and a general nervousness about the future mix uneasily with a superficial self-assuredness to degrade democratic tendencies within the body politic.[94]

Even the most ardent Islamic radical gives substantial support to equal rights for individuals, but Israelis eye the same principle with caution. Mounting concern over state security, buttressed by the intifada, has convinced governmental authorities in Israel that granting full equality for all citizens under Israeli jurisdiction (including Palestinian Arabs) would be premature.[95] Portions of Israel's Jewish population have also felt unequal treatment. Israel has moved from a nation unified by its pioneering spirit to a state with a surfeit of ethnic, religious, and generational differences.[96] Its early period bears witness to a program disfavoring those who came to Israel from Arab North Africa and the Middle East as well as the ultrareligious, the apolitical, and the nontraditional woman.

More recently, a transformation in society has resulted in increasing services and extending educational and occupational opportunities to the Oriental- or Sephardic-born (North African or Middle Eastern) resident.[97] An upsurge in religious membership and appeal has meant a reduction in the level of unfairness the state metes out to the devout. But new zealousness by a growing movement of religious extremists has enabled them to exert their own form of discrimination against more common elements in the society. The transition from a center-left–wing dynamic in the political process to a right-wing orientation coincided with, and helped to consolidate, a drift in the direction of Jewish fundamentalism.[98] Neither the older variant of arbitrariness, which enforced a trend against the religious, nor the newer shape of prejudicial conduct on behalf of unconstrained faith can be seen as a healthy sign of equity arrangements in Israel's body politic.

Political elites have historically been held to be a positive and impartial force in society. However, when Jewish voters came face to face with their government in the past two national elections, they found a system badly in need of repair. The routinization of politics had given rise to economic favoritism and privilege, and the citizen without party stature or influence was left merely to complain about an administrative structure gripped by a paralysis that only worsened with time. The electorate struck back in 1984 and again in 1988, producing a deadlock in the governing process and thereby restraining the growth of elitism as well as attempting to restore the pattern of egalitarianism the nation's founders had intended.[99] Although it is much too early to offer final judgment, recovery of equity in the management of Israel's politics may be a long way off.

Israeli citizens nonetheless participate in an array of freedoms unavailable to Palestinians under military administration. A free press, with an exceptional reputation for criticizing the government, provides the public a lively forum for debate and a way to be informed on all matters affecting their lives.[100] A truly representative Knesset, moreover, ensures that liberties that are inherently a function of citizenship are safeguarded.[101] The ability to vote, hold office, and speak without fear of retribution on issues of small or great consequence are among the freedoms most strongly valued by Israelis as they wait out the long ordeal from war to peace with troublesome neighbors.

Arabs and Israelis have shown they have mixed feelings about the US creed and about each other. Equal rights took on new significance for Muslims when fundamentalist attitudes on fairness grew to be more attractive in the Middle East. Egalitarianism has attained a wide appeal in the region, except in Israel, which believes itself vulnerable to Palestinian exploitation should Jews behave impartially toward Arabs under occupation.

Although liberty has not gained as comprehensive a foothold in the thinking of Arab elites, the principle has been powerfully felt by most Israelis. Yet, freedom for each Jewish citizen is imperiled when any person has his or her rights stripped away through arbitrary acts, no matter how justifiable. The Jewish state's handling of the intifada, therefore, threatens to tear apart basic liberties in the Holy Land, whether or not Israelis enjoy freedom of the press, the right to vote, or any other right associated with democracy.

How effective the United States may be in establishing a better role for itself in the Middle East, therefore, could depend on the care and attention given to understanding fundamentalism, populism, and the region's need for equity arrangements. Will the United States be able to confront the theme of Arab alienation that Saddam Hussein has so successfully (and hypocritically) played upon? How will the United States deal with the millions of citizens who go hungry daily because of poor conditions and lack of employment, as well as diminished hope in a decent future? Can the United States adopt a new wisdom for the Middle East that is balanced in favor of treating the homeless and dispirited with sensitivity and compassion? Or is the United States doomed to repeat the errors of the past and defend a status quo—a conventional wisdom—that ensures order and stability alone for the leader, and maximizes the threat or use of force and ignores people's most basic rights—to enjoy life, liberty, and the pursuit of happiness?

Because conventional wisdom figured in so many US Middle East decisions, succeeding chapters will focus on how Henry Kissinger, Jimmy Carter, and Ronald Reagan saw the challenge of bringing peace to the region. Chapter 1 addresses these leaders' philosophical approaches to peace; Chapter 2 focuses on how and why fundamentalism plays an important role in the area, thereby proving the need for a "new wisdom" on the part of US mediators. Chapter 3 examines how and when "conventional wisdom" worked to achieve peace and where it failed. Chapter 4 discusses the risks of Gulf thinking in the United States regarding "ally" and "enemy" patterns. Chapter 5 identifies how and why a "new wisdom" might provoke success for the United States in the Levant. Finally, Chapter 6 offers the Bush administration a prescriptive agenda to follow in the Middle East during the first half of this decade.

1

Philosophies of Peacemaking:
The United States in the Middle East

To develop a new wisdom, we must thoroughly understand the strengths and weaknesses of the conventional wisdom that has determined US policymakers' actions and reactions in the recent past. US efforts to shape the peace process have, on occasion, earned it gratitude and a richer place in the world. What were the philosophical convictions, ingratiating styles, peculiar forces of personality, special tactics, strategies, and powers of persuasion that led to favorable Middle East negotiations by three US administrations during two decades? At the risk of some recounting of events well known to scholars in the field, it may be useful to recall the realpolitik of Kissinger, the pragmatism of Carter, and the populist approach of Reagan.

THE REALPOLITIK OF HENRY KISSINGER

Realpolitik advocates have much to say about the nature and disposition of power. They strategize about the need to calculate force, a presumed national ambition to survive, an imperative for a balance of power, an ethic of responsibility over one of conviction, the significance of geopolitical factors for assessing goals, and the role states play as actors on the world stage.[1] How states determine the balance of forces arrayed against them, what constitutes standards of behavior on the part of regional players, where stronger states prevail over weaker ones, and whether peace can ever be guaranteed continue to worry US negotiators as they seek to bring peace to the Middle East. A commitment to help states harmonize their influence, however, contradicts the essence of a US value system that binds citizens to a distrust of power. US peacemakers, therefore, have stepped into the position of Middle East mediator with a certain wariness about achieving peace at once consistent with US ideals and capable of gaining the parties' acceptance.

The central figure in formulating and implementing US goals in the Middle East during important stages of the Nixon and Ford presidencies was Henry Kissinger. His conceptualizations were better developed, more vivid, and more celebrated than those of perhaps any other senior diplomat in recent service to the federal government. The future national security adviser and secretary of state initially drew inspiration, as a mature Harvard undergraduate, from self-study of man's nature—his relationship to life, death, culture, and historical consciousness. Kissinger's mastery of the historical theories of Oswald Spengler and Arnold Toynbee, and the metaphysics of Immanual Kant, enabled him to confront the dilemma between freedom and necessity.[2]

Kissinger began his search for the meaning of freedom by rejecting Spengler's deterministic view of history. He saw Spengler's preoccupation with decline among civilizations as an unrewarding basis for demonstrating leadership and an inhibiting factor in the development of a normative philosophy of history. Yet Kissinger was pulled toward Spengler's "intuitive perception"—the leap of creativity that sought to capture the real meaning of events. His grasp of Spengler's intention to regard every event as an "inward experience" liberated Kissinger to argue, much later, for the notion of freedom as intuition, provided the limits of knowledge were understood.[3] Kissinger was also attracted to Toynbee's belief in historical purpose, but the British historian's reliance on empirical research repelled him. He found Toynbee's theology devoid of normative patterns and lacking a "profound metaphysics."[4] The mixing of religion and science to help man keep in touch with his environment, as well as to describe how civilization evolved, was incompatible with spiritual freedom.[5]

Kissinger's probe for the inner meaning of freedom and necessity was to be reconciled through an adaptation of Kantian metaphysics. The eighteenth-century Prussian had divided reality into two spheres: that which can be apprehended by pure reason, or the world as it appears through sensation, known as phenomena; and things in themselves, the objects of speculative reason, or the world in and of itself, called noumena.[6] The realm of noumena held great importance for Kissinger. It was a world that contained man not as a thing but as a spiritual and moral being endowed with freedom and bound by duty and responsibility. Kant's moral law, the categorical imperative, rested on the Protestant notion of conscience and "inwardness," but he also believed that as man passed from the phenomenal to noumenal state his existence went beyond categories of time, space, and causality.[7]

Kissinger was unprepared to accept a transcendental dimension to the human spirit. He envisioned man as a historical being, destined for death but attempting in life to surmount his circumstances and culture. Kissinger was, as one biographer recently noted, a "lapsed Kantian"—a believer in the existence of human freedom but unable to share in the Prussian's regard for the purpose and progress of human history.[8] The future statesman was caught in a paradox: He could equate freedom and morality with the historical process—a philosophy that emphasized each person's uniqueness and finite quality—but at the same time he recognized that man's experiences lifted him above nature. Value and purpose were, nevertheless, considered by him to be relative to the individual and his specific culture.[9]

The implications of Kissinger's "existentialism" were grave for the governing process: If man were involved in an endless historical search, then the human will could not receive direction from a divine or moral law; an immanent will necessarily intended man to create his own meaning, values, and reality. A Nietzchean concept of survival and the will to power would therefore seem the most likely result of such thinking.[10]

Kissinger's historical relativism, moreover, had profound significance for his political philosophy. He would soon come to understand that nations, like individuals, must accept limits on their ability to compete. Otherwise, instability and disorder would arise. The notion or doctrine of limits therefore formed the core of Kissinger's performance as statesman, even though its philosophical origins were somewhat obscure.[11] Kissinger has maintained that Kant and his prescription for "perpetual peace" were the cause of his enlightenment;[12] others have charged that its content was Weberian but also influenced by Reinhold Niebuhr's writings.[13] In any case, Kissinger's historicopolitical philosophy can be fairly summarized as a belief in man's freedom resulting from an inner experience within conditions of human limits. "Inwardness" alone allowed for apprehension of the meaning of history and recognition of the ethical content of one's actions.[14]

Kissinger's later writings, particularly on nineteenth-century European diplomacy, incorporated his rules for effective leadership. An exceptionally qualified statesman, he believed, must be able to recognize the relationship of means to ends, analyze forces at his and the adversary's disposal correctly, as well as gauge how such elements may be utilized to serve short- and long-term goals.[15] He should not only be capable of judging the balance of forces but be successful in implementing his vision. And he ought to accomplish his tasks within the context of a domestic structure that supports immediate objectives.[16] Crucially, the leader must not be deterred by bureaucratic inertia or administrative blockage.[17] In point of fact, Kissinger was to conclude that his preference was that statesmen should "act as if their intuition were already experience, as if their aspiration were truth."[18] The leader must be an educator, must "bridge the gap between a people's experience and his vision, between a nation's tradition and its future."[19]

Henry Kissinger attempted to become the consummate statesman dutifully described in his doctoral dissertation, published as *A World Restored*. His intellectual capital, however, was to be consumed by a US national character that declined to subject itself to the premises that he rigorously held. Kissinger was, for all his merits, neither wholly American nor decidedly European. The hybrid nature of his status as a Jewish émigré from war-torn Germany, uncomfortable in the wellspring of either heritage, allowed the future diplomat to choose his own cultural métier. The attention showered upon him by mentors of his deepening intellectualism at Harvard and earlier during his military career bolstered an otherwise limited appreciation of the Lutheran-Kantian theme of inwardness.[20]

Although to a certain extent the idea of God's having died at Auschwitz symbolized Kissinger's feelings as a nearly lone survivor in the German town of Furth, his subsequent cultural choices were not uncommon. Many prominent nineteenth-century orthodox Jews were drawn to the German idealist school of thought championed by Kant, Hegel, and others. The poet Heinrich Heine and economic historian Karl Marx are just two examples of Jewish thinkers caught up in the drama of high German culture premised on the ideals of Lutheran Protestantism.[21] Moreover, in the twentieth century neoidealists or historicists—such as Dilthey, and Ortega y Gasset—sought to reform Kant's philosophy, and their novel values had an exceptional appeal for the young Kissinger.[22] They and he spoke of a course of action based on "power" and "survival" that would indeed prove alien to the US creed. That is reason enough why Kissinger's conduct as chief US envoy to the Middle East during the early 1970s would become controversial and yet so ironic. His shuttling to and from the region to bargain with enigmatic leaders was, additionally, a sobering reminder of the significance that one's strongly held philosophic convictions may have on the practice of international bargaining.

THE PRAGMATISM OF JIMMY CARTER

Pragmatists see the world differently from proponents of realpolitik. They do not view power politics and international relations as synonymous; power is regarded solely in terms of improving the human condition. Power for its own purposes is unwise and objectionable on moral, ethical, and practical grounds. Values are not irrelevant to the conduct of international affairs. Rather, scientific understanding must begin with questions about *whose* values, or *what* values, need examination.[23]

The rights of individuals, groups, and society as a whole must be respected if the state is to grow and prosper, according to pragmatists. A necessary degree of human development, therefore, thrives in a pluralistic, democratic environment in which equality is emphasized. Change may come about, but it should be gradual, with a minimum of disruption to society and in ways that preserve its most valued features.[24] Thus, pragmatism as a philosophical concept stands apart from realpolitik, in which power is held to be an end of international society, bound to a diplomatic strategy in which the outcome of conflict is determined by the strongest party or the one creating a "balance of power."[25]

Jimmy Carter's presidency was marked by an energetic pursuit of Middle Eastern peace. His effort was an intensely personal one, and, despite the presence of remarkably gifted Middle East experts in the administration, Carter took direct control of the details necessary for a successful negotiation. This extraordinary effort was due in part to circumstances arising from unresolved tensions in the Arab-Israeli quarrel, but the zeal Carter displayed in his management of the peace process was largely a consequence of his philosophy, which blended traditional US pragmatism and Niebuhrian Christian ethics.

William James, a Harvard psychology professor, in writings at the turn of the century, coined many of the elements composing the singular US philosophy that would attract a farm boy growing up in rural Georgia during the Great Depression. James's *Pragmatism* was based upon a perception of truth that relied upon verification through experience,[26] and young Carter's daily tasks of planting, harvesting, and marketing the peanut crop, and later, obtaining a military education and serving in the US Navy's nuclear submarine program, were great levelers.[27]

James believed in the human mind as a "fighter for freedom," in the creative personality's reaching its highest potential within a pluralist society. His invention of the "stream of consciousness"—later popularized by Irish novelist James Joyce— permitted an emphasis on *process* instead of fixed views on such subjects as the difference between fact and value, mind and matter, experience and nature, or religion and science. It was the interaction between mind and environment that determined consciousness, according to James.[28]

Jimmy Carter's bids for office in local, state, and national contests, often against great odds but nevertheless winning, demonstrated that his egalitarian habits were not the hindrance that some wished for or warned against. He accepted Jamesian views that the environment's plasticity did not necessarily reduce mankind's challenges to alter it, lessen the setbacks one would likely undergo, or limit the time required to achieve beneficial results. Carter's presidential bid was premised on James's optimism that, with hard work and creativity, a good chance existed for ultimate success.[29]

James's lavish praise for the individual, his inventiveness, forcefulness, and vitality, were kindred emotions to Carter, who as a youth of twelve had been infatuated by Tolstoy's characters in the epic *War and Peace*. The Georgia farm boy had been most impressed by the Russian storyteller's presentation of students, barbers, farmers, housewives, and common soldiers affecting the course of history, rather than the usual portrayal of generals and statesmen determining events.[30] And if, indeed, the inclinations, passions, will to power, courage, and prejudices of ordinary people could manage change in an otherwise dogmatic era, then Carter may have reasoned as an adult and future leader that he could decisively shape the tone and substance of major occurrences.[31]

Making decisions, even on the flimsiest of evidence, was an imperative of James's philosophy of pragmatism. He believed that individuals could not avoid becoming involved in the solution of social, economic, and political problems of the day, and he regarded the suspension of judgment, on the theory that a more complete basis for decision would emerge later on, as putting pressure on events equal to acting in the first place. Skepticism, for James, was laced with immorality. The moral person based his judgments on the best scientific evidence available and responded on the supposition that an approach of this kind stood a reasonable chance of affecting the course of the universe. James, in fact, reminded his countrymen that "sins of omission" were just as devastating as "sins of commission."[32]

James was convinced that human thought was purposive and goal oriented. Solving concrete problems was, to him as to Carter, an act conducive to human well-being. James termed such mental activity "meliorism," and Carter regarded this function as a rational process in which the most beneficial course of action would be chosen among likely alternatives leading to good governance.[33]

War and interventionism occupied the thought of William James in his later years as he attempted to deal with US liberation of Spanish dependencies in Latin America. James urged the setting up of a kind of forerunner to the Peace Corps, which would engage youth in a program of public service and thereby ward off natural proclivities toward violence. He called this effort "the moral equivalent of war"—a term that Jimmy Carter would use as president to redirect public attention toward energy conservation.[34]

Carter welcomed the "pluralistic" vision that James formulated as a commonsense approach to human affairs. The Harvard psychologist recommended toleration of opposite views as appropriate for a political order in which the search for truth and application of scientific knowledge were deemed essential. Carter, as a state legislator and as governor of Georgia, was able to use these maxims as a prod for the civil rights movement during a time when others in the South were inhospitable to the struggle for equality.[35]

Carter's evangelism, his repeatedly criticized preference for born-again Christianity, was a manifestation of a standard of moral responsibility called for in the teachings of Reinhold Niebuhr. Niebuhr, a pastor, theology professor, and theoretician of Christian social ethics, was perhaps best known for his portrayal of man as a transcendent spirit and a creaturely sinner.[36] Niebuhr's neoorthodoxy, explaining man as having a dual nature, clashed with a more liberal church tradition that took the human race to be theologically improving with age. Moreover, there were cleavages within the fundamentalist movement, and between it and those espousing neoorthodoxy over an error-free scripture, separatist behavior, and the relevance of the gospel to the sociological, economic, and political arguments of the day.[37] Niebuhr's emphasis on literal interpretation of the Bible troubled many evangelicals and separated them from Carter, who was charmed by an ideological kinship on social matters with the Missouri-bred theologian. Furthermore, the religiously conservative Carter was interested in neoorthodox positions critical of the historical relativism and sentimental morality favored by Christian liberalists.[38]

Jimmy Carter was heard frequently quoting Niebuhr's aphorism "The sad duty of politics is to establish justice in a sinful world." Others regarded Niebuhr's judgment about Christian goals to be more representative: Members were to avoid establishment of "a loving society" and, rather, seek "a relatively just order maintained through a balance of forces."[39] Niebuhr's thought, distilled and applied to the field of international politics, therefore took account of man's imperfections and guaranteed that national pride would ensure a will to power even as the state sought to approximate justice. Applying his doctrine to US-Soviet relations, Niebuhr warned of the excessive power motive behind the Kremlin's policies. Containment, he argued, would be a reasonable method of curtailing Soviet aggressive intentions.[40] Niebuhr nevertheless was prevented from recommending a solution to the Cold War based solely on national interest as a result of his confidence in, and respect for, US justice. The United States could choose policies encouraging self-protection, but an implication of justice along with temperance must undergird its effort. Containment was reserved for Soviet behavior because the Soviet government was prouder and more sinful, whereas the US response was likely to be just. Moreover, a pluralistic United States contained sufficient bases of independent power to ensure moderation and self-restraint in its response to potential hostilities.[41]

Jimmy Carter's spiritual and intellectual odyssey was masked by incongruities in James's *Pragmatism* and Reinhold Niebuhr's Christian social ethics. Both twentieth-century philosophers were comfortable with an activist moralism and agreed on the desirability of a pluralist society with an emphasis on justice and equality. Both were against military solutions to conflict. But James and Niebuhr diverged over the place of sentimentality in an antiwar posture, as well as whether a real danger existed from totalitarian rule. Niebuhr—like Kissinger much later—worried that the structure of the international system was becoming unstable as a consequence of the sweep of communism. He believed it imperative that balanced order be maintained so that the dissolution of international society could be prevented.[42]

Carter's ambivalent behavior in the foreign policy arena—what some would refer to as inconsistency or, worse, schizophrenia—may be regarded as a natural result of the contradictory solutions to concrete situations offered by James and Niebuhr. For example, President Carter supported a program of human rights in nations subject to conflicting international pressures, yet he was sympathetic to a policy of containment in the Gulf as a response to the shah's ouster. He could defend allies who distanced themselves from US goals out of national pride, internal contradictions, or questionable obligations. However, the same sensitive US leader might be filled with rancor against those who dismissed claims of equal justice, invoked historical necessity, or proposed inevitable consequences. The social dimension of Carter's philosophy—its Niebuhrian quality—enabled optimism about the inequities of life; however, his pragmatism—the Jamesian outlook—ensured an astute regard for the limits inherent in contentious matters. An unbridled faith in the power and appeal of the individual, moreover, encouraged Carter's belief that one's presence could make a difference. Bargaining at the Middle East table would be an especially useful testing ground for Jimmy Carter's particularist approach toward resolving disputes.

THE POPULISM OF RONALD REAGAN

Ronald Reagan's foray into Middle East peacemaking during 1982 pointed up the stake that US ideals had in the peoples of other nations. Reagan had based his career upon the goals of populism, but his opinions were not the result of a deliberate philosophy, as were Kissinger's, or drawn from roots deep in the soil, as were Carter's. A Midwestern sports announcer turned actor, labor negotiator, and public figure, Reagan relied on traditional values conceived at the workplace: liberty, freedom, patriotism, morality, religion, self-help, and civility. His ethos of hard work, duty, and consistency was the consequence of a working-class environment and economic depression as a youth.[43] Having grown up immersed in the detail of how to get ahead, Reagan was poised for a promising career as an actor and defender of private choice. He was favored with good looks, charm, a winning smile, and the confidence born of a consumer-oriented postwar boom that rewarded independence. Self-assertion and continued personal success led Ronald Reagan publicly to advocate issues associated with traditional US precepts, first as a guild leader, then as a politician and statesman.[44]

There were nearly always forebodings among the professional party elite regarding Reagan's sincerity. Nevertheless, the US public lined up on election day to support Reagan's conservative ideology, with glowing results. The "teflon-coated" president took pleasure in projecting an image of what was best about the United States—its generosity, persistence, and ethics—as compared to his predecessor, who had berated a nation newly addicted to relativism.[45]

Ronald Reagan was known to cherish a boyhood romanticism and the heroic image of himself as well as others. This "Jack Armstrong" image in fact emboldened the White House to attempt to regain the US way in the world, an objective that Reaganites claimed had gone all but unnoticed by earlier administrations.[46]

The "Reagan Revolution"—its rising tide of conservatism and its corporate resilience—was forever subject to proof about the vision, vitality, or performance of the United States. The central notion in the Reagan ideology, however, was to raise the United States to the position of number one, to work at removing obstacles to national success, to adhere to no limits on options or opportunities, to be assured of the nation's destiny as surely as Hollywood moguls had been confident of the profits to be made in the wake of a world at war.[47]

"Reagan's America," as one author dubbed the phenomenon, was born of a period in US history nourished by faith in the individual and uplifted by a Mark Twainesque view of leadership. Twain was fond of feigning an untutored, genteel, pleasant exterior to confuse the nearest adversary, while all the time he was laying siege by artful strategy. Ronald Reagan, with a twinkling of the eye and a calm presence, would approach bargaining in

UNITED STATES IN THE MIDDLE EAST   25

much the same manner. He would appear to be the bumbling, distracted, uncultured personification of US obtuseness. In fact, Reagan was a study in contrasts. In the finest US tradition, he held his cards close to his vest and played for the moment of retribution.[48] This style—perfected by Eisenhower—and method of negotiation was greeted by some shock in the Middle East, which was used to careful attention from high-level personages such as Kissinger and Carter.

Reagan's philosophy (some would say ideology) was really a despoiled pragmatism, leavened by aspects of realpolitik, that went far beyond the teachings of Reinhold Niebuhr. The ex-governor of California was viscerally anti-Communist, but so was Niebuhr. However, Reagan believed that national interest was at the heart of any moral crusade. He considered the Kremlin to be truly an "evil empire," and he would protect the United States from its folly by drawing away from weak, knee-bending leadership that regarded peace as worth any price. Niebuhr had divorced intrinsic US goals from his suspicions about the Soviet Union because of his confidence that justice would persevere over pride and sinfulness. Ronald Reagan could not bring himself to be that trusting.

Reagan's approach to international politics and to the Middle East arose from a Hobbesian concept of society. He was committed to hard work and the triumph of the individual but recognized that the other side at a negotiating table may not be so motivated. It was a nasty, brutish world, and the just might not ever gain simply as a result of righteousness. Calamities observed no limits, and the just might have to fight to retain even a semblance of their world.[49]

Terrorist activity rekindled Reagan's distrust of Middle East politics and reminded him of the strength of his ideological convictions. He was insensitive to the goals of rebellion when rebellion inevitably led to violence. In fact, he rewarded antiterrorist campaigns in other nations and shepherded his own country toward eliminating any further military successes by guerrillas.[50]

Reagan was willing to work toward peaceful resolution of the Middle East conflict only if a way could be found to protect US standards of life and liberty. Hard bargaining could not be carried out in the face of armed hostilities. Satisfactory negotiations must give consideration to each side's minimum goals while ensuring an end to violence.

Finally, Reagan pragmatically assumed that although egalitarianism was a valuable commodity, it would not be assured in an environment in which the significance of the ideal was underrated. The "fighter for freedom"—in this case, Ronald Reagan—would not be persuaded to engage in a peace process where hopelessness remained a surer guide for the future. But, as Jimmy Carter had demonstrated at Camp David, sometimes good governance required the setting aside of predictable consequences. Renewed energies could unleash new opportunities, and Ronald Reagan, in the spirit of individualism, wished to be in the forefront of novel efforts to induce change in the conditions for Middle East conflict.

PHILOSOPHY AND PRACTICE:
THE PURSUIT OF MIDDLE EAST PEACE

The depth of resentment felt daily in the West Bank and Gaza and the nature of violence occurring there have led some to wonder whether Henry Kissinger's gamesmanship could work as effectively in the 1990s as it did a decade and a half ago. He was then a tireless devotee of melding strategy, tactics, and realpolitik philosophy on behalf of Middle East peace. His energy and skills produced comfort and trust in states used to dealing with each other under a regime of mutual suspicion and antagonism, and the character of his mediation inspired confidence in peace during moments of high drama and tension when war in the region appeared to be the greater possibility.

Israelis and Palestinians recently have been quarreling as they never have before. The consequences of their cycle of retribution may be less predictable and more uncontrollable than at any time in the history of the West Bank and Gaza occupation. That is precisely why a "leap of creativity" may be the only means left to achieve an effective US policy. Henry Kissinger's approach to peace in the area embodied what Spengler called an "intuitive perception." Therefore, his most authoritative statement on what the shape of a Middle East peace could look like might appear to be instructive.

The extraordinary favor that has been shown in the capitals of Europe, the Middle East, and at the United Nations to the convening of an international conference prompted Kissinger to offer a critique. He questioned the conventional wisdom that emphasizes the machinery of a global meeting—as if conflict were merely a legal condition. He pointed to the Indo-Pakistani and Iran-Iraq hostilities, in which death and destruction exceeded the casualties inflicted throughout the Arab-Israeli struggle despite the presence in the subcontinent and Gulf of a contractual peace. He cautioned that peace would not emerge from documents, but solely as a response to concrete situations. The immediate goal of any Middle East diplomacy, he believed, must be to define substance.[51]

Kissinger regards the task of the United States as obtaining the parties' agreement to compromise and sacrifice in advance of any international conference; his list of prerequisites is therefore revealing. The former secretary of state offered first his version of an ideal solution: a unilateral Israeli initiative to place the Gaza District and heavily populated areas of the West Bank under Arab control, subject, of course, to negotiations respecting governance and security. Kissinger, however, realized that until new elections were held the Israeli government was incapable of making that choice.[52] Nevertheless, he felt the modalities of any future peace in the Middle East ought to include relinquishing Israeli control over large segments of West

Bank territories; setting up defensible borders in lieu of a return to 1967 lines; forgoing external guarantees as a substitute for regional compliance; excluding a redivided Jerusalem but providing for special access to the holy sites of all faiths; demilitarizing those areas ceded by Israel; and arranging for Jordanian or joint Arab state—not PLO—responsibility for the civil administration of those parts of the West Bank and Gaza given up by the Jewish state.[53]

Kissinger preferred a unilateral US approach but recognized differences between the present era and the period of the 1973 war. There was no Arab leader ready to undertake a solitary initiative, as had Sadat; Israel, unlike its state in the mid-1970s, was deeply divided; and US mediation no longer had sole claim on the parties.

Kissinger was also convinced that an international conference would result in a deadlock. He believed that the United States would be called upon to impose a settlement on its ally Israel, whereas the Kremlin was likely to avoid seeking the same degree of sacrifice from its Arab clients. Soviet attendance at a Geneva-style meeting, therefore, was viewed as originating from a simple desire in its leaders to regain a central role in the Middle East.

In any case, Kissinger was left wondering whether an appropriate formula could be found to couple answers to troubling questions: What area (in the West Bank and Gaza) was subject to self-government; who shall govern it; and how can Israel's security concerns be fully met?[54]

Henry Kissinger's sense of the future conformed to his conception of the past. The modern history of the Levant, he found, was a timeless search for reconciliation of two people's aspirations and perceived rights. Few real solutions had been presented over the decades and even fewer had been acted upon. Conflict resolution, whether past, present, or future, depended greatly upon how each party understood the other. Constraints, moreover, were imposed by the states' delicate domestic need for survival; a successful mediator would have to travel very carefully between Arab and Israeli constituencies in order to achieve even modest progress.

Kissinger furthermore recognized that instability arose whenever disparities in the parties' positions were overlooked. Thus, barring Israeli adoption of his interim solution, a substantive framework of Middle East peace was to be built upon the creation of tolerable limits. Kissinger's proposal avoided specifics, was offered at the height of Palestinian travail on the West Bank, and promoted neither unqualified positions nor ones totally favorable to either side. In addition, the skeletal outline omitted discussion of issues certain to be too costly by internal standards and externally fractious. He did provide a general structure that could tie narrowly conceived purposes into broader objectives. Kissinger did not exclude the use of private channels of communication, offers of economic and military assistance, loose construction of terms to convey flexible meanings, or highly public diplomacy as proper incentives to achieve peace. He was entirely comfortable with the secretary of state conducting any or all of these activities separately, simultaneously, or in sequence. He was mostly concerned that the cause be undertaken, and US ingenuity and perspicacity displayed while events that had created the opening were still fluid.

Carter, as private citizen, has refused to be passive about finding a solution to the Arab-Israeli conflict. He has spoken out against US disentanglement from the region's chaotic condition; has held private meetings with areawide leaders who vigorously tested methods of bringing chronic adversaries together; has publicly hosted seminars and consultations devoted to sharing different visions of the future; and has written and lectured widely to audiences capable of understanding how peace might be conducted within a US value perspective.[55]

In nearly all of these forums, Carter has sounded a singular theme: The most universally accepted route to peace lies within the bounds of an international conference sponsored by the five permanent members of the UN Security Council.[56] For ex-President Carter, the shape of comprehensive peace has been somewhat altered, but not its essentiality. Moreover, the recurring idea was of particular significance, according to Carter, because of the latest outbreak of violence in the West Bank and Gaza.[57]

Carter was sure that angry, disadvantaged Palestinian youth would be unwilling to engage in talks with Jordan, or in any other context acceptable to Israel, while the Jewish government was responsible for daily acts of hostility to West Bankers and Gazans. He placed confidence in the ability of the UN Security Council to perform as a conduit for direct talks between Arabs and Israelis, although these seem impossible while West Bank and Gaza rioting continues. The former president rejected any likelihood that the international meeting would be able to impose solutions unacceptable to even a single party.[58]

Carter expected that when Israel could be enticed into selecting measures to defuse the volatile situation in the occupied territories, restoration of goodwill among the parties would be possible. The ex-president listed freezing Israeli settlements on the West Bank, opening Jewish markets to the manufactured goods and agricultural produce of Palestinian Arabs, and holding municipal elections in the territories as among the most important moves that a government in Jerusalem could take.[59]

Carter also understood that until a new Israeli national election had been held, or in the unlikely event that the Labor party formed a working coalition, those confidence-building efforts would go unrealized. It was therefore especially important that a US chief executive refuse to allow obstacles to Middle East peace to go unchallenged. For example, flexibility could be accomplished during an international conference by permitting US professors of Palestinian origin to represent the PLO. The forum could adjourn after opening speeches, while direct negotiations between Israel and Syria, among Israel, Jordan, and the PLO, as well as between Israel and

Lebanon, went on in private[60]—a formula concocted in the Begin era by the late Foreign Minister Moshe Dayan and agreed to in principle by the current Israeli government.[61]

Carter thought that a group of mediators approved by the parties could stand between deadlock and uncertain support for questionable propositions. Should an impasse be reached in the two-party negotiations, then the plenum powers—the United States, Britain, France, China, and the Soviet Union— would intervene and establish new options. In this way, the former president believed, the bargaining could be framed without the Arab states appearing to be aligned on one side and Israel on the other.[62]

Jimmy Carter's advocacy of a Middle East peace settlement held under the auspices of the five permanent members of the UN Security Council was consistent with a decade of his recommending a comprehensive answer to the region's problems. Nevertheless, as president, Carter had been willing to bend toward pragmatic solutions in order to rescue peace from the hands of would-be supporters of conflict. For example, he accepted the form of a bilateral agreement between Egypt and Israel when their enthusiasm had waned for fastening Sinai withdrawal to a favorable West Bank result. His pragmatic outlook was once again visible during months of "rug-merchant" negotiating with a divided leadership in Iran to secure the release of US hostages. In each of these episodes, Jimmy Carter remained steadfast in applying the moral principles and ethics taught by protégés of William James and Reinhold Niebuhr. Moreover, Niebuhr's advice increased the weariness that he felt as a result of betrayal in the Gulf and the waterway's susceptibility to Soviet influence.

The surprising tenacity of young Palestinians, unconnected to the PLO and unaffected by superior Israeli force, equally worried Carter when he surveyed the damage that the months of West Bank and Gazan rioting had produced.[63] The world community was quick to register its outrage as hundreds of Palestinians and Israelis squared off in a David-and-Goliath–like struggle. The repeated outbreaks of serious internal violence offered those like Carter an opportunity and a platform for new efforts, even if they were wrapped in old solutions.

Carter hoped to bring the force of global opinion to bear on Israelis who have persistently refused to accept advice. Israeli leaders have generally been impervious to international opinion, mostly because they believed that officials of Third World and certain developed nation-states were intent on dismembering the Jewish state. Jimmy Carter's appointment of a group of mediators who would receive their cue from the five permanent members of the UN Security Council hardly provided the assurances that Israel has been eager to receive. Furthermore, his concept of PLO admission to the international conference—in whatever guise—was proof to the Likud portion of the electorate that a Palestinian state would emerge as a third force in the corridor between Jordan and the Mediterranean. Such a development has been viewed by nearly all shades of opinion in Israel as a "mortal danger."[64]

Jimmy Carter remains strongly opposed to a return to the step-by-step strategy of Henry Kissinger. At Camp David, symbolized by the smiling faces of Sadat and Begin clasping hands, Jimmy Carter's flexibility and magnanimity as a mediator was best exemplified. The ex-president still carries with him the darker side of Niebuhr, suspicious about a world held at bay by totalitarian dictatorship. William James's pragmatism nevertheless enabled Carter to raise the level of sensitivity to how the two sides in the Arab-Israeli conflict face their pain, fears, and assumptions about each other. Carter's wisdom and his experience in gaining support among the peoples of the area place him among a select few who could offer any elected president clever options for promoting regional peace. The advice may be more hopeful and lasting, however, if, in the dialectic between James and Niebuhr, Jimmy Carter enlists the former as a more powerful influence on shaping future strategies as well as tactics for securing peace in the Middle East.

The Reagan administration's lackluster approach to Middle East peace changed at the beginning of 1988, as it contemplated the outbreak of Palestinian riots in the West Bank and Gaza. Still, Reagan's uneven strategy of setting out US standards to guide future discussions in the West Bank and Gaza during 1982 gave way to soporifically glancing at events, and sustained tactical effort rarely materialized through the intervening half decade. This neglect of issues just beneath the surface in the occupied territories, moreover, assured a bubbling up of anger on the part of frustrated Palestinian youth.[65]

Secretary of State George Shultz's shuttle diplomacy during March and April 1988 was intended to help the peace process come unstuck, but it failed for several reasons. First, the formula for peace was built on a series of steps that were impractical within the time period set for implementation. Shultz's plan envisaged an interim stage of self-administration for Palestinians on the West Bank and Gaza, to be followed by Jordanian-Palestinian-Israeli negotiations for withdrawal from the territories under the rubric of an international conference. The entire package of agreements was to be completed by the end of 1988, just prior to the conclusion of Reagan's second term.

Second, the Shultz scenario took account of, but was insufficiently attuned to, constraints on Israel's cabinet as a result of elections coming at the end of the year. The Likud government led by Prime Minister Yitzhak Shamir was unwilling to contemplate negotiations during a preelection period in which it would be punished for making too many compromises or not enough, depending on the character of the US and Arab proposals. In addition, Shamir was locked in a tight struggle for control of the right-wing Likud movement, and spectators such as Ariel Sharon would be encouraged to challenge the prime minister if he were perceived to be leaning toward moderate positions. Moreover, months of rock throwing by Palestinian youths, emboldened by the international outcry against toughened Israeli military measures, with the corresponding increase in Jewish casualties, had made the majority of the state's electorate more strident.[66]

Finally, the Palestinians in the camps of Gaza and in the villages dotting the West Bank and Galilee were convinced that their cause would grow in intensity and scope should they accelerate their rioting. Even the April murder of Khalil Al-Wazir, Arafat's second in command and the coordinator of PLO activities in the territories, seemed to stimulate a sense of purpose and trial ahead for the chanters of retribution. Whatever the practical consequences of the assassination, Jordan's role in the fortunes of the West Bank had become less influential. Shultz's plan, based as it was on arranging an international meeting of Jordanian, Palestinian, and Israeli delegations, had been overtaken by events.

George Bush may find final outcomes offered by others—Henry Kissinger, Jimmy Carter, or Ronald Reagan—unsuited for slowing up the events on the ground that still give Middle East peace less chance than before. He might see, though, that parts of peace plans or newer proposals brought by the parties would be a help toward bargaining now made exceedingly difficult as a result of the intifada, and further complicated by the new Gulf conflict. President Bush should reexamine his style, temperament, roots, and philosophy of history before embarking on a mediation that could place his presidency in some jeopardy at home.

When George Bush has reconciled his talents and traits with the uncertainties that accompany the making of Middle East peace, he may come away wondering how previous US negotiators managed to stave off renewed armed hostilities for over a decade while promoting limited agreements and a single treaty for ending war between two of the parties. He might be reminded that Henry Kissinger's performance depended on an understanding of how to observe the limits inherent in state behavior. He should remember, however, that Jimmy Carter's and Ronald Reagan's care in applying egalitarianism was responsible for the Camp David Accords and the hospitality tendered US mediation since. President Bush may also want to recall that it was flexibility and pragmatism that accounted for Carter and Reagan administration triumphs in the least promising of circumstances.

The way toward influencing how to unstick the Middle East peace process, therefore, could be for George Bush to look on Israel's holding elections on the West Bank as being as controversial a matter inside the Jewish state as it has been for Palestinians, both within the territories and outside. Kissinger's preference for accepting national limits, moreover, would have to be coupled with some practical considerations about how to negotiate. An international forum, favored by Carter and opposed by Kissinger, may not fit with bargaining that places less emphasis on the skills of a negotiator and more on whether decisions at the table mesh with fundamentalist assertiveness at home. Bush thus will need to demonstrate adroitness in fielding talks—formal or informal, face-to-face meetings or proximity discussions—as well as in what manner to worry about issues— one at a time or in packages. Whatever the choice, the peoples of the Middle East will profit if the Bush government keeps a keen eye on delivering a peace based on the values it shares with many in the Middle East: equal rights to live without fear of retribution, to have one's voice heard, and to be able to enter into the fruits of life that a society must offer.

US PERSPECTIVES ON FUNDAMENTALISM

Since pragmatic-minded US leaders, former Presidents Carter and Reagan, have made populism and equality easier to fathom, and George Bush stands ready to give ethically bound moves a chance to work, then fundamentalism as a phenomenon for the United States and the Middle East may have gained in importance. How are we to understand fundamentalism? The concept comes out of the experiences of the evangelical movement in the United States following Prohibition. When breakaway elements in mainline Protestantism needed to express their opposition to changes in the fundamentals or traditions of true religious faith, they did so militantly.

Prior to World War II, US citizens were traumatized by the issues of the Scopes trial and the threat posed there to the concept of modernism. Since the war's end, fundamentalism as an active church movement has almost disappeared, split apart by denominational stress and doctrinal disagreements with larger and more mainstream Protestant groups.[67] The conservative trend that fundamentalism was popularly associated with, however, has been taken over by the more socially and politically acceptable evangelicals.

Evangelicalism was legitimated in the Cold War climate of the 1950s when evangelists performed differently from fundamentalists: They were less spiritually pure, more willing to work for change from within the Christian church, and looked for members among secularists and liberals as well as conservative churchgoers. Evangelicals sought to achieve harmony and cooperation within Christendom instead of the separatism that characterized fundamentalists.[68] Evangelicals, as a result, drew their strength from the urbanized metropolitan centers across the country instead of the southern and midwestern population that characterized the fundamentalists' narrow rural constituency.[69]

A skillful and populist image, promoted by the campus appearances and radio ministry of Billy Graham, the anti-Communist crusades of Billy Hargis, and those who were to argue against the Vietnam War and segregation,[70] enabled religion and politics to mix more easily in the amoral climate of the post-1960s. And the millions of middle-aged people, who were responding to the ills of drugs and a freer society, may have been more open to evangelicalism as they elevated born-again Christian Jimmy Carter to the presidency in 1976 and contributed to the primary victories of Pat Robertson in 1988. Along the way the "tel-evangelists"—such as Jerry Falwell, Jimmy Swaggart, and Jim Bakker—aided by shrewd packaging, touched a nation that momentarily had lost its moral address. Disclosures of personal immorality and corruption that confounded the ministries of Swaggart and Bakker nevertheless came at the start of a downward slope in the appeal of evangelicalism and led many to rethink the proper place of religion in US society.[71]

Whatever improvements evangelicals may be able to make in their image, deep differences exist in the United States and the Middle East about how conservative religion is regarded. Evangelicalism represents a rich moral order for those wishing its embrace. But evangelicals travel in a pluralistic culture, and the United States withholds sanction for any individual faith or its mores. Moreover, a tradition of ecumenism in the United States has led many evangelists toward a greater degree of hospitality to fellow Protestants and to members of other faiths. The better-educated evangelicals—seminarians and college students—are questioning their movement's theology on such traditional subjects as biblical inerrancy, the integrity of the gospel, and salvation solely through the teachings of Christ.[72] Doubt has also arisen over orthodoxy relating to family practice, social issues, and political disposition, as these younger members confront the diversity of present-day US society.[73]

Some evangelicals want to use political action to further their goal of a moralistic universe. Their attempt to do so, however, occurs within the political system, especially now that boundaries have eroded among religious conservatives and secularists, and evangelicals are in the midst of redefining their orthodoxy.[74] The activists in the movement have been suspicious of communism's reach and of the attraction of secular humanism. They react positively to the moral majority and remain politically conservative on major issues of the day. But as a whole, evangelicals are content to have the government speak for them on affairs of state, the economy, education, and other public matters.[75] Religious conservatives may be willing to engage the forces of modernism on issues of family, sexuality, and the private sphere generally. But even where they have taken their strongest stands—abortion, women's rights, and homosexuality—evangelicals have exhibited nonextremist, tolerant behavior.[76]

Consequently, what some have called an "ethic of civility" governs the conduct of a majority in the evangelical movement.[77] Civic culture in the United States requires a discourse in which religious beliefs and political convictions are shared, but with a sensitivity to taste and approved norms. Society in the United States does not condone belligerent obsessive behavior. Therefore, religious groups are circumscribed in their roles and expected to perform tactfully, keeping public and private spheres separate. The moral majority's efforts to politicize morality have been considered by many evangelicals and others within the nonevangelist population as unbecoming this ethic of civility.[78]

Evangelicals are somewhat embarrassed by the moral majority's breach of civil norms. And they are offended by secularists' perceptions that conservative religion is radicalist and fanatic, ready to use unprincipled measures to achieve desired goals. Thus they search for ways in which to defeat unfair labeling and charges of violating the spirit and substance of church-state separation.[79]

The US fundamentalist perspective shares with the Middle East a set of common features: (1) a scriptural- or oral-based transcendental message of truth conveyed by a charismatic or prophet; (2) a group of the chosen who believe because they are deemed to be both good and clean; (3) an enemy who is sinister, evil, faithless, and reactionary; (4) a promised land—a veritable "heaven on earth;" and (5) a commitment to radical conversion, revivalism, and militant separatism.[80] Converting the godless means a complete transformation from a previous set of beliefs to a fundamentalist worldview. Reviving institutionalized tradition requires a strategy for restoring what once was by bringing back old vitality. And militant separatism calls for a rhetoric of external warfare against all comers, thereby ensuring that purity can never be compromised. Separation from the conventional protects the identity of true believers and conveys strength.[81]

The quality and intensity of fundamentalism may be gathered by how determined and how involved its members are—whether both leaders and followers are so committed that they will die for their cause. Martyrdom or heroic self-sacrifice is the ultimate test of an extremist, fundamentalist ethic. Therefore a representative description of fundamentalism may be the following: a distinctly extreme type of militant religious conservatism that courts separatism, growing out of a radical reaction to ideological and institutional changes perceived to be in profound opposition to clear and dogmatic fundamentals of the truth.[82] How has this phenomenon manifested itself in three crucial areas of the Middle East—Iran, Israel, and the West Bank?

Fundamentalism: Middle Eastern Values and US Perspectives

It is safe to assume that the appeal of fundamentalism in Iran will survive Khomeini's death,[1] and it is no less correct to believe that religious conservatism will become the basis for Israeli governance or that Islamicism can be an attractive alternative to PLO influence among Palestinians on the West Bank. The United States has spent nearly a decade trying to limit the spread of fundamentalism in the Gulf and may be quite unprepared for its growth in the Levant. What will be the character and likely status of fundamentalism in a post-Khomeini regime, within Israel, and under an increasingly non–PLO-led West Bank Palestinian movement? And can the depth of fundamentalist appeal thus far recorded help the United States understand that it needs to convert a conventional wisdom approach in the Middle East to a new wisdom?

THE MEANING OF KHOMEINI TO IRAN

When Ayatollah Ruhollah Khomeini is discussed in the West, it is largely within the context of a political legacy that spawned brutal repression in Iran and terrorism abroad.[2] Iranians, however, have been especially grateful that the Imam restored tradition and honor to their society. They welcomed Khomeini's call for removing foreign influence, they understood his commitment to recapturing religious values, and they were tolerant of his effort to bring Iraq to heel after that country's 1980 invasion of Iranian soil, despite the costs of massive casualties, economic disruption, and social unrest.[3]

The disparity of impressions concerning what Khomeini has wrought continues to be at the core of Western disbelief in the staying power of Islamic fundamentalism. Although any assessment of Iran's future course is problematic, the cohesion of a successor regime, its probable worldview, and its style of leadership will undoubtedly emerge from the dynamic bequeathed by Khomeini. His meaning to Iran, therefore, could determine the longevity that Islamic fundamentalism may have both within and without Iran.

Khomeini's sense of timing, his perception of Iran's ruinous past, and the depth of his commitment to a future based on Islamic purity combined to animate a series of tactical moves intended to bring about a thorough revolution: He concentrated on developing a constitution dedicated to Islamic principles; chose a president and new parliament, trusting both to rule according to Islamic law; offered measures designed to provide equity for a generous portion of the population; and even announced his choice of successor in hopes of curbing factionalism at the time of his death. Yet, he was unable to assure that his designated successor would reach jurisconsult status—a perch from which Khomeini had ably pressed for absolute power—or follow a purist approach to life after his demise.[4]

Khomeini's extraordinary hold on his people, however, was not simply a function of steady gains for society, the lure of economic justice, or grand military success, although the government has made claims—however dubious—in all these areas.[5] Rather, the force of his personality and the compelling nature of his message aroused the populace and helped secure widespread approval for fundamentalist solutions, despite the pain of war and the corresponding decline in productivity.

Khomeini's charisma rested upon the emotive force of a moral injunction—that each person should conduct his life according to an ethical code, aspiring to a higher morality (he was particularly critical of Mohammad Reza's venality during the shah's final days in power). Khomeini's focus on the importance of values as a demonstration of national will grew out of his teachings at Qom and more than a decade of exile in Najaf, Iraq. He is remembered in both locales for his interest in and lectures regarding Erfan or mystical philosophy.[6]

Erfan—sharing much with Sufism—bases its millenarian outlook on the apprehension of God. The practitioners of Erfan strongly believe that God is immanent and that his face can be seen in each individual. Collapsing eschatological doctrine in this manner requires the mystic to adopt ascetic habits, such as nightly prayer, a vow of poverty, and fasting. The mystical philosopher, a master of Erfan, besides preparing his students for the pitfalls of a materialist existence, also instills a sense of fearlessness about the external world and its habit of procuring political power.[7]

The scale of casualties suffered by Iran's population as a result of excesses by the shah's ubiquitous security forces enabled Khomeini to plumb issues central to the followers of Erfan as well as important to the families and friends of those already martyred. Khomeini was the legatee of a three-generation teaching tradition of providing assistance to those who sought mystical salvation. He had been taught by the student of a disciple of Jamal ad-Din, a leading mystic of the nineteenth century.[8] But in 1978–1979, Khomeini found himself at the center of opposition, first to the shah's corrupt rule, then to the court's having turned Iranian society into a replica of the West. Both themes were welcome to mystics, the disenchanted, and nationalists alike.[9] The nationalists could recall earlier admonitions spoken by intellectuals such as Al-e-Ahamad, who warned of submitting to "Euromania" or "Westoxication"—terms used to denote the replacement of Persian values with Western ones.[10]

Khomeini was later to retreat from a nationalist pose, but he used the power of the anti-Western, anticolonial metaphor as a basis for engineering his own universalistic and strictly Islamic revolution.[11] Some were struck by his reluctance to present antishah themes in Iranian terms; others were puzzled by his desire to draft a constitution that did not ensure that the presidency was held by a Persian.[12]

Although he may have temporized with respect to Iranian symbols, Khomeini was clear about what transcendental factors ought to be present in his revolution: He created Islamic courts; he built a revolutionary army (the Pasdaran); he imposed a hierarchal domain on both politics and religion, reserving for himself the position of jurisconsult—*velayat-e faqih*—while appointing an assembly of experts to confirm his selection of a successor.[13]

Khomeini's explanation of *velayat-e faqih* (guidance of the learned) was broader than traditional Shiite doctrine called for and therefore troubling to many in the clerical establishment. He extended the concept to political matters, whereas historically *faqih* merely referred to the exercise of jurisprudence in areas relating to the property of the victimized, the awarding of religious endowments, the advancement of theological education, or the enforcement of social mores. However, during a 1971 lecture series on the value of Islamic government, Khomeini offered a definition of state authority that depended on the guidance of either an individual jurisprudent or a collective composed of several senior clerics. Nevertheless, when it came time to rule, Khomeini chose to stand alone, thereby becoming unpopular among his peers and running counter to Islam's sacred principle of consultation (*shura*).[14]

But Khomeini's linkage of religious and political matters—said to have been in the interest of assuring internal order—helped prepare the public for claims of his being presumptive heir to the Hidden Imam. He was able to strengthen that image by remaining above the rough-and-tumble of daily politics, husbanding his role carefully and intervening only at the final hour when it appeared that chaos would otherwise ensue. He was truly the arbiter of national policy, balancing left and right, avoiding the extremes of both sides, and speaking a language pleasing to the masses.[15]

His themes of distress and deprivation resonated most among the poorest elements of society. Khomeini played on the martyrdom of Ali and Husayn, around which Shiism is built, to remind his audiences of the sacrifices still necessary to complete the revolution. Thus, Khomeini was able to inspire loyalty and support for policies normally deemed too controversial. Among the most celebrated issues that had been long deferred by Khomeini were how to effect peace with Iraq while continuing to assist revolutionary Muslim regimes in Lebanon and elsewhere; whether to improve relations with Arab states—chiefly Saudi Arabia and Kuwait—as well as the United States or the Soviet Union; when to establish limits on prices, food, trade, and land distribution; and where to cut private wealth and promote public sector development.[16]

Khomeini's instincts for touching the lives of ordinary Iranian citizens and for being able to speak directly to their natural concerns sprang from his preoccupation with a regenerative future. His was a world in which revitalization would occur through journeys to God. He therefore chose a successor, Ayatollah Husayn Ali Montazeri, who he believed was committed to religion and the place it ought to have in the affairs of the common man. Montezari had been the leader of Friday prayers, first in Qom, then at Tehran. He had been a loyal, sometimes indefatigable, proponent of much that Khomeini spoke for regarding political activism, and he saw politics and religion as a unitary phenomenon. Yet, he was less disciplined on social matters, favoring private initiatives, particularly in the realm of land distribution and trade implementation. And when he publicly urged the government to climb down from a program of repression and arbitrariness against its citizens, Khomeini removed Montezari from the post of presumptive heir.[17]

IRAN UNDER KHOMEINI'S SUCCESSORS

Khomeini's death, nevertheless, focused greatest attention on the problems of the present. Foremost among the matters being scrutinized is how to pursue the revolution while promoting equity at home and association abroad.[18] Khomeini was able to land on each side of almost any issue because of his enormous reputation in the nation. His successors, individually as well as collectively, have not—and possibly cannot—achieve the same esteem,[19] but neither are they able merely to stand aside and allow the situation in the country to deteriorate.

Hojjat al-Islam Ali Akbar Hashemi Rafsanjani, three-term speaker of the parliament and newly elected president, is said to be pragmatic, moderate, and resourceful, but he is inadequate as a direct replacement for Khomeini. Although he is touted as a worthy successor in temporal matters, Rafsanjani has little or no standing in the well of the puritanical. He is a minor cleric without the training, position, or background to give promise of his holding together the religious fabric of society. Moreover, Rafsanjani's support for public sector intervention—endorsed during the 1988 parliamentary elections—came under broad attack from the same technical elite that the government expects to help resolve the nation's economic problems; the middle-class technocrat and the bazaar merchant share an urgent need to protect and advance private investment.[20]

The issue of *faqih* and Khomeini's inability to confer his position on anyone else was especially comforting for the older generation of clerics. Those ayatollahs, more prominent than is Rafsanjani, opposed his using the title of jurisconsult and declared the position vacant until such time as the

Hidden Imam returns from occultation. Moreover, since Rafsanjani himself, or any other of Khomeini's advisers, were unnamed as jurisconsult, the new president accepted their decision.[21]

Separating politics from religion will also impinge on alienation themes, once so important to Khomeini. Efforts under way to cure the diseased economy, whether by private or public means, will necessarily rely upon strengthened ties with the West and moderate states of the region. The passion and excitement that Khomeini drew upon to whip up popular indignation and animus against the "oppressors"—the United States, the West, and Iraq—have been set aside by a government now intent on waging peace and securing commercial advantage.[22]

A post-Khomeini government, therefore, formed from collective rule, with a division of responsibilities, may be capable of producing a greater democratic and populist spirit in Iran.[23] This could mean that fundamentalism will be demystified and less anti-imperialist. This style of operation, moreover, would permit the flowering of an already rich and vigorous Persian culture. The nature of fundamentalism in Iran might at last be able to escape its negative reputation—an image cultivated by Khomeini for more than a decade.

This rather pristine and optimistic portrait of Iran, however, could give way to tougher, less pragmatic leadership that would be required to revive the threat of Western interventionism in order to assure even the most tenuous hold on power. In that event, a populace reeling from war and economic dislocation can be expected to resist additional suffering by moving against leaden leaders. Whatever the outcome, the struggle will be fought out within the context of a liberalizing trend in fundamentalism inside post-Khomeini Iran.[24]

THE NATURE OF JEWISH FUNDAMENTALISM IN ISRAEL

A more moderate approach to fundamentalism on the part of Iran's leaders is not likely to be matched by Israel, as the government there shares in the territorial objectives of an influential body of messianic-nationalists known as Gush Emunim (Bloc of the Faithful). The Gush Emunim was given impetus in the afterglow of the 1967 war but was not officially formed until 1974, following the Yom Kippur war. Its organizational ethos was based on secrecy, especially while the group was being challenged to build a parliamentary constituency for exercising Jewish sovereignty over the whole of "Judea and Samaria"—the West Bank and Gaza.[25] However, despite earlier Israeli cabinet approval of the Gush Emunim's political agenda, no government—including the latest one, framed at the midpoint of 1990—has been impressed by the movement's theological premises.

Gush Emunim's leaders derive their ideology from the teachings of rabbis Abraham Isaac Kook and Tsvi Yehuda Kook. The elder Kook was appointed chief rabbi by the British soon after they assumed responsibility for mandated Palestine in the wake of World War I; his son Tsvi Yehuda managed, by the mid-1960s, to revive a religious center for learning that had languished for nearly thirty years.[26] Both rabbis drew their inspiration from Kabbalistic mysticism—a Jewish liturgical tradition dating from the second century.

The ancient mystical practice of Kabbalism involved two separate paths: Theosophic Kabbalism, which emphasized detailed scriptural study of the Torah and Talmud; and Ecstatic Kabbalism, which specified the recitation of sacred hymns and special names to honor and bring forth a mental image of the divinity.[27] Ecstatic Kabbalism, which failed to come into its own until the thirteenth century, was the more dangerous of the two and was performed ritually only by the priestly elite of the Second Temple period.[28] Theosophic Kabbalism was a more intellectual and acceptable method of reaching a spiritual vision of the deity and achieved greater popular appeal. Crucially, it carried neither the stain of magic nor the presumption of exclusionism that was central to the ecstatic type. Moreover, it aimed at restoring divine harmony—disrupted by the sin of Adam—through the performance of good deeds.[29]

Each of the Kooks was to exhort his followers to travel the path of Kabbalism toward redemption, but differences in generation and temperament, and the challenge to Jewish existence, conditioned their separate approaches to salvation. Abraham Isaac Kook belonged to an era that regarded Jewish experience as a model for others to imitate; he therefore hoped that Jewish redemptionism would become but a prelude to deliverance for all mankind. As a result, the elder rabbi was reminded that the faithless—those resisting the mandate of the Torah—could take part in a Jewish reawakening. He believed in a concept of holiness that was latent, coming from within. He thus called upon all Jews, observant and nonobservant alike, to settle the land of Israel and defend Jewish sovereignty over it. Rabbi Kook was convinced that redemption required an avoidance of compromise so as not to interrupt the messianic impulse of satisfying the commandment of God.[30]

Tsvi Yehuda Kook took issue with his father's desire for religious and nonreligious Jews to cooperate. He had witnessed the Holocaust and Zionism's struggle to achieve statehood for Israel; Abraham Isaac Kook had died in 1935, before the Nazi onslaught on Jewish life. Moreover, Tzvi Yehuda saw the process of securing redemption for Jews occurring in several stages, each tied to seminal changes in the landscape of the Middle East.[31]

The messianic era, according to the younger Kook, had begun with Jewish independence and the creation of the State of Israel, an event marked by physical danger for Jews residing in the diaspora. A second step in the move to redeem a Jewish future would be to join the people with their promised land, Judea and Samaria. The revival of a bond between Jews and the land foretold in the Bible was already under way. The third and final

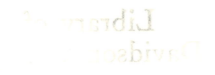

fulfillment would come when the Jewish people, reunited with the land, would observe God's commandments, thereby placing themselves in a position to receive the Messiah and final redemption.[32]

Both Kooks wrapped their messages in alternate forms of Theosophic and Ecstatic Kabbalism, ranging from emanations of the Torah to preparations for psychic phenomena borne by charismatics in direct touch with the divine spirit. The fact that theosophy was supposed to benefit the deity, whereas ecstasy shored up the mystic alone, did not seem to bother the younger Kook as he went about translating his father's theoretical formulations into a pragmatic political agenda devoted to retention of biblical lands.[33]

Tsvi Yehuda Kook was quick to take advantage of incidents attributed to his mysticism as he sought to widen public approval for resettlement in Judea and Samaria. His forecast of the extent to which Israel's military would be victorious in 1967, as well as the popular but apocryphal story concerning Menachem Begin's kneeling before him after selection as prime minister in 1977, were welcome images through which to gain sympathy from an otherwise skeptical audience.[34] In fact, a few conversions were obtained among those normally opposed to mystics and at a time when signs of general acceptance for territorial compromise were on the increase. But the most impressive support for values consistent with redemption—particularly after the younger Kook's death in 1982—came from a younger generation of biblical scholars traditionally found within Zionism's religious subculture.

Nearly a third of Israel's educated adolescents attend the state-supported religious school system. The Mizrahi, as it is known, has given rise to a steady stream of recruits for Gush Emunim in the decade after the organization's formation. These high school–age Talmud-Torah students are socialized through shared military service and national land resettlement experience, and they renewed Yeshiva training prior to taking up more worldly activity. The schools are modeled after elite boarding academies, and their graduates—or "Knitted Skullcaps," as they were called—are the core support for an expanding number of Jewish settlements on the West Bank as well as a crucial political strength for parties springing up after 1981 on the far Right and dedicated to retaining all the Land of Israel in perpetuity.[35]

Politicization of the fundamentalist movement began with Menachem Begin's experiment in Palestinian autonomy following Camp David. Gush Emunim activists, especially those seminarians grouped around Tsvi Yehuda Kook, were fearful that uprooting Jewish residents, such as had occurred at Elon Moreh in 1979 and the Sinai town of Yamit in 1982,[36] would become commonplace. Their leaders broke with Begin's Likud party and, in the 1981 parliamentary election, fielded a political grouping composed of both religious and nonreligious territorial nationalists. Tehiya, as it came to be titled, was neither officially endorsed nor supported by Gush Emunim, but the new organization's close identification with the fundamentalists was widely known.[37] Tehiya, led by a secular ultranationalist who had received the younger Rabbi Kook's blessing, polled well in its first public outing and placed three deputies in the 1981 Knesset.[38] The ultra–right-wing party increased its representation to five members three years later,[39] but in the 1988 contest returned to its earliest form, garnering three mandates.[40]

A deadlock in the 1984 formation of Israel's government, with corresponding paralysis in improving Jewish West Bank settlement, spawned extremist solutions as a legitimating context in which to realize messianic goals. Fringe politicians, such as Meir Kahane (head of the Jewish Defense League), found a simple but effective message to transmit during the election campaign: Was the land theirs (the Arabs) or ours (the Jews)?[41] The overwhelmingly positive response to Kahane's question enabled the violence that had accompanied Jewish vigilantism to attain a more mainstream acceptance, particularly when Gush Emunim's appeal had scattered to newer political groups of the far right, religious and nonreligious. Jewish terrorists carried out a number of attacks directed against persons and property, including spectacular efforts such as the foiled bombing of five Arab buses and an attempt to blow up the famed al-Aqsa Mosque and Dome of the Rock.[42] Gush Emunim leaders lobbied hard and successfully for the commuted sentences that were eventually handed down to many of the two dozen zealots who belonged to their movement.[43] Meanwhile, the principal fundamentalist organization searched for ways to reconcile elite differences on how more smoothly to manage retention of the land ordained by God and believed to be essential for the redemption of the Jewish people.

JEWISH FUNDAMENTALISM'S CONFRONTATION WITH THE FUTURE

Although Gush Emunim members continue to quarrel over how to manipulate theological constructions of reality, they have refused to be confounded by a political agenda subject to the vicissitudes of the intifada as well as Israel's 1988 election contest. The sense of extraordinary struggle over leadership—intensified by Tsvi Yehuda Kook's untimely death—or unusual acrimony over how to advance the redemption process was absent during moments when the movement chose to confront critical issues such as land, peace, relations with Palestinians, and democracy.

Fundamentalists as a whole have long regarded the land as a central element in their quest to prepare the Jewish people for redemption. The intimate relationship among land, population, and the divinity has been the subject of several tracts, essays, and lectures given special honor by the movement. The younger Kook, just prior to his death, noted that the land was "chosen even before the people" and that together they constituted "divine unity, joined . . . at the creation of the world and the creation of history."[44] Other nationalities may have believed land to be important to their destiny (e.g., the US pioneer push westward), but according to this view no people other than Jews were intended to see these ties as ordained by God. Moreover, Gush Emunim leaders hastened to add that because territorial questions were filled with such cosmic significance—promoting God's covenant with his people—the prospect of trading land for peace could only be regarded as unthinkable. The entire Land of Israel, not a portion of it, therefore has been marked by the fundamentalists as the Promised Land and may not be divided or subdivided without disregarding the transcendental will of God.[45]

More extreme members of the fundamentalist movement also challenged the notion that the Land of Israel could be confined to existing borders of the Jewish state. Those Israelis, including important leaders of Tehiya, envisioned boundaries of the Promised Land to include present-day Iraq, Syria, Jordan, and Egypt. A more sobering assessment of the biblically important territory would provide for stretches east and west of the Jordan River. However, many of the faithful in the movement could be satisfied with an irreducibly minimum control of the area between the Jordan and Mediterranean or the West Bank and Gaza, thereby fulfilling the purposes of Zionism.[46]

An even smaller number among fundamentalists, shattered by the Lebanese experience, believe that prospects for peace and the saving of Jewish lives make it worthwhile to delay extending rule over the territories. But, although this viewpoint retains the support of some prominent members of present and former governments, postponing Israeli sovereignty over the West Bank lands—central to the Camp David formula—or ceding modest portions of the disputed territory has been outside the pale of serious advocacy.

A more widely held opinion within fundamentalism has relied upon peace as a temporary expedient in order to solidify Israeli power. The deep and everlasting enmity between Israel and its neighbors—as understood by a growing majority within Gush Emunim—ensures that peace will be maintained alone through Israeli military success, which Begin had attempted but failed to achieve in Lebanon during 1982–1983.[47] On the other hand, according to this view, permanent or "real" peace would come about only as a result of reaching the messianic age. Meanwhile, wars will likely persist until either the Arab world is subdued by superior arms or transformed through acculturation.[48]

Others in the fundamentalist camp have theorized, en route to redemption, that informal instruments as well as limited proposals should be floated as a means of inducing calm. Ariel Sharon's plan for territorial contiguity with a Maronite-run Lebanon or his labeling Jordan a rightful Palestinian state falls into this category; the influential Moshe Levinger has also proposed de facto arrangements with Syria to pacify the common border.[49]

Fundamentalists have persuaded themselves that interim solutions designed on the basis of Western humanism are not only bound to fail but could retard ultimate salvation.[50] Negotiations could smooth the way toward redemption, but they, too, would be offered within a context that carried acceptance of traditional law, thereby prompting the spirit of moral change with a correspondingly better opportunity for improved Arab-Israeli relationships.[51]

Nevertheless, fundamentalist ideas were to be most powerfully felt in regard to how Jews sought to treat Palestinians in the land they had come to share. Israelis used to a history of joint occupation were committed to avoiding the transfer of Arabs from the territories, but the prevention of future violence would depend on strict Jewish enforcement of security laws, the banning of sloganeering or other inflammatory political activity, closure or direct supervision of Arab higher educational institutions, and minimizing contact between the two opposing groups of West Bank residents.[52]

Palestinian-instigated bloodshed resulting in deaths of Jews justified, according to every fundamentalist account, collective punishment against refugee camps and Arab extended families. And in certain cases where repeated offenses occurred—stone throwing or bus burnings, for example—Israeli authorities were expected to deport the offenders.[53] Should government officials take even harsher measures, it might discourage renewed efforts by squads of Jewish citizens to pursue vigilantism and terrorism against selected Palestinian targets. However, the removal of Meir Kahane from the 1988 ballot for operating a party dedicated to racism[54] seemed actually to do little to quell rising sentiment among fundamentalists for a policy of expelling Israel's Palestinian population.

The Israeli electorate's increasing attraction to Palestinian expulsion raises disturbing questions about the future of democracy in the Jewish state. Fundamentalists have already passed on the virtue of majoritarianism by their strong opposition to jailing Jewish terrorists held responsible for conspiring to commit murder. Crucially, some within Gush Emunim have argued that democratic trends run counter to Jewish tradition and law.[55] Others are prepared to defer settling the issue until redemption arrives. These same procrastinators, however, see the leftists among Zionism as harming the structure of Judaism with their spasmodic approach to supporting the rights of Palestinians.[56] Jews living in the diaspora are also criticized for courting moderate Arabs, who fundamentalists say favor selective justice.[57]

The events of the 1988 political calendar—beginning with the intifada and concluding with Israel's double burden of an inconclusive election and Yassir Arafat's becoming a moderate—exerted a decisive influence on fundamentalist outcomes, despite Gush Emunim's preferring to avoid such a result. The spontaneous, youth-led Palestinian uprising on the West Bank has reawakened Israeli society to the awful prospects that, according to Gush Emunim, accompany efforts to revive Arab-Israeli contacts.[58] Moreover, although Israeli security officials could take a certain comfort in their ability to counter or punish acts of violence committed by known PLO activists—especially by those belonging to elements easily penetrated by the military—the impulsive nature of terroristic acts now directed against Jewish citizens by relative unknowns has required countermeasures usually associated with the conduct of a full police state.[59] Revolutionaries, after all—particularly those acting out of desperation—rarely know limits to their attempts to change the landscape.

The more rabid fundamentalists, quite naturally, welcomed the intifada and Arafat's newfound magnanimity about Israeli recognition. These overzealous representatives readily believed that events, taken together, signaled an imminent appearance of the Messiah, and although messianists traditionally have been concerned with "forcing the end"—taking deliverance into their own hands—this "age of glory" is supposed to be ushered in by a period of destruction.[60] For many in Gush Emunim, Israel's five wars constitute the apocalyptic era. Fundamentalists regard the 1967 war, especially, as a modern-day symbol of the biblical conflict of Gog and Magog (after which the Promised Land was restored to Jewish control)[61] and a sign of the dawn of the messianic age. When coupled with Arafat's episodic handling of UN Resolution 242, the intifada has become for Gush Emunim radicals the equivalent of apocalypse.

Whether or not Israel's fanatics succeed in their aims, the Jewish state's haphazard formation of a government in mid-1990 offered fundamentalists a golden opportunity. Making an Israeli cabinet has always been a dicey matter, and the selection of a right-leaning governing coalition in 1990 means that Israel's religious minority enjoys the largest influence imaginable. Zionist and non-Zionist religious parties now make up a full 15 percent of the Knesset.[62]

Religious non-Zionists and the Gush Emunim have disagreed in the past over how to reconcile the obligation to serve in the military with daily practice of prayer and study, as well as over questions of land resettlement and development of separate educational and social institutions. Although differences have not been profound, they have been conspicuous.[63] Any uneasiness felt could certainly be remedied by regarding future contests over the Land of Israel and its devolution to a life of sanctimony as falling within the terms of a movement toward salvation. The other worldiness factor found in non-Zionist ultrareligious existence, moreover, enables the setting of an agreed agenda with the fundamentalists around such shared objectives as constructing an orthodox community in the center of the West Bank, dismantling Muslim shrines on the Temple Mount, or building a third Jewish synagogue on the same site[64] (or possibly both of these latter two).

Although the creation of a third Jewish commonwealth is an unlikely event in the near term, a national dialogue on its merits would have a corrosive effect on the stability of the Middle East peace process as well as ruin prospects for latent tendencies that may exist toward liberalizing Israel's society.[65] The impetus to open the debate, however, can be expected to receive encouragement from the strength achieved by a tactical political alliance of Gush Emunim sympathizers and the religious community of Zionists and non-Zionists, who will count on their renewed ability to marshal a Knesset majority for discussion. Whatever may result, fundamentalism has become so integral to Israel's political culture that it is likely to be a powerful force in shaping the Jewish state's national will in the coming decade.

THE PROMISE OF FUNDAMENTALISM ON THE WEST BANK AND GAZA

Whereas Israelis and Iranians seek ways of becoming accustomed to new forms of fundamentalism, Palestinians in the West Bank and Gaza turn to Islam as the surest path toward a more tolerable existence. The work of diplomats to ease Palestinian pain, as well as the question of whether to establish one, two, or three states west of the Jordan River, no longer holds strong appeal for West Bankers and Gazans. A hazardous two decades has convinced most Palestinians that the censure of the international community, pan-Arabist gestures, or pressures instigated from outside the territories by nationalists do not produce meaningful results when opposed by intimidation and physical abuse at the hands of Israelis. Moreover, the PLO and its steadfast supporters among the urban elite and old-line landowning politicians, as well as newer, pragmatic professionals, have been largely content to issue an occasional threat, adopt public stands of indignation, and privately accept accommodation with Israeli security officials.[66] Meanwhile, a lesser cast of youths, women, shopkeepers, and rural poor vent their anger and frustrated hopelessness.[67] The intifada arose partly from insensitivities exhibited by the PLO, Jordan, and other Arab players toward disadvantaged groups of Palestinians as well as from Israeli-inflicted injuries.

The stone throwers and the hurlers of Molotov cocktails, who at first aimed at Israeli riot forces in Gaza during December 1987, were a special kind of Palestinian youth. They were high-schoolers who had been abandoned to a fate of permanent deprivation, the result of unexpected change within the broader regional economic structure.[68] Palestinians who aspired to a higher education soon found that attending university—itself an opportunity disappearing from the West Bank—did little to guarantee employment in Jordan, the Gulf states, or Israel. Sharp declines in revenues from falling oil prices led Gulf countries to retrench their hiring of foreign labor at home and subsidization of employment in Jordan.[69] Corresponding losses in job opportunities in neighboring Arab states forced the upwardly mobile Palestinian to fall back on the prospect of finding suitable work in Israel, but the Jewish state sought an Arab work force only in the construction trades, industry, and the service sector.[70] University-educated Palestinians found blue-collar jobs objectionable. Even without such reservations, Palestinians would have been working in an Israeli economy where real wages barely equaled price rises and in some cases fell below them.

Highly educated Palestinians, deterred by a complicated Middle East job market, therefore found it more desirable to emigrate to the United States, Latin America, or Europe.[71] When added to the 50 percent female and one-third male population that has left the West Bank since 1967,[72] this latest exodus opened up a serious void in the stock of potential Palestinian leaders. Single women in their late twenties—abandoned by heavy emigration or else regarded by bachelors at home as an unwelcome financial burden—soon joined with adolescent stone throwers and moved into the vacuum created by an absent male stewardship.[73]

Disaffected women and secondary students, however, are merely the tip of a mass-based institutional network that includes labor union and university committee members. The first months of the intifada saw the formation of a United National Command to meld together elements of these populist groups. The command was able to draw in an especially diffuse representation that extended across ideologies from Marxists to Islamicists.[74] The PLO, though, did not become integral to the command structure until the planners of the uprising were well into seizing the initiative inside the territories.[75]

Yassir Arafat's personal popularity remained high on the West Bank and Gaza, but the PLO's reputation was sullied by its being seen as more devoted to the intricacies of international diplomacy and less to using armed struggle for liberating the territories.[76] The military capability of the organization that spoke for all Palestinians was shredded during Israel's 1982 Lebanese invasion. Since that time, Arafat has attempted to rebuild his forces and renew armed strikes against Israel from the outside. Except for an infrequent success, neither Fatah nor any of the more radical elements within the umbrella organization have been able to erode public confidence in the Israeli government's protective ability.[77] Moreover, the PLO has not aimed its founding of social service institutions—day care centers, workers' alliances, schools—at the development of independent, indigenous leadership.[78] Instead, Arafat's lieutenants hoped by these acts to demonstrate to their Jordan-backed rivals a plausible alternative. The youths, women, and tradesmen on the West Bank and Gaza thereby received the unmistakable signal that the PLO was only marginally concerned about altering Israel's disposition of the territories but did feel a substantial interest in maintaining sole political control of the Palestinian movement.[79]

The skepticism that PLO acts evoked in those taking part in the intifada pushed many Palestinians toward Islam. Over half the population in the West Bank was raised in villages where Islamic prayer, fasting, and dress were customary. Some Palestinians shrugged off their traditional roots when attending college or journeying to look for employment in Arab cities. An even larger group held back fundamentalist tendencies in order to embrace the nationalism that had burst forth on university campuses during the 1970s and early 1980s. Still others heeded a call for ascetism and remained at home tending to family farming. A smaller number took to activism, forming and reforming units of popular Islamic organizations ranging from moderate to the very radical.[80]

The growth of fundamentalism in Iran as well as successes against US and Israeli forces by militant Lebanese Shiite factions encouraged a certain buoyancy among Islamicists on the West Bank and Gaza. Resentment of interference in Palestinians' daily life by Israeli military administrators nevertheless followed upon the PLO military breakdown in Lebanon, and a corresponding confusion in the political identity of Palestinians caused similar concerns in West Bankers over the maintenance and vitality of Arab tradition. Islam, with its emphasis on purity and cultural unity, exerted a powerful draw upon those discouraged by what they saw as the extension of a valueless, Western-influenced society. Jewish extremist solutions to the question of landownership on the West Bank, moreover, stimulated an equal intensity among Islamic revivalists for Arab control of the same territory.[81]

The spread of ideas associated with an Islamic rebirth on the West Bank and Gaza was aided by Israeli and Jordanian tolerance for the creation of Islamic religious colleges and observance of Friday prayers. The Jewish state and the Hashemite kingdom were both interested in weakening the appeal of Arafat's PLO and, in any case, assumed that Islam would face difficulties among a largely secularist West Bank and Gaza population.[82] However, with the buildup of educational, social, and cultural institutions determined to offer instruction in Islamic law and history as well as provide for the needy, fundamentalism flourished even among those unreconciled to religion.

The student movement at leading West Bank colleges and universities led the Islamic political movement. A half dozen organizations vied for the attention of those no longer committed to nationalistic solutions for reestablishing authority over the West Bank.[83] Islamic-run bookstores brought magazines and political tracts to the rural masses, whose access to these materials would otherwise have been limited.[84] The young were soon joined by a broad constituency of landowners, merchants, shopkeepers, and workers from the towns, who—together with university faculty—were exposed to lectures, study groups, and a wide circulation of literature distributed to major cities.

The mosques, too, served as rallying points for an Islamic takeover of the West Bank and Gaza.[85] In language strikingly similar to that employed by radicalists belonging to the camp of Jewish fundamentalists, Friday prayer leaders proclaimed an uncompromising stand on developing a theocratic state. Moreover, the Muslim clerics offered their followers absolutely no latitude to deal with Israel over any part of the disputed West Bank and Gaza territories and specifically condemned PLO efforts to orchestrate such a move.[86] The

Islamicists struck against Israeli targets even before the intifada, selecting Jewish troop concentrations at the famous Western wall for attack in October 1986, and thereafter spurring demonstrations and strikes in Gaza.[87]

The intifada prospered from a perspective sympathetic to fundamentalism. The stone throwers began challenging Israel's military in order to dramatize how desperate their living conditions had become. They were not choosing tactically to improve their negotiating positions toward a peaceful resolution of Palestinian rights on the West Bank; rather, the leaders of the uprising showed unusual capacity for demonstrating Israeli maltreatment and PLO-Jordanian disregard for their plight. The stone throwers hoped by their acts of resistance to compel Israel to loosen its hold on the territories. If the Jewish state were sufficiently unwise to tighten its grip, these same rock hurlers would offer their opposition in the most culturally authentic terms— denial, self-sacrifice, and martyrdom—thereby proving the struggle to be a spiritual one.[88]

The rural strength of the uprising enabled a string of early victories despite the widespread use of counterterror by Israeli forces, intended to dull the intifada's effect. Mass resignations by Palestinians serving on the Israeli police force, as well as large-scale support of Israeli Arabs and stateless West Bankers who had closed their shops, were featured aspects of the shadowy command's call to service. The intifada heads also successfully asserted authority over local sanitation matters, while the youngsters gained familiarity with other administrative areas.[89] Meanwhile, the PLO's discovery of how popular the intifada had become in West Bank villages stirred Arafat to order financial and organizational support.[90] Some of the wealthier Gulf states and a few rich Levantine communities also tapped their coffers once the PLO had endorsed the intifada's goals. But, at West Bank universities—shut down repeatedly by the nervous Israeli military—and in the rural-based mosques, fundamentalism was held to be the locomotion for future armed resistance to a harsher Jewish rule.

Nevertheless, internal strife among Islamic groups, lack of an agreed-upon leader for the uprising, and Arafat's potential as a worthy diplomatic partner for the West will have to be overcome if fundamentalists hope to succeed in regulating opposition to Israel's West Bank and Gazan policies. A Muslim impulse to outstrip its nationalist rivals for the souls of urbanites may dampen Islamic disunity, which had grown to epic proportions before the uprising. And, although a solitary charismatic figure has failed to emerge as the intifada leader, the youthful command has been able to exert an exceptional degree of cohesion in planning and carrying out a profusion of activities on the West Bank and Gaza.[91] That consensus, however, will be challenged as temporary interruptions of Israeli civil administration become insurrectionary. The clandestine nature of the intifada's command will undoubtedly assist early progress against superior Israeli military capability, but the acid test of leadership may well come when the full might of the

Jewish state's security apparatus, with its incomparable assets on the West Bank, is exerted to smash the uprising.

Arafat received a good deal of notoriety for supporting Resolution 242 and for recognizing Israel's right to exist, as well as for forswearing terrorism,[92] but his ill-fated mission to obtain diplomatic participation for the PLO in the Middle East peace process, when combined with Israel's uncontrollable behavior on the West Bank, will surely unleash a new spasm of discontent among Palestinians. The immediate respondents for those dispirited Palestinians will be Israelis, both peace loving and warmongering. The United States, moderate Arab nations such as Egypt and Jordan, and Arafat's cohorts among the elite landowning class of the West Bank all will come in for substantial criticism if they embrace a negotiated solution to the Palestinian problem.

In this set of circumstances, Arafat will likely be denied the unflagging support previously given him by a majority of West Bank and Gazan Palestinians. Moreover, he can be expected to receive the strongest disapproval yet for his governance of the PLO, both from inside the movement as well as from Syrian-influenced elements outside the umbrella organization.[93] Arafat's ability to structure additional West Bank and Gazan moves will be extremely limited, thereby opening up a rather significant leadership vacuum in the area.

Fundamentalists, under such a scenario, have demonstrated an important counterpoint to the discredited PLO: First, they have initiated a platform of unswerving dedication to the removal of the Israeli presence from the West Bank; and second, the Islamicists could be seen as offering the return of Palestinian dignity if their religious revival reaches full bloom as a result of the Jews' ouster from lands belonging to Arab citizens. Moreover, the fundamentalists could then say that they alone are capable of restoring sociocultural unity by proposing linkage of rural and urban elements. In short, Islamic ritual may be the single most potent force for the recreation of Palestinian identity on the West Bank and Gaza, in what many regard as an enduring struggle for survival against an unshakable enemy.

THE CASE FOR A "NEW WISDOM"

Meanwhile, fundamentalists throughout the Middle East realized their worst fears about Western practices when the United States came to the Saudi desert in the fall of 1990 to wrest Kuwait from Iraqi hands. Fundamentalists worry about the West's undermining traditional values as a consequence of the large US military force so near Mecca—home to the holiest Muslim shrine. Fundamentalists are angered about the West's double standard. The United States and its allies are seen as eager to punish the regime of Saddam Hussein for moving into Kuwaiti territory while they shrink from doing anything about UN resolutions calling upon Israel to relinquish land held illegally.

Fundamentalist audiences from Jordan to Algeria also grow in response to the power of a simple message that asks the world to provide equally for all states and their citizens who have suffered repeated indignities and usurpations.

The United States, however, may be positioned poorly to heed the call, to seize the initiative, until it is able to show both resolve and sensitivity to the fundamentalist perspective already overtaking local politics in Iran and Israel, and among West Bank and Gaza Palestinians. How the United States manages to put its case for resolving the Arab-Israeli conflict, whether it agrees to link ending Iraqi aggression in the Gulf with preventing Jewish maltreatment of Palestinian youth, how it tests when and where to negotiate with governments hitherto deemed too radical, how it recognizes (or fails to recognize) a relationship of faith to power in the Middle East could for some time to come determine whether Washington has any authority over events in the region. A new wisdom that translates into a keener appreciation of how popular the equity issue may be in Middle East politics could help free Washington from the position it is improvidently stuck to. When the United States did focus its energies on how values related to policy performance during the 1970s and 1980s, its reputation in the Middle East was enhanced. Those successes deserve a new evaluation in light of our understanding of events on the ground and in the perspective of how values operate in international dialogue.

3

Success at Camp David, Confusion in Lebanon and the West Bank

The salience of certain US values to Middle East problems is complicated by regional tensions arising out of religion and politics and over which strategy—realpolitik or pragmatism—works best. This uneasiness makes it necessary to discover how and when US policies have historically led to peace and how and when they have led to armed outbreaks of conflict.

VALUES AND ACTION: CARTER CONFRONTS THE PALESTINIAN PROBLEM

In the spring of 1977 the Carter administration worked toward dramatic evidence of the timelessness and universality of the US creed—a peaceful settlement on the West Bank and Gaza. Jimmy Carter was convinced that he had a responsibility to assist Palestinians in their quest to vote, assemble, own property without fear of its confiscation, discuss the future openly, and live free of military rule. He was also drawn to the notion of Israelis functioning in peace within secure boundaries while sharing in rights accorded to all states of the region; that is, participation in trade, tourism, and cultural exchanges. The concept of egalitarianism was a matter of faith to Jimmy Carter; it had informed his Southern Baptist heritage and flowed from a reading of the Bible that was devoted to a Jewish homeland as well as to ensuring a devolution of moral and ethical privileges for others.[1]

The specifics of who the Palestinian leaders were, how they could participate in their own future, and whether peaceful relations in the West Bank and Gaza could really be attained consumed Carter administration energies during the balance of its term. The president and his advisers were troubled by an ill-defined Palestinian entity as well as by Israel's inflexible opposition to PLO representation in any internationally convened conference. Carter searched for some way to describe Palestinian aspirations to US citizens favorably. His efforts, particularly at a town meeting in Clinton, Massachusetts, in March 1977, only served to evoke emotional responses from normally prudent and patient audiences. The public outcry, coupled with the proclivity to suspect Soviet exploitation of a Palestinian state, prompted Carter to accept Palestinian alliance with Jordan as the most suitable method of achieving equity in the West Bank.[2]

53

The Carter administration hoped to orchestrate a conference to be held in Geneva at the conclusion of the year, in which Palestinians would participate as members either of the Jordanian delegation or of a pan-Arab group. The United States preferred the latter and sought Israeli concurrence to seat Palestinians as part of a grouping representing all Arabs. Foreign Minister Moshe Dayan approved in part, but his price for the compromise was to invalidate an earlier and controversial US-Soviet commitment to force the parties to Geneva by December 31, 1977.[3]

The Carter administration's backpedaling from its agreed October 1 communiqué with Moscow was played out against both frustration at having a Palestinian solution elude its grasp and the larger drama of Egyptian-Israeli and inter-Arab relations. US officials feared that links between Cairo and Jerusalem would be established at the expense of the Palestinians. The White House suspected that Sadat's grand initiative to visit Jerusalem on November 19 would be met with Israeli plans to return only the Sinai, producing a separate agreement with Egypt.[4]

Secretary of State Cyrus Vance was dispatched to both capital cities in early December, charged with the responsibility for gaining approval of a "declaration of principles" that would confirm both parties' resolve to seek progress on the Palestinian issue as part of any Sinai talks. Such a declaration could also serve as a rallying point for support from Arab moderates, who were otherwise convinced that Sadat's surprise Jerusalem visit betrayed the Palestinian cause.[5]

The Carter administration initially viewed Israeli Prime Minister Begin's "home rule" plan—brought to the White House in mid-December—as an unwelcome development, especially because Jerusalem had failed to embrace the declaration of principles. The president, nonetheless, gave qualified approval to this proposal of Palestinian autonomy within Israel, expecting that a positive response would lead the Israeli premier to be more accepting of the transitional self-government that US, Egyptian, and moderate Arab leaders intended for Palestinians living on the West Bank. Carter and his national security team banked on the belief that US mediation could, in time, soften the Israeli design and achieve the inclusion of a Jordanian role in an interim West Bank government; an international or joint Arab-Israeli authority to choose an autonomous council to administer contested areas; the substitution of UN peacekeeping forces as a guarantor of security in portions of the area vacated by the Israeli military; and the transformation of the West Bank and Gaza, during a five-year period in which Jewish sovereignty would not be exercised, into a region of self-rule for Palestinians.[6]

Carter had, during his first year in office, established a process that would factor in consideration of equal rights for Palestinians on West Bank and Gaza lands. The most serious test of US negotiating skill, however, would come months later when natural optimism evaporated and hard bargaining proved fruitless. Then, movement on the Palestinian matter would appear to be insubstantial and achievement inconsequential.

In large and small ways, the Carter administration during the first half of 1978 moved to achieve a more equitable existence for Palestinians residing on the West Bank and Gaza. Carter declared that the burgeoning Jewish settlements were contrary to international law and a barrier to peace, and he approved new objectives requiring clear recognition of the "legitimate rights of the Palestinian people" as well as a solution that would enable them to "participate in the determination of their own future."[7] In addition, he became a party to a deliberate scheme to confound the Israeli prime minister into making more generous compromises on peace than Begin would otherwise find agreeable.[8]

US strategists decided on a plan that outlined the steps that could resolve the status of the West Bank. An attempt to refashion Begin's December 1977 home-rule plan was formulated in February under National Security Adviser Zbigniew Brzezinski's authorship. Its main points were a transitional period of five years in which to achieve Palestinian self-rule; an interim arrangement, designed by Egypt, Jordan, and Israel (negotiations would be conducted among these parties and Palestinian representatives from Gaza and the West Bank); an authority, freely elected by the inhabitants of Gaza and the West Bank, to govern during the interim period (its responsibilities would be defined by mutual agreement of the parties); forfeiture of both Israeli and Jordanian claims of sovereignty over the West Bank during the transitional period; withdrawal of Israeli forces to specified locations in the West Bank; and negotiations among the parties (West Bank/Gaza authority, Israel, Jordan, and Egypt) to establish secure and final boundaries, including modifications of lines consistent with pre-1967 borders, during the five-year interim period.[9]

An unpublicized strategy group drawn from the White House, State Department, and National Security Council staff began meeting in Middleburg, Virginia, on June 1, 1978, to chart the basis for determining a US peace program.[10] The secret planning effort followed a particularly disappointing period in which neither Sadat nor Begin was ready to accommodate on the West Bank and Gaza. Central to the planners' task was managing a reconciliation of all parties' views on Palestinian aspirations, security, and recognition, as well as a return of occupied territories. Those themes ricocheted from session to session during bargaining in Washington, Jerusalem, Cairo, and Leeds, England, but without serious advance toward even modest agreement. The State Department, meanwhile, strung together elements of Begin's home-rule plan, Brzezinski's February scheme, and the July 1978 Leeds Castle discussions into a grand, three-stage negotiation scheme for Carter to present at Camp David in September.

The US proposal offered at Camp David was revised twenty-three times before formal acceptance by the parties on the thirteenth day of their historic meetings. Assistant Secretary of State Harold Saunders developed the initial draft; many of its provisions regarding a West Bank and Gaza solution survived. Key to ultimate success at the presidential retreat was insistence that negotiation in the territory take place in stages with widening participation of Arab states. The staggered deliberations over the future of the West Bank and Gaza were to commence with Egyptian and Israeli agreement on a set of principles regarding the interim period, elections to a self-governing body, and withdrawal of the military administration. A second level of discussions, perhaps with Jordanian participation, would focus on creating the transitional regime, selecting its officials, and forming security arrangements. The third and final stage would witness, no later than the third year, four-party talks (among Israel, Jordan, Egypt, and the Palestinians) determining the final status of the West Bank and Gaza—this aspect to be concluded by the end of the fifth year.[11]

US commitment to applying Resolution 242 to all fronts, however, was rescinded in the flurry of compromises exacted during the final moments of the Camp David talks. Subscribing to the implementation of UN Resolution 242 in the West Bank and Gaza would have meant that Begin would have to withdraw entirely from the areas he called Judea and Samaria. This he could not do. Carter therefore approved wording to circumvent the issue: Resolution 242 would apply to the negotiations without precisely spelling out any set of future agreements. Israel could claim that the resolution was to be used as a basis for its peace treaty discussions with Jordan, whereas the United States and Egypt were free to claim its application to the West Bank and Gaza. The Israelis were mindful of the markedly weaker Jordanian claim to both areas and believed that the subject of Israel's withdrawal from the occupied territories would not arise between Jerusalem and Amman.

A paragraph inserted late into the Camp David Accords reflected its ambiguity both on negotiations—West Bank and Gaza or Jordan-Israel—to be applied under Resolution 242 and respecting the Palestinian people. In order to obtain Begin's agreement to wording that incorporated reference to Palestinian legitimate rights, Carter endorsed changes in the draft statement that added new vagueness to already compromised language. The change from applying Resolution 242 to the *results* of the negotiations to applying it simply to negotiations underscored the Israeli belief that, although each of the parties retained the right to raise the principles of the UN resolution, final agreement need not be rooted in those precepts. Enumeration of the points contained in Resolution 242 were also omitted to preclude from the final agreement mention of withdrawal.[12]

The compromise struck at Camp David in September hardly satisfied administration doubters who had counted on a demonstration of US strength and resolve to achieve a reasonable settlement on the West Bank and Gaza. In point of fact, the Aswan formula of January 1978 was preserved; that is, legitimate rights of the Palestinians and their participation in the determination of their future were recognized. But the Camp David Accords were unspecific on the nature of a final peace; procedures and arrangements were to apply only during a transitional period. Moreover, full Israeli military withdrawal was conditional, the status of the West Bank Jewish communities unsettled, and Jerusalem unmentioned in the text of the accords. Linkage between the two framework agreements (the one ceding Sinai and the other calling for West Bank and Gaza resolution) remained unestablished.

Carter saw the Camp David Accords in stricter terms than did some of his closest advisers. He regarded the summit as having produced a process inextricably linked to promoting peace rather than war in the Middle East. He preferred to believe that despite differences in attitude, demeanor, and style, Sadat and Begin had laid a foundation for ensuring that the largest Arab state would be unlikely to go to war with Israel—its historic archenemy—for decades to come. Although the accords revealed a preference for stripping away Palestinian rights, prudent conduct by Israelis governing the West Bank and Gaza could in time create a more agreeable climate in which to foster equity arrangements.[13]

In the meantime, the Carter administration continued to press for implementation of the accords, arguing that resolving the issues on the West Bank and Gaza could best occur if Israel would hold elections in East Jerusalem with Palestinian residents voting, and if a self-governing council were set up to administer rights to public lands and water in the Gaza–West Bank area.[14] Carter was unwilling, however, to threaten an aid cutoff in order to ensure Israel's compliance with measures intended to make life more convenient in the occupied territory. Consequently, the interregnum between the September 1978 Camp David meetings and signing of the Egyptian-Israeli peace treaty in March 1979 provided little evidence to Jordan or others in the Arab world that their participation in the peace process would yield beneficial results.

Some have attributed President Carter's unsteady hold on the attempt to reach peace in the Middle East during the first months of 1979 to domestic pressures; others believed that his commitment to help Palestinians achieve their rights lacked sincerity; still more have charged that Carter was convinced that a rapprochement between Egypt and Israel would relieve a jittery US electorate and assure his victory in a second presidential bid. The steady, commanding presidential presence was indeed absent during the lengthy negotiations between Egyptian and Israeli representatives in the six months between Camp David and the signing of their peace treaty. The US president had performed brilliantly, cajoling and challenging, inducing compromise from very tough leaders who were used to satisfying their own wills and desires. Carter had unstintingly devoted time and resources to resolving the Arab-Israeli quarrel. The thirteen days spent at Camp David as well as weeks of preparation earlier had taxed the energies that any US chief executive could bring to bear. Carter's domestic agenda had sputtered to a near halt; details of normalization of relations with the People's Republic of China had not been fully attended to; and the shah's hold on stability in Tehran was fast crumbling.

The most persuasive reason for Jimmy Carter's distancing himself from a final West Bank and Gaza settlement may have been sheer exhaustion and frustration at doing battle with Israel's wily and skillful premier. President Carter was leader of the worlds' most powerful nation. The United States was engaged in manifold issues having to do with the safety of its hemisphere, economic stability for industrial states, inadequate food and shelter in the nations of the Third World, and the mix of weaponry for defense of NATO partners. Menachem Begin, by contrast, was at home with the steady drumbeat of threatened security in the Middle East, as well as being an exceptional expert on the legalisms, justifications, and juxtapositions of the various entreaties for solution to the Palestinian problem.

Carter had adeptly mastered many of the technical aspects and nuances of the quarrel over the West Bank and Gaza. The toll that it took, however, to defend, debate, and deter Arab and Israeli conclusions regarding the future of the territory was not sustainable. The president was aware of the clock that ticked toward the November 1980 US elections; Begin was unhurried by either a test of political strength or the necessity to resolve matters on the West Bank and Gaza. The Israeli leader was furthermore unruffled by favor or intimidation from the United States or Israel's Arab neighbors. He was unsparing in vitriolic comment where he deemed the expression appropriate to the circumstances. Jimmy Carter, in short, was "outgunned" by a very nimble, ably prepared Israeli prime minister who was overzealous in guarding interests perceived to involve life-and-death concerns.[15]

The US president, therefore, selected the most satisfying as well as most suitable method of approaching peace in the Middle East. He decided to concentrate on removing the threat of war from the area by enabling Egypt and Israel to resolve their differences on the Sinai territory while settling for appearances on the West Bank and Gaza. Jimmy Carter supposed he would be in a stronger position to move toward a real solution for Palestinians residing in the territory during his second term. Meanwhile, the US government would use its good offices to encourage movement in the unresolved matters affecting the quality of life in the West Bank and Gaza. The signing of the Egyptian-Israeli treaty on the White House lawn in late March 1979, therefore, inaugurated a thirty-month search for ways to implement provisions relating to the West Bank and Gaza. Egypt, as promised, stood in for Jordan and bargained with Israel on behalf of the Hashemite kingdom as well as the Palestinians.

However, shifting fortunes in the Iranian revolution and the subsequent hostage crisis so absorbed the White House in 1979–1980 that it relinquished exclusive control of West Bank–related matters. Restoration of Palestinian rights in the territory was placed in the custody of a succession of special presidential negotiators. Carter's last-named envoy, Sol Linowitz, who had successfully managed approval of a new Panama Canal treaty, teamed with the State Department to reduce Egyptian and Israeli concerns to five critical issues:

1. How can Israel be assured of the protection and preservation of its security?
2. What arrangements can be satisfactorily concluded that would result in a fair distribution of water resources between and among Palestinians, Israelis, and others in the region?
3. How should the problem of public lands in the West Bank and Gaza as well as multiple rights and claims be dealt with equitably?
4. What should be the nature of the power exercised by the self-governing administrative authority?
5. What role should the Palestinian inhabitants of the West Bank and Gaza, including residents of East Jerusalem, play in the election of the self-governing administrative authority?[16]

The Carter administration left office in January 1981 with an extraordinary if incomplete record of accomplishment in moving the Palestinian problem from the periphery to center stage. Jimmy Carter's religious training, his sense of mission, and worldview beckoned toward equal-mindedness. In US terms, equality meant having the same value as another, being fair, just, impartial. When Carter became president he tapped the roots of US egalitarianism to give Palestinians political, economic, and legal rights equal to those enjoyed by others who occupied the same land. But even as he performed the rite expected of a US leader who is devoted to bringing decency and humanity to the inhabitants of the Middle East, Jimmy Carter knew that standards would be improved in the area only when Arabs and Jews held direct substantive talks with each other. So the president of the United States found himself marshaling a peace between Palestinians and Israelis but not deciding how the effort would reach a conclusion.

Movement toward equity in the West Bank and Gaza—that is, toward an arrangement pledged to be fair, just, and impartial—was pragmatically and convincingly demonstrated by Carter before the Middle East erupted into Iran's fundamentalist revolution. Carter became absorbed by the US embassy takeover and unable to sort out the heinous nature of the Iranian deed from the reasoning that brought the fundamentalists to power. He could not separate how the fundamentalists had come to govern arbitrarily from their need to assert a blend of social justice and religious authenticity severely lacking in the body politic—the result of egregious action on the part of the shah and his cohorts. Indeed, during those first few months of Khomeini's power grab there were so many excesses committed in the name of faith and justice that the Carter administration was simply unable to penetrate the traditional basis for the fundamentalist claim. Instead, Carter and his advisers saw that militancy as being associated with a breakdown of order and resulting terrorism.[17] This legacy of hate and suspicion of fundamentalists as a group spawned a counterproductive set of policies on the part of Ronald Reagan and his team when they encountered violence in Lebanon during the very first foreign policy test of the new US government.

VALUES AND ACTION: REAGAN CONFRONTS THE LEBANESE PROBLEM

US policy toward Lebanon and its civil war had developed in the late 1970s mostly as a response to Israeli support for the Christian Maronite faction's attempted containment of PLO military forces. The United States had strenuously objected to Israeli incursions across the Lebanese border, such as those in the fall of 1977 and spring of 1978 to punish PLO terrorism. Carter, Sadat, and Begin, en route from Camp David to the White House to sign the September 17, 1978, accords, had agreed that the Lebanese conflict would have to be dealt with; no party, however, had addressed the issue before Carter's leaving office or Sadat's untimely death.

The Reagan administration's attention was also diverted from Lebanon toward other pressing matters in 1981; however, a negotiator was dispatched to arrange a cease-fire in the Beeka Valley during April. The gifted former State Department undersecretary, Phillip Habib, remained in the area through midsummer, successfully negotiating a curtailment of military action between Israeli and PLO forces, which had been bombarding each other's positions on the Lebanese border.[18]

Israel remained dissatisfied with the emplacement of Syrian missiles in the Beeka Valley, lodged there to protect PLO and Syrian main force units from unlimited air reconnaissance and attack directed from Jerusalem. Moreover, during the first months of 1982, PLO raids across Israel's northern border intensified, and through late spring the Jewish state's cities nearest Lebanon were under constant rocket barrages.[19]

Controversy and angry denials persist even today in Washington and Jerusalem over the silence or warning that accompanied Alexander Haig's successive meetings with Israelis at the State Department over the wisdom of an Israeli military invasion of Lebanon. In any case, Haig's last days as secretary of state were spent attempting to minimize the effects of Israel's massive land, air, and sea border crossing, launched June 6, 1982, and intended to eliminate the PLO's military infrastructure.[20]

The presence of bogged-down Israeli units in West Beirut who threatened to mount a house-by-house search for wavering PLO commandos, the assassination of Bashir Gemayel—the Israeli-supported, recently elected Lebanese government head[21]— and the subsequent murders of Palestinian civilians at Sabra and Shatilla[22] combined to draw the Reagan administration directly into the crisis in the summer of 1982. Habib was called back to service, journeying between the Middle East and Washington, and to the UN offices in New York, while arranging for an international peacekeeping force, including US troops, to safeguard the evacuation of PLO forces from West Beirut.[23] Reagan's announcement of his peace plan, therefore, coincided with the successful removal of the PLO fighters to Tunis and other locations. Meanwhile, US marines took up positions guarding Beirut's international airport,[24] while French, British, and Italian units strengthened the Christian Maronite–led government of Amin Gemayel—brother of deceased Bashir—in other important ways.[25]

The Begin government, during the spring of 1983, moved to shore up its political relationship with the shaky Lebanese government. Israel had offered assurances upon the election of Bashir Gemayel[26] and, after his death, supported Amin, based on understandings relating to the sanctity of an inviolable border as well as a peace treaty between the two states.[27] Israeli pressures on Amin Gemayel to normalize relations, together with bombing at the entrance to the US embassy in Beirut—resulting in the loss of sixty-three lives, including seventeen US citizens—drew Secretary of State George Shultz, successor to the resigned Alexander Haig, to the area in early May.[28]

Shultz hoped to achieve simultaneous withdrawal of Israeli and Syrian forces from Lebanon and return the country to normalcy. Efforts at shuttle diplomacy to and from Damascus, Beirut, and Jerusalem convinced him that he could not manage a removal of external forces from Lebanon. Because there was considerable US suspicion that the bombing of the embassy in Beirut on April 18 was the work of a Syrian-backed Iranian faction, Shultz acquiesced in the Lebanese-Israeli peace treaty signing on May 17, 1983, despite unalterable opposition from Damascus.[29]

The protocol agreement with Israel now became such a sufficiently contentious and unpopular issue that Sunni and Shiite Muslims as well as Druze groups vied in their opposition to the government of Amin Gemayel. Syrian president Assad further polarized the PLO by summarily dismissing Arafat from Damascus and fielding his own loyalists in Lebanon, who sought to prevent the return of Fatah leadership. The factional Druze militia located in the Shuf—a mountainous area controlling the Beeka Valley—began a lengthy and effective counterassault against Israeli forces in the region.[30]

In the middle of the summer, Israel, suffering from a bewildered leadership and a dissatisfied populace reacting to mounting casualties from the onslaught of Druze forces, abandoned the Shuf.[31] The Lebanese army remained no match for the Druze militia, and Shia, also located near the Shuf, were threatening to join in the fighting against the Gemayel government's battered forces.

Exposed US marines seeking to maintain an open international airport at Beirut came under heavy fire from Druze-directed artillery, as well as Shia-inspired sniper attack. The Reagan administration, split between soft-liners searching for a rapprochement with Syria and hard-liners who argued for holding Assad responsible for deteriorating conditions, decided on a controlled use of force as a response to the attacks.[32] The United States became a combatant in the middle of September 1983, directing return fire on Druze positions and mounting a defense of the Lebanese army caught in the Shuf.[33] At the end of September a cease-fire was negotiated with agreement to convene an all-party conference in Geneva and press for a broadening of the base of Amin Gemayel's government.

A week prior to the contemplated start of the political conciliation conference, on October 23, a truck packed with explosives entered the marine compound near the Beirut airport, exploded, and killed 241 US soldiers.[34] The Reagan administration regarded the terrorist attack as a Syrian-directed conspiracy and promptly renewed its strategic cooperation agreement with Israel.[35] Thereafter, Israeli aircraft struck at Syrian sites in the Beeka Valley. US naval-based F-14 Tomcats flew reconnaissance over the bombed area, exposing them to Syrian antiaircraft fire. The United States responded with attack from two fighter wings; two aircraft were downed, with one pilot killed and another captured. Eight marines were killed on the ground in a related action.[36]

Despite calls for Amin Gemayel to continue his effort at sharing power as well as toughening the Lebanese army, Reagan began the new year by acceding to congressional criticism and preparing to withdraw marines from Lebanon. The United States covered its retreat by announcing, on February 7, 1984, a "redeployment" west of ships of the Sixth Fleet. Meanwhile, the battleship USS *New Jersey* masked the withdrawal by sending sixteen-inch shells indiscriminately against unprotected Shia villagers, adding new virulence to the charges of US insensitivity to the Arab world.[37]

By 1985 the United States was becoming less central to a Lebanese peace. Stationing US forces in Lebanon, ostensibly for peacekeeping purposes, had resulted in a belligerent status. Shia and Druze factions were convinced that the Reagan administration was intent on perpetuating the conflict and taking sides in Lebanon's war. The United States was viewed as part of the problem instead of as a contributor to a Lebanese solution.[38] The disdain for the United States expressed by a large number of Lebanese groups ruled out any role for Washington.

The Christian Maronite leadership was now forcefully committed to strengthening its hold on government and the capital, Beirut. Moreover, the appearance of new Shiite factions, guided by Iran and devoted to militancy, pushed Gemayel's regime toward heavier reliance on externally supplied solutions. Syrian President Assad was seen to be consolidating military positions in the Beeka Valley that would increase the security of nearby Damascus. Meanwhile, Israeli assistance to an inexperienced Southern Lebanese Army command assured a stalemate in the war, which worked toward preventing a resumption of PLO presence near the Jewish state's northern border. Crucially, US personnel resident in Beirut and its suburbs were subject to the vicissitudes of shifting alliances in the struggle for advantage among contending Lebanese factions. Hostage taking had become both a sport and a reflection of the sharpening divisions in Lebanese society, as well as a signal of contempt for the inability of the United States to put a stop to deteriorating conditions.[39]

The wreckage of lives and fortunes strewn over Lebanon's mountainous landscape for more than a decade attests to a tragedy of near-classical proportions. With it all, sectarianism has continued to flourish, in fact resembling the pattern during the nineteenth century. Then as now the dynamics of intersectarian competition provided for two ascendant communities—Druzes and Maronites in the earlier period, Maronites and Shias at present. It took the Maronites nearly forty years, from 1825 to 1861, to replace the Druzes as the most powerful Lebanese force.[40] Shias have converged today to claim preeminent status a mere decade and a half since the start of their campaign to supplant Christian protagonists.

Confessionalism—a system of government established nearly forty-six years ago through an unwritten pact that allocates national offices accord ing to 1932 demographic proportions among sects and minorities—has been legitimately argued by Shias to be irrelevant to the Lebanese society of today. Although population figures have generally tended to be unreliable, most observers seem to agree that Shia figures have climbed by about 15 percent to their present level of a third of the country's 3 million people. Meanwhile, Maronite Christian representation has correspondingly fallen approximately 5 percent to about one-quarter of Lebanon's inhabitants. The Christian community accounts for nearly a third of the state's population, but this figure includes Greek Orthodox, Greek Catholic, Nestorian, Chaldean, and other sects. Sunni Muslims and Druzes compose the final third of Lebanese society with the latter making up about 7 percent of the total.[41]

Shias, unlike other Lebanese communities, have avoided geographic concentration. They are dispersed into three parts of the country: the south, the central mountainous region in and near the capital, and the northern portion of the Beeka Valley toward the east. Shias have also been well integrated into the national economy. Profiting from offers of steady enrollments in a heavily subsidized higher-educational program at Beirut's national university, Shias had managed to combine professional opportunities in the fields of teaching, law, and business to dominate a growing commercial sector before the advent of internal conflict during the mid-1970s. A decade more of social mobilization to the urban center has brought cohesion and a sense of national identity for the more than 300,000 Shias drawn from each of their more traditional locations and now living among the carnage of suburban Beirut.[42]

Amal was organized by Musa Sadr—an Iranian-born cleric from Qom—
and was intended as a political-military response to the social injustices suffered by Shias during the 1970s. Sadr espoused fairness and equity for all
sects but in terms inoffensive to the entrenched Christian establishment. He
spoke to the deprived and the disinherited, emphasizing authenticity,
tradition, and the martyrdom associated with an exclusive Shiite heritage. He
reminded his listeners of the wish to make women equal, told of the necessity
to improve conditions for the poor, and showed that it was essential to create
a new life for the children, who otherwise stood to inherit squalor and self-
pity. He endeavored to bring cohesion and self-respect to a people inured to
grief and exploitation.[43]

Sadr's suspicious disappearance in Libya during a 1978 visit[44] sparked a
leadership struggle, settled only in part by the succession of southern-born
lawyer and activist Nabih Berri. Berri's opposition within the Shia sect came
from hard-liners, influenced by Iran's Khomeini, who were critical of Amal's
secularization and failure to display sufficient militancy against the movement's natural enemies. Berri's support within Amal has been drawn from
among a core of professionals, moderate clerics, and long-time regulars
committed to the pragmatic middle.[45]

Repeated calls to reassemble the structure of government have gone
unheeded by a Maronite-led national apparatus, with resulting radicalism
among a younger generation unforgiving of the past and uncomfortable with
the future. Criticism has been showered on the more conservative of Shia
leaders as well as on the despised Gemayel clan. Amal has been unable to
relieve the unrelenting and indiscriminate violence and terror, which a noted
Lebanese sociologist has called the "demoralization of public life"[46] besetting
ordinary Lebanese citizens.

Nonetheless, Amal under Nabih Berri has shown itself to be a loyal and
creative force for strengthening national will and protecting Lebanon against
external forces. Often caught in the cross fire between Israeli and PLO
military forces in the late 1970s, and in some cases preferring Jewish victory,
Amal nevertheless joined the resistance to Jerusalem's occupation once it
became clear that the basis for invading—pushing the Palestinians out of
Lebanon—had been overextended. The Amal leader also declared equal
opposition to the return of PLO influence in Lebanon by attacking
Palestinian guerrillas south of Beirut.[47] In fact, Berri managed to assume
official custody for the fate of south Lebanon—a traditional base for Shias—
as a condition of joining a new cabinet formed in 1984 by arrangement with
Syria to forestall the demise of Amin Gemayel's regime. The Maronite
government had been toppling as a result of an Amal-inspired decision by
Muslim troops to desert from the Lebanese National Army.[48]

In any case, Nabih Berri has insisted all along that all Lebanese,
belonging to each sect and minority, were entitled to equal rights as well as
obligations. The Amal leader's spoiling operations against both Israeli and

Syrian hegemonic aspirations are convincing evidence that he did not wish to establish what some have labeled a condominium approach to Lebanon's future. Similarly, the widespread geographic distribution of Shia home bases, and in particular Berri's demonstration of paternalism in south Lebanon, make it highly unlikely that Amal would ever consider partition. Nor is the Amal leader likely to accept an Iranian-style Islamic government in Lebanon, in spite of the movement's adoption of less intrusive models of dress and comportment.[49]

Lebanon, already fractured by a fifteen-year-old civil war, reached new heights of disruption in September 1988 when factions belonging to the Christian Maronites could not agree upon a candidate to succeed President Amin Gemayel. Gemayel, constitutionally unable to succeed himself, at the eleventh hour appointed Major General Michel Aoun, a Maronite commander, to form a provisional military government. Aoun was under attack by various elements—including civilian leader Selim al-Hoss, who set up a countergovernment—resulting in some of the bloodiest fighting of the entire Lebanese ordeal.[50]

VALUES AND ACTION: THE REAGAN PLAN FOR THE WEST BANK AND GAZA

US involvement in Lebanon at the outset of Reagan's first term postponed his handling of the Palestinian situation. But on September 1, 1982, barely two weeks before the infamous Sabra-Shatilla massacre in the Palestinian refugee camps near Beirut, and three months after Israel's invasion of Lebanon, President Reagan announced a comprehensive program for solution of the West Bank and Gaza problem. The White House viewed its proposal as restarting a peace process that had fallen into disuse. Reagan built his plan on the foundations of the Camp David Accords, but he was unwilling to be bound by all of their limitations. While the accords spoke of a transition period during which Palestinian dwellers on the West Bank would enjoy autonomy, details governing their existence had not been spelled out. The Reagan plan provided specificity: Inhabitants of the territory were to have real authority over "themselves, the land and its resources, subject to fair safeguards on water." Additionally, formal economic, commercial, social, and cultural ties between West Bankers, Gazans, and the Kingdom of Jordan were to be maintained.

Palestinian residents in East Jerusalem, moreover, would be able to participate in electing the West Bank–Gaza self-governing administrative authority. Jewish settlement on the West Bank was to be frozen, and the Palestinians living in the area were to achieve progressive responsibility for their own internal security based on "capability and performance." Reagan promised, however, that he would oppose any measure that called for dismantling existing Israeli settlements or sought to threaten the Jewish

state's security (reasonably defined) as well as isolate the Jerusalem government from the West Bank and Gaza. He was similarly against allowing either
Palestinians or Israelis latitude to trumpet sovereign rights, with the ex-
ception of external security, which had to remain in Jewish hands during the
interim period.

The Reagan plan reiterated previous US positions that UN Resolution
242 was the agreed basis for achieving peace in the Middle East. However,
the president noted that the resolution clearly meant withdrawal from the
West Bank and Gaza, and he stipulated that the pace of Israel's leaving
would be linked to the nature of the peace and security arrangements concluded among the parties. Reagan rejected any solution that entailed
permanent Israeli sovereignty over the territories or the establishment of a
Palestinian state. Nor would the US president recognize and negotiate with
the PLO unless prior conditions of acceptance—acknowledgment of
Resolution 242 and abandonment of the organization's covenant—were
satisfied.

Reagan preferred to associate the West Bank and Gaza with Jordan. He
understood the desire and obligation (according to the Camp David Accords)
of the parties to arrive at a negotiated settlement that incorporated a policy of
self-determination for Palestinian residents of the area. Self-determination
according to the Reagan administration, however, was not to be confused
with a presumption of Palestinian statehood. Instead, Reagan was agreeable
to Palestinian involvement in their own future status, with elected
representatives deciding how best to engage in self-government consistent
with final-status negotiations.

The thorniest issue—Jerusalem—was left unexamined, although the
Reagan documents contained a statement referring to conditions in the city
being determined by discussions alone. Israeli settlements were similarly to
be finalized through bargaining arrangements, although the United States
would not support their continuation as "extraterritorial outposts."

The Reagan plan was set within a context that deserved a more
considered hearing than it received in Israel, or among Arab moderates, or, in
particular, from the Palestinian people. Reagan did not claim to be unique
among US peacemakers: He, as well as others, spoke with vigor and
forcefulness about a vision of the future that encapsulated US ideals and
values—particularly equality. The president, though, was more specific than
his predecessors had been regarding the quality of life extended to Palestinian
inhabitants of the West Bank and Gaza: They should be able to vote, whether
as residents of East Jerusalem, Jenin, or Ramallah; they should share in the
resources of the area, both land and water; they should have rights to govern
themselves; and they should enjoy cultural, economic, commercial, and
social relations with East Bankers, if desired. Care and responsibility for their
daily lives should in time yield opportunities for them to shoulder the
burdens of internal security.

Israelis also received assurances of equity under the Reagan plan, whereas without it the temporary expedient of military arms protected an otherwise risky existence. The Jewish state and its leaders had hungered for recognition and international approbation for thirty-five years. US statesmen from Jimmy Carter to Ronald Reagan had sought to deliver the political guarantees that would free Israeli governments from dependence on arms for peace and security.

The Reagan administration did not expect Israel to dismantle its settlements, only to refrain from building new ones; the president did not ask Israeli leaders to abandon their interest and presence in the West Bank and Gaza, only to permit the logical extension of rights to Arab residents in the territories; the US government did not suggest to the Israeli premier that he should entertain the development of a third state in the limited territorial confines of the West Bank, only that self-governing Palestinians join in association with Jordan; US officials did not declare Jerusalem an open city with questionable jurisdiction by its Jewish occupants, only that it remain undivided and subject to future negotiation.[51] In short, the Reagan plan was a gallant attempt to devise a compromise solution for peace in the Middle East.

Nonetheless, the presidential proposal restated an old theme all too obviously unsuccessful in the Middle East: trading land for peace. No one had pointed to this flaw during the summer of 1982, when the White House had labored hard, before announcement of the Reagan plan, to draw together the widest approval and the most expert bipartisan advice for developing a useful peace program. Administration efforts resulted in the forging of a remarkable domestic consensus behind the tenets of the president's September 1 announcement. US Jewish leaders and organizations across a wide spectrum voiced their approval of the Reagan plan; Arab-American support was more muted, but officials within that community, too, expressed general belief that conditions had improved for an overall settlement.[52]

US ambassadors were dispatched to meet with host government leaders in Tel Aviv, Cairo, Amman, and Riyadh—even prior to Reagan's televised statement—to elicit detailed reactions to the new proposal. Predictably, Israel was most upset by Reagan's departure from the letter of the Camp David Accords. A September 2, 1982, cabinet statement took issue with Reagan plan pronouncements on the participation of East Jerusalem Palestinians in the election of a self-governing administrative authority, as well as eventual Palestinian responsibilities for internal security and land-water resources.[53] Begin's government was equally hostile to clauses committing Israel to a freeze on new villages in the occupied areas while allowing for the improvement of services between West Bank and Gaza Palestinians and Jordan. The Israeli premier was convinced that such arrangements would encourage the formation of a Palestinian state, thus eliminating any possible claim of Jewish sovereignty over Judea and Samaria—a move the Camp David Accords did not prohibit.[54]

US explanations were more warmly received but not endorsed in the capitals of Arab moderate states. Monarchs such as Fahd and Hussein regarded the Reagan plan as containing encouraging elements toward a workable peace settlement, but neither leader was prepared to sacrifice Arab unity by embracing the document.[55] Instead, at an Arab summit meeting convened in Fez, Morocco, during the second week of September, traditional hard-line positions were blended with less extreme ones. Creation of an independent Palestinian state with Jerusalem as its capital and identification of the PLO as the sole legitimate representative of the Palestinian people were emphasized. Israel was called upon to evacuate the West Bank and Gaza, and the United Nations was to supervise a transitional period of several months as a step in the evolution of a PLO-controlled state. The Arab document did not exclude Israeli participation in the benefits of UN peace guarantees accorded to all states in the region, nor was the Fez plan specific on the question of whether the Jewish state was to coexist with a newly developed Palestinian state or be replaced by it.[56]

The US Department of State was confused and discouraged by the tepid Arab response to President Reagan's peace proposal. Assistant Secretary of State Nicholas Veliotes had learned in August 1982 that King Hussein was prepared publicly to support a US plan dedicated to Palestinian-Jordanian association.[57] Nevertheless, at Fez in September the diminutive Jordanian monarch was unable to dissuade core Arab leaders from once again conferring Palestinian representation on the ungainly PLO or from promoting acceptance of US willingness to separate itself from immoderate Israeli positions regarding the West Bank settlements.[58] The specter of an Israeli military using US weapons to crush PLO and Syrian troop locations inside Lebanon, without Washington's putting a stop to the conflict, was too frightful for even moderate Arab states to ignore.

Eradication of the PLO's ability to wage war tempted the organization to patch up its quarrel with Jordan and seek ways to join talks on the West Bank. Yasir Arafat was, however, incapable of smoothing over differences among competing groups in the fractious organization, and the PLO ended up declining any arrangement to enter broader discussions on the future of the West Bank and Gaza.[59] King Hussein promptly notified the United States on April 11, 1983, that he could not subscribe to the terms of Reagan's proposal.[60]

In the spring of 1984 King Hussein wondered if a US government, burdened by an obvious taste for continued Israeli intervention in Lebanon as well as its own recent retrenchment there, could be true to commitments or neutrality in any forthcoming Middle East peace effort.[61] The resilient and indefatigable Jordanian monarch pressed for a second reconciliation attempt with the PLO at the end of that year. King Hussein organized a meeting of the Palestinian National Council (PNC), the Palestinian parliament-in-exile, at Amman during late November. This time the strategy was intended to force the PLO away from Syria while strengthening Arafat's bonds with Egypt and Jordan (Amman had reestablished ties with Cairo in September).[62] Holding the seventeenth session of the PNC in Amman also revived sagging PLO fortunes among West Bankers after a hiatus in which Arafat had had to travel from capital to capital. The proceedings of the parliamentary body were in fact broadcast to the territory's inhabitants over Jordanian television.[63]

The most important outcome of the PNC meeting was the start of a full-year dialogue between Hussein and Arafat on establishing agreed positions on Middle East peace. The tough, pragmatic, and always Byzantine talks began on February 11, 1985, and concluded on February 19, 1986. They started on a high note with a communiqué committing the two sides to confederation while implying joint agreement on accepting Resolution 242 and a peace delegation made up of non-PLO members, and they closed with displays of acrimony and mutual recriminations of bad faith. Arafat was hemmed in by a series of PLO Executive Committee declarations disallowing both schemes for association with Jordan and meeting US and Israeli objectives for conference representation and recognition.[64] King Hussein, for his part, spoke of creating new leadership on the West Bank and reserved to Jordan the right to reach separate decisions regarding the future character of social, economic, and political patterns in the territory.[65]

Meanwhile, the Reagan administration had been battered by terrorist incidents with Syrian, Iranian, and PLO complicity at Lebanon's international airport during the hijacking of TWA flight 847, and on the high seas against an Italian cruise ship, the *Achille Lauro*. Both events had resulted in the murder of US citizens and the mental anguish of those threatened but physically unharmed. Moreover, the US government's outrage seemed to increase Washington's sympathy for the plight of Israel, which had also suffered attacks against its civilians in Cyprus and chose to respond with a bombing run against PLO offices in Tunis.[66]

Reagan and his closest national security advisers were so thoroughly engaged in a campaign to whittle away Muamar Qhadafi's power in Libya during 1986—first severing economic ties and freezing assets, then conducting military exercises in the Gulf of Sidra, luring Tripoli into aerial dogfights, and finally making a mid-April bombing run on key sites[67]—that events relating to the West Bank and Gaza escaped their notice. The Libyan campaign was waged in retaliation for separate terrorist incidents in a West German discotheque frequented by US military personnel and at the Viennese and Roman airports, during which many US and Israeli citizens had died. All the while, US officials were crudely dealing with Iranians in an attempt to retrieve hostages held in Lebanon by forces friendly to Ayatollah Khomeini.[68]

The Reagan administration, however, was reminded of the volatility of the West Bank in March 1986 when the Arab mayor of Nablus, Zafir al-Masri, a member of a wealthy Palestinian clan, was brutally murdered for defying a PLO ban on improving relations with the Israeli military administration.[69] The United States was further made aware of the capriciousness of inter-Arab relations when it noticed an improvement in communications between Syria and Jordan with the visit of President Hafiz Assad to Amman during May.[70] King Hussein, in fact, followed his February termination of talks with Arafat by closing down the Fatah leader's Ammanese office in July—no doubt a symbolic gesture directed toward Assad, who sought to drive the PLO head out of a job.[71]

While the Reagan administration and its detractors, both at home and abroad, became fixated on the sordid details of the secret arms sale to Iran, Jordan and Egypt attempted to press Shimon Peres's successor, Yitzhak Shamir, as well as the United States, for approval of a Geneva-style comprehensive peace conference to take place some time in 1987.[72] US officials at first were in tandem with the Likud leadership's rabid opposition to the move, despite calls for support by Peres, now the Israeli foreign minister. However, US-Israeli discord began to be noticed when it became clear that the government led by Shamir was intent on furthering ultranationalist goals: resuming Jewish settlement in the West Bank on a grand scale, toughening Israeli military measures in the territory, and relaxing restraints on Jewish extremism.[73] Meanwhile, active pursuit of glasnost in the Soviet Union and hints of a more flexible policy on Jewish emigration, as well as the improved atmospherics of détente with the signing of the INF treaty during December, were to make convening an international peace conference with Moscow's participation a less odious task for the United States.[74]

Ronald Reagan finished his two terms in office still facing a conundrum in the Middle East: how to fulfill the promise of bringing peace, order, and stability to the West Bank, Gaza, and Lebanon. In many ways the mistakes that the Reagan administration made in Lebanon prohibited improvements in the US effort regarding the West Bank and Gaza. When the United States became too closely identified with the Christian Phalangists in Beirut, Washington took on the persona of a Western imperialist power. Ronald Reagan worked hard to build a reputation for moral-mindedness and pragmatism. The Reagan plan for the West Bank and Gaza established a role for Palestinians in keeping with equity arrangements. Proposed association with Jordan was a reminder of how Palestinians might contribute to order and stability in the region. And provision for Israeli security and for Jews to have the same rights in the territories as Palestinians was evidence that the United States had respect for an ally.

But when fundamentalist assertiveness appealed to the Lebanese as a method for driving the United States from the Middle East, Reagan gave way on an imperative to create equitable conditions for those most in need. He instead demonstrated his anger and frustration at the carnage that resulted from civil conflict in Lebanon and itself acted as a tripwire for fundamentalist-inspired terror elsewhere in the Middle East and in Europe. He was as definite about fundamentalist insensitivity toward decency as Shias, Druzes, and others in Lebanon were convinced of US insincerity regarding fair outcomes for the Christian Phalangists and their Israeli supporters. The Reagan people saw any Muslim-Christian separation as untidy and an uncomfortable dividing line. But they also expected all fundamentalists to be fanatics. And they were nearly certain that in time the cycle of violence and repression in the West Bank and Gaza would spin out of control and into the hands of those able to cause a level of destruction equal to that in Lebanon during a decade or more.

Fundamentalist arguments and disagreements with the United States, therefore, seemed to be at the heart of Reagan and Carter perceptions about the Middle East. Carter devised a set of arrangements for Palestinians on the West Bank and Gaza that were rooted in egalitarianism, but saw them disappear entirely after Khomeinism swept the region. Reagan offered a credible alternative to the Camp David proposals, but he too witnessed his peace plan flounder when the terror that accompanied events in Lebanon grew out of control.

It might be said about US behavior toward the West Bank, Gaza, and Lebanon during the 1980s that when Ronald Reagan gave pragmatic consideration to the rights of all citizens, peace in the region was nearer. But when order and stability were thought to be paramount, and the religious fabric, upon which was organized so much of Muslim life, was ignored or viewed as a harbinger of disorder, then conventional wisdom or realpolitik set in, and the United States seemed to be much farther from its Middle East goals.

VALUES AND ACTION: THE CASE FOR CIVIL RELIGION

It should be noted that in the 1970s and 1980s the United States missed chances to test whether civil religion could be a bellwether for discovering how US values and those of West Bankers as well as Lebanese might have converged. For example, because neither Palestinian nor Jewish life on the West Bank and Gaza was governed by ecclesiastics, and both groups subscribed to religious folkways as well as the primacy of a moral transcendental order, civil religion could be thought of as adding some meaning to their existence. And, because fundamentalists were prevented from making inroads among Palestinians until late in the 1980s, and Jewish fanatics achieved mainstream acceptance from the Israeli electorate only after 1984 and then with modest gains until 1988, a window of opportunity opened mid-decade for a dialogue about the sociopolitical order in moral terms. What could Palestinians and Jews in the territories have said to each other and under whose auspices?

The violence that resulted in inestimable destruction and death in both communities could have become a focal point around which to investigate how to construct a moral universe. In the workings of civil religion, the United States possessed a conceptual device for arriving at some common ground, even among humans in conflict. The Reagan plan, when it was offered on September 1, 1982, treated the civil side of relations on the West Bank and Gaza: who should vote, how to divide water resources, what type of relations to establish with East Bankers. But nowhere in the Reagan plan, or for that matter in US peace efforts before or since, was there any mention of a moral compass to guide the parties.

Civil religion undoubtedly had its problems in the period around 1982–1983, as it most certainly would today. Then as now the West Bank and Gaza were not an area where religion was conducive to homogeneity. Then as now, society in the West Bank and Gaza was split several different ways, with a pervasive sense of disunity even among citizens in a single community—Palestinian as well as Jewish. Then as now, particularly as a consequence of the terrible loss of life, many had lost their moral desire. And then as now, a few were intent on secreting themselves in a religious experience that gave both social and personal fulfillment and with which civil religion could not hope to compete.

However, the standard life-style of both Palestinian and Jew on the West Bank and Gaza during 1982–1983 was a highly politicized one. Both groups were especially conscious of their social and historical attitudes, and desperate to arrive at a way to deal with one another and yet still protect their unique sense of culture—myths, rituals, ceremonies, and stories. Land issues had been transformed to people concerns, but the Reagan plan spoke solely about how citizens should extend their political lives. Daily existence was crumbling in the West Bank and within Lebanon as occupier and occupied strove to retain some semblance of sociocultural continuity. Fundamentalists among Jews and Palestinians on the West Bank and Gaza, and Shias in Lebanon, saw that tradition would receive a proper due in society only when religious custom was reestablished. The struggle then between a fundamentalist pattern of living—a response to the foreigner in society, Jews on the West Bank, US citizens in Lebanon—and a secularist one was thought about in terms of polar opposites with no insight into possible compromise.

Palestinians and Jews on the West Bank, and eventually most Lebanese, surely could have been made to understand that they shared some common symbols and beliefs. The communities might have reacted positively to an emphasis on familiar concepts such as respect and reverence for the place of religious values, the unique worth of each individual, and the legal right to be heard and live without fear of retribution. Had the United States insisted on specifying similarities in national group ideals and cultural preferences instead of behaving as though equal rights grew out of the barrel of a gun, then peace in 1982–1983 might have been easier to achieve. In the absence of a US civil religion made distinct to the peoples of the region, Palestinians,

Jews, and Lebanese found themselves unable to reconcile attachments that had grown more emotional than real. In any case, the United States had distinguished itself during 1984 by sending sixteen-inch naval shells into Shia villages off the coast of Lebanon, instead of taking advantage of the window of opportunity when fundamentalism had not yet managed to fill a religious vacuum in the Levant. And in the wider region, particularly in the Gulf, US policy seemed equally wedded to realpolitik, perceived as overriding self-interest.

4

Crosscurrents of US
Strategy: The Gulf

When the United States faced off against Iran in 1987, Washington gave a strong impression that it preferred a policy based upon the conventional wisdom of realpolitik rather than one organized by pragmatic moral considerations. More recently, a massive multinational US-led land and sea force located in the Saudi desert and in the waters of the Gulf drove Saddam Hussein out of Kuwait. The United States must ask itself: What are the costs of policy in terms of US reputation and influence in the region when Washington doggedly pursues the old pattern of "ally or enemy" in the Gulf? The question cannot be answered until we understand the behavior traits most common to national decisions taken by Gulf states. A brief review of recent events may serve to illustrate.

THE IRAN-IRAQ WAR

The Iran-Iraq war began in September 1980 when Iraq, seeking to enhance its leadership of the Arab world, invaded southwestern Iran in response to Tehran's weakened military condition, which had been brought on by internal revolution and the withdrawal of US patronage. The pretext for Baghdad's initiation of hostilities was a dispute over boundary claims in a narrow river channel that travels along a common shoreline and empties into the Gulf.[1] Despite substantial loss of Muslim life and property on both sides in the see-saw conflict, the West, and in particular the United States, was unaffected by the stalemate through 1985. Beginning in 1986, however, a tanker war ensued, interrupting the delivery of oil through the Strait of Hormuz. Iraq had been able to secure French-made Exocet missiles for its more capable air force, and it successfully bombed Iranian shipping and oil platforms. Iran responded weakly with air raids against civilian populations inside Iraq's major urban centers. Baghdad's major oil supply moves through pipeline and is thus less vulnerable to attack.[2]

Iran's repeated land offensives against Iraqi territory failed, and popular dissatisfaction with economic dislocations fed by the war grew. Tehran, accordingly, sought to increase international attention to the important Gulf waterway and began to target Kuwaiti shipping in the summer of 1986.[3]

Kuwait, a member of the Saudi-led Gulf Cooperation Council (GCC), waited until November before announcing that it would seek assistance from either superpower to ward off continued Iranian attacks.[4] Public exposure of a secret but failed effort to trade arms to Iran for the return of Lebanese-held US hostages led a discredited Reagan administration to accept the Kuwaiti plea. The proximate cause for the United States to move a naval flotilla of twenty-four ships and 15,000 personnel into the Gulf area during the latter half of 1987 was the threat of Soviet aid to beleaguered Kuwait.[5]

THE UNITED STATES REFLAGS KUWAITI SHIPPING

The Kuwaiti request for protection was at first handled routinely within the US bureaucracy, but once the Iran arms scandal was disclosed[6] high administration officials grasped the gravity of the issue and moved to grant approval.[7] Whereas US dependence on imported oil had fallen considerably after worldwide disruptions in 1978–1979, Western Europe and Japan remained large recipients of Gulf-originated petroleum for industrial and private consumption.[8] The United States, arguably, could not be viewed as a credible leader of the Western alliance as well as a vital superpower intending to project military capability into a region crucial to its security if it chose to ignore the Kuwaiti tanker imbroglio.[9]

In January 1987 Mikhail Gorbachev had offered Soviet help to the emir of Kuwait to ensure free tanker movement through the Gulf.[10] US officials rushed to prevent the Soviet move and detailed, on February 6, a plan whereby Kuwait would reflag its eleven tankers as US shipping, entitled to US naval protection.[11] President Reagan formally adopted the reflagging policy on March 4, after being told that current naval assets—four ships in the Gulf and five more on standby—were sufficient to carry out the mission.[12] Congress was notified of the plan a week later, and through April and part of May technical support preparations were negotiated with friendly states in the area.[13] On May 17 an Iraqi pilot, without warning, fired several Exocet missiles at the US frigate *Stark* on patrol in Gulf waters. Damage to the unprotected ship was considerable, with a loss of thirty-seven sailors. A Baghdad government statement immediately acknowledged pilot error and regretted the incident.[14]

Iran was now in a position to manipulate US public and congressional opinion, distressed over US casualties and worried by an open-ended Reagan administration commitment in the Gulf. Tehran mined the waters close to Kuwait, and on July 24, two days after the first US-escorted convoy of reregistered Kuwaiti ships entered the Gulf, a lead supertanker, the *Bridgeton*, was struck and damaged by an exploding World War II–vintage mine.[15]

The US Navy and Joint Chiefs of Staff had severely misjudged Iran's ability to mine Gulf waters free from detection, and scurried during August to engage the superior minesweeping capability of the European allies of the

United States.[16] Most of the European states resisted the call to support US operations, but on August 10 a Panamanian-registered vessel hit a mine in the Gulf of Oman, just south of the Strait of Hormuz, suffering a twelve-foot hole below the waterline.[17] The incident—a first outside the Gulf—caused a reversal in British and French attitudes. The two European states dispatched minesweepers to the area—but as a defensive measure to protect their own shipping, not as a shield for Kuwaiti reflagged vessels.[18]

During September and October, a pronounced escalation in US-Iranian military activity transformed the reflagging matter into a major US responsibility for Gulf security, thereby providing a close reminder of other watershed periods in the Republic's history, notably Lebanon and Vietnam. US forces on nighttime patrol discovered an Iranian ship laying mines on September 20 and proceeded to blow the vessel out of the water, retrieving and repatriating survivors of the incident. US helicopters returned fire on Iranian gunboats that same month, and in October US operations resulted in the destruction and capture of patrol craft outfitted by Tehran.[19]

The Iranian leadership from mid- to late October responded by sending Chinese-made Silkworm missiles into a docked Kuwaiti reflagged tanker as well as holding platform.[20] And the United States, with a twenty-minute warning, conducted a retaliatory operation with the participation of destroyers and navy frogmen to obliterate oil-rigging platforms in the Gulf that served as housing for Iranian speedboats.[21] Toward the end of October Tehran announced that it possessed US-made Stinger missiles—undoubtedly acquired from US-backed Afghani freedom fighters—and threatened their use as a deterrent against US control of the Gulf.[22]

Congress was smarting from its sidelined position in what was rapidly becoming an "Americanized" Gulf conflict. The War Powers Resolution of 1973, unrecognized by every US president since Richard Nixon, was at issue. Reagan refused to invoke the provision that would trigger a stipulated period of ninety days in which the president would have to seek congressional authorization for the Gulf convoys or face a cutoff in funds. By the close of 1987 the Reagan administration was therefore confronted with a Solomonesque choice: manage a Gulf venture that at the least would involve military action against Iran and deteriorate into a wider war, or back down gracefully as a result of congressional mandate. Either move would endanger the international position of the United States and generate uncertainty and instability at a crucial moment in the history of the Middle East.

In the meantime, Reagan administration officials received yet another jolt on July 3, 1988, when the US cruiser *Vincennes* shot down an Iranian commercial airliner, apparently mistaking it for an F-14 attack fighter.[23] The incident, which resulted in 290 Iranian lives lost, was a somber reminder of how quickly the threat of escalation could arise. The Gulf states were quite naturally left to wonder whether US military operations had improved or worsened chances for long-term safety in the region.

Cleverly managed diplomatic negotiations nevertheless led to a satisfactory conclusion in the Iran-Iraq war. The offices of the UN secretary-general and representatives of the parties to the eight-year-old Gulf war spent much of 1988 working out details for an effective cease-fire,[24] but resolution of the war clearly was not the result of either a show of preponderant US military power or an attempt to portray the Soviet Union as endangering area stability. Instead, Iranian willingness to end hostilities stemmed from forces operating in the country's complex domestic politics—infrequently examined within US government circles. Although many US officials continued to question Soviet intentions in the Gulf, an even larger group had been embittered by images of a deceitful Iranian leadership bent on erasing Western influence from the region. The Khomeini regime's behavior in the Gulf, however, can be more easily understood if considered within the context of an interelite effort to preserve the revolution.

THE POLITICS OF IRAN'S GULF STRATEGY

Iraq took advantage of its superior weapons-delivery capability to rain scores of missiles on Tehran during 1987–1988. The Soviet-made Scuds caused massive casualties among Iranians and, together with a downturn in the nation's economic prospects, produced alarm in the core of support for Khomeini.[25] Revelations of a scheme to lure the United States into covertly selling military arms further enflamed the atmosphere. A decision to enter into a formula for peace with the Iraqis, therefore, seemed to be the most sensible way for Iran to escape from large-scale bombing as well as to begin recovery.[26] Khomeini, nevertheless, was always on the lookout to protect the essence of his Islamic revolution, especially if it meant playing on the moral weaknesses of others. A scaled-down conflict with Iraq set new challenges for those closest to the ayatollah. Quarrels had already broken out over how to keep the revolution pure and still deliver on economic and social improvements largely denied to a population ravaged by war. A powerful group of clerics led by parliamentary speaker and presidential candidate Rafsanjani backed a relaxation of hostilities with Iraq; their adversaries at the Ministry of Interior, in the prime minister's office, and among the Pasdaran (Revolutionary Guards) strongly opposed ending the war.[27]

Although Khomeini eventually accepted the advice of pragmatists such as Rafsanjani, he allowed an escalation of military attacks against Iraq's more vulnerable neighbors, therefore also giving in to the hard-liners.[28] Khomeini must have known that conducting raids on Kuwaiti vessels would provoke a forceful reaction from the superpowers. Although he may have hoped that mutual Soviet-US suspicions could be exploited to prevent the use of joint sanctions, he surely reasoned that uncorking the Pasdaran to prey on reflagged shipping would serve essential domestic needs. The move would remind an otherwise docile Iranian audience how the "Great Satan" had ignored fundamentalist aims in the region, thereby making a future US role there inconceivable.[29]

Khomeini, however, was to sink into solitude as a slackening in the contest with Iraq yielded temporary improvements in relations with Great Britain, France, West Germany, and Canada.[30] The lull in the war also permitted the Iranian regime to wrestle with political reforms. Ayatollah Montazari—Khomeini's designated successor until March 1989—reminded the public how loathsome executions were to the civilized world. A band of advisers loyal to Khomeini's son Ahmad soon coaxed the elder leader into taking issue with a reassertion of Western influence. Those grouped around Ahmad Khomeini—Prime Minister Mousavi and Interior Minister Mohtashami—desired to limit foreign credits and technological assistance as well as to prohibit negotiations leading to a release of Lebanese-held hostages.[31]

The publication of Salman Rushdie's *Satanic Verses* in early 1989 snapped Ayatollah Khomeini out of his somnabulist state. He was obviously revolted by the novel, which he claimed blasphemed the Prophet Muhammad, but Iran's spiritual head also saw the book's notoriety as a way of binding the nation during a period strained by the losses of war.[32] Because Khomeini was a steadfast revolutionary, he sided with those who found a revival of Westernism objectionable. The Iranian leader broke with Montazari at the end of March and ordered the reform-minded cleric to step down from his position as heir presumptive.[33] Montazari's resignation concluded a bitter campaign to curb the regime's excesses. Opposition to arbitrary arrest and torture had earned Montazari public recognition as a symbol of change. Khomeini and his cohorts, however, were not receptive to altering the essence of their revolution. They believed that Iran's fundamentalism was sustainable only by rooting out doubters and traitors.[34]

The pragmatists, for their part, were unprepared for the furor that erupted in the Muslim community in response to the publication of *Satanic Verses;* they were astonished by Khomeini's call to kill Salman Rushdie. Rafsanjani and his supporters saw the necessity to work their way back into Khomeini's good graces, so, in the first half of 1989, charges were leveled at the United States for conspiring against the Iranian government. The United States was linked to Great Britain, France, and Israel in an alleged plot to mistreat West Bank Palestinians. Rafsanjani issued instructions during May for US, British, and French citizens to be killed fivefold for every Palestinian martyred in the intifada. The repugnant statement was later retracted, but the vividness of the speaker's language and his insistence on punishing the Western "demons" led to speculation that Rafsanjani would become Khomeini's successor.[35]

Although renewed radicalism may have helped to stabilize Iran's government, the abuse it engendered sowed mistrust among Gulf leaders who expected a better tone of area relations in the aftermath of the war. The six

Arab monarchies that made up the GCC were looking to regain a more placid atmosphere. They hoped to replicate the 1970s, which had seen amicable settlement of disputes among Gulf neighbors as well as a promising beginning to regional cooperation.[36] When the GCC was formed in 1981, it had competing goals, the most enduring of which was to manage commercial, cultural, and technological linkages. But the 1979 Iranian revolution stirred such unease in Saudi Arabia, Bahrain, and Kuwait that their rulers spent much of the 1980s ensuring against internal upheaval. Uncertainties over the rise of Communist influence in neighboring Iran also frightened Gulf monarchs, especially the Saudis,[37] but the most worrisome aspect of Khomeini's power grab was its implications for exercising a conservative-based hegemony in the Gulf.

Although neutrality marked the GCC's official attitude to the Iran-Iraq war, some GCC members strayed to Iraq's side. Saudi Arabia, Kuwait, and the United Arab Emirates provided Iraq with a plentiful supply of arms and finances during its eight-year effort to subdue Khomeini's forces.[38] Saudi behavior during this period was often ambivalent, allowing Iran to think that any postwar recovery could be independent of trends in Gulf cooperation. Iran, for example, was forgiven for inciting Hajis (religious pilgrims) to political sloganeering, for authenticating Khomeini's form of Islam without granting equal status to others, for claiming territories in the western portion of the Gulf. Moreover, an exchange of visits by the Saudi and Iranian foreign ministers to each other's capitals resulted in expanded trade and cultural relations. The Saudis acquiesced in excluding outside powers from the region under foreseeable circumstances.[39]

Even when the Iranians and Saudis had fundamental differences over the course of the Iran-Iraq war, diplomatic rather than military means were generally used to settle matters. Interruptions in free shipping brought about by the tanker war were condemned by resolutions in the GCC and the Arab League, and through UN resolutions. Meanwhile, the Saudis prepared for a spillover of conflict by dramatically increasing their defense preparedness. Weapons systems—AWACs, streamlined F-15s, Stinger missiles, aerial refueling—were added to the Saudi inventory, making the Arabian kingdom a powerful regional adversary. Nevertheless, except for an occasional mission to protect air space, the Saudi military showed compliance when faced with Iranian aggressiveness.[40]

The Saudis' conciliatory tone toward Iran probably stemmed from a variety of reasons. Although they differed vigorously over Khomeinism, the Saudis and Iranians shared the view that religion was a core value of society. The two states came to recognize that the Soviet Union was a hostile influence better opposed than ignored. Similarly, they partially agreed that US military intervention in the Gulf was destructive for the region. Saudis and Iranians saw the Palestinian problem in much the same way, and disagreed only over the use of armed struggle as a solution. They looked at

Iraq with equal suspicion, believing that the secularist, nationalist regime in Baghdad was still politically ambitious and a threat to regional security.[41]

The Saudi government's attempt simply to contain Iran's radical impulses, however, was in sharp contrast to Western expectation. The United States, in particular, regarded Iran as a conspirator in the bombing of Pan American Airways flight 103, an instigator of the 1987 Mecca riots, a producer of chemical weapons, and a perpetrator of Lebanese instability. Although each charge had a measure of validity, the Muslim states in the region were far more concerned about foreign meddling. The Saudis, for example, had been outraged by Iran's involvement in the deaths of 400 pilgrims during the 1987 Haj,[42] but they showed even greater displeasure for the clumsy manner in which the United States behaved after the Iran arms sale, betraying both Tehran and Baghdad as a convenient means of limiting domestic damage from the scandal.

US dissembling in the Gulf made it easier for the Saudis to accept new arms suppliers now that Washington had demonstrated a cavalier attitude toward supposed allies. Chinese East Wind surface-to-surface, inter-mediate-range ballistic missiles, capable of reaching targets 1,800 miles distant, were bought, along with $20 billion worth of British-manufactured aircraft and the bases to house the planes.[43] Iraq, for its part, diversified its sources of weapons, mixing Soviet-made Scud Bs with French-supplied Exocets. The Scuds' range had been extended with the combined assistance of Egyptian, East German, and North Korean technicians. Iraq, moreover, possessed the most extensive holdings of chemical weapons in the region.[44]

Iran had worked its way toward a political strategy in the Gulf that depended more upon the fears of big power interventionism than a temporary risk to comity and good neighborliness. Khomeini was able to portray the US deepening Gulf commitment as the prelude to imperialism because Ronald Reagan's men badly misjudged the temper of GCC members. US officials slavishly followed the concept of Soviet encroachment in the area, but the Gulf states showed greater interest in preserving their individual cultural identities. Iran's leaders may have given the Gulf monarchs some scary moments as they went about ensuring their revolution, but the value premises of each society were never at issue. The United States, meanwhile, was known for its insensitivity to peoples who embraced standards other than its own.

Khomeini's wish to punish Rushdie and his promotion of the puritanical in Iran's internal struggle for power were welcome signs to the conservative Gulf states, who were mostly concerned that Khomeini should refrain from exporting his revolution. Still, they saw advantages in Iran's commitment to the sanctity of the Muslim faith. Gulf leaders as a whole were especially conscious that the power of their appeal rested upon the familiarity of religious observance and respect for Islamic tradition.[45]

THE UNITED STATES AND THE GULF IN THE BUSH ERA

The Bush administration in its early months was unprepared to examine the cultural exigencies of the Gulf states. A team assembled from the Departments of State and Defense, the National Security Council, and the Central Intelligence Agency spent most of the initial period devising a foreign policy to accompany the strategic review already under way. The nature of the Soviet threat, whether Gorbachev could successfully induce reform in the archaic system of the Soviet Union, how NATO should respond to change in the balance of forces—these matters consumed the full attention of security planners and defense consultants.[46] Regional matters were thrust forward either as a consequence of crisis—for example, the student revolt in the People's Republic of China, or Noriega's ballot stuffing in Panama—or because of their centrality to bilateralism with the Soviet Union.[47] Linkage—a discredited concept during the Carter and Reagan presidencies, although stylized in the Nixon-Ford period—was once again to be applied in specific cases where Soviet leverage could improve chances for peaceful conditions. Because the Gulf neither fit the crisis category nor was an appropriate area for settling differences with Moscow now that a cease-fire had quieted Irani-Iraqi conflict US officials became rather blasé.

A curious mixture of skepticism and eagerness greeted Iran's talk about repairing relations at the beginning of the Bush presidency,[48] but hope gave way to despair when the ayatollah ordered the execution of Salman Rushdie and otherwise threatened the United States over a string of imagined plots against Islam. Nevertheless, Iraq's apparent turn toward moderation in its relations with the West and the Arab world bolstered the impression of a Gulf at rest. Strongman Saddam Hussein let it be known that Iraq needed friendly ties with France, West Germany, the United States, Egypt, and Jordan. Despite a record of human rights abuses, including the use of chemical warfare against the Kurds, Iraq believed itself ready to be counted as a reasonable member of the family of nations.[49] Bush officials hoped that Iraq's latest role as chairman of the Arab Cooperation Council—an economic union with Egypt, Jordan, and North Yemen—could be used as a wedge to bring about tighter control over its missile development, chemical weapons program, and human rights effort.[50]

President Bush's decision to continue lowering the US profile in the Gulf by stripping the Kuwaitis of tanker protection was further evidence that the area had become, in Washington's view, a less dangerous place.[51] Informing the Saudis that they could not buy newer and more sophisticated weapons from the United States was yet another way of drawing away from Gulf matters. Riyadh's influence with the PLO, controversial and unproven as it was, was similarly not sought by US officials, who in 1989 had opened direct talks with Arafat's lieutenants in Tunis.[52] The Omanis and Bahrainis were also quite confused by the US de-emphasis on the Gulf. These smaller

Gulf kingdoms had willingly participated in basing agreements for the US rapid deployment forces, and it would not have been surprising if they had chosen to modify refueling arrangements as a result of US insistence on devaluing the significance of the Gulf region.

Although Bush officials believed their foreign policy fit a broader canvas than had predecessor Reagan's, programmatic choices concerning the Gulf continued to depend on how the United States thought about the Soviet Union. The Reagan administration's determination to reflag Kuwaiti vessels and otherwise respond to regional provocations grew from a strong sense that events had been planned by an aggressive, close-at-hand Soviet Union. The Bush government acknowledged that a reform-bound Gorbachev might be keen to dampen regional conflict and maintain flexibility in the face of localized flare-ups, even those taking place in adjacent territories. Beyond that, the most militarily capable Gulf states—Iran and Iraq—were war weary and, at least in Tehran's case, preoccupied with future leadership. Neither the United States nor the Soviet Union appeared to have a direct stake in the Gulf.

US officials had gained satisfaction from seeing Iran at bay, a decreased Soviet intrusiveness in the Gulf, and a Kremlin under some regional restraint. But how did the United States see cultural and religious revival in the region? For example, was there a presumption that fundamentalism acted as a deliberate brake on geopolitical considerations?

George Bush had been active in the previous administration, which had been unforgiving toward Iran. As vice-president, he had been convinced that the revolutionary regime that overthrew the shah intended to work to oust moderate, pro-Western governments throughout the region. Overtures to Khomeini for a transfer of arms had been meant as an enticement to release Lebanese-held hostages. When the deal went sour as a result of public exposure, the vice-president had merely resumed his expression of distaste for Iranian fundamentalism. And as president, George Bush had carefully to weigh outrageous Iranian conduct—for example, complicity in blowing up Pan Am flight 103, lobbying against a Middle East peace, taking an unbending position in the Rushdie affair—against the riveting success of revivalism.

The United States, galled by poor experiences with Iran, grew increasingly intolerant of fundamentalism, but it failed to recognize that conservative religion had found its way to the Gulf more than a century ago. Saudi orthodoxy was a pervasive force in Arabia long before Khomeini entertained millenarianism. Most of the GCC states owed their formation to traditional, tribal-oriented value systems. Political change took root in several of the monarchies as they borrowed early forms of constitutionalism, but Islam remained a powerful institutional force. It spread among the populace even as Iranian-bred Shiite dogma became unwelcome to the predominantly Sunni residents of the Gulf following Khomeini's political consolidation. Theological differences aside, the Gulf states shared a dedication to the centrality of the Prophet Muhammad, the Koran, and Sunna (traditions), principles of equality and social justice, opposition to corrupt and repressive government, and freedom from external interference in the makeup and conduct of their societies.[53]

The US relationship to Iraq, meanwhile, has been a curious one. Successive US governments treated Iraq with scorn, resenting Baghdad's hostility to a US-brokered Middle East peace and its status as a Soviet client arms recipient. Once the Iran-Iraq war broke out, Iraq found Soviet supplies inadequate and turned to the West. The Saudis acted as a conduit for very small amounts of US weapons until Baghdad opened an embassy in Washington. Thereafter, US-Iraqi relations took on an inverse proportionality to US-Iranian dealings, until the secret arms deliberations with Tehran were uncovered.[54]

Iraqi outrage at the sordid US-Iranian arms dealings nonetheless became moot when the Reagan administration furnished Baghdad with intelligence data and allowed them an update in their spare-parts inventory near the close of the Iran-Iraq war in 1988.[55] US-Iraqi relations steadied throughout 1989 as the White House viewed as positive Saddam Hussein's effort to build economic ties with moderates in the Arab world and US allies in Europe. US-based businesses were encouraged to join with other international firms and aggressively participate in the postwar reconstruction of Iraqi industry.[56]

Suspicions remained, though, about the Iraqi leader's military development plans, especially in light of Saddam Hussein's emphasis on long-range missile research.[57] The Bush administration continued to condemn Iraqi human rights abuses and found Saddam Hussein's gassing of the minority Kurds abominable.[58] Nevertheless, George Bush refused through the middle of 1990 to go along with congressional efforts to impose economic sanctions as a way of interfering in the Iraqi strongman's preparation of chemical and biological agents, as well as applying brakes to his missile program.[59] Each type of offensive weaponry was a serious threat to Iraq's Gulf neighbors and to the State of Israel.[60]

In the meantime, Kuwait decided not to forgive Iraq's $65 billion war debt.[61] GCC members, including Kuwait and Saudi Arabia, took the lead in improving ties with Iran.[62] And overall Gulf revenues stayed low as a consequence of an oil glut on the spot market in the late 1980s.[63]

The combination of these pressures pushed Saddam Hussein to reassess Baghdad's role in the Gulf's future. The Iraqi leader at first blustered his way toward OPEC readjustments in overall production allocations.[64] And when that netted Baghdad some added income, he targeted lower productivity levels for Kuwait and the United Arab Emirates.[65] But Saddam Hussein was still unable to coerce his Arab neighbors to release Iraq from its massive war debt or grant him territory as compensation for the war he claimed to have waged on their behalf against the fundamentalist-inspired Iranian regime. Saddam

Hussein was also unconvincing about alleged Kuwaiti improprieties in siphoning local oil supplies while the Iraqi strongman was otherwise engaged in fighting off Iranians.[66]

IRAQ INVADES KUWAIT

Iraq's government readied plans for a military assault on Kuwait as Saddam Hussein feigned an agreement with the Egyptians and Saudis to mediate an end to the quarrel.[67] The United States was drawn into the Iraqi leader's ruse, although warnings conveyed during the summer to the US ambassador in Baghdad take on a more ominous tone in retrospect.[68] On the morning of August 2, 1990, a large Iraqi armored force spearheaded a lightning invasion of Kuwait,[69] and after a few days' mopping-up operation, the units regrouped to make it appear as though an attack on Saudi soil was imminent.[70] The United States responded by accepting a Saudi request to place its military forces in the desert opposite the Iraqis.[71] Within several weeks President Bush managed to assemble, under UN provision, matériel and personnel support from a wide array of nations, including the Arab states of Egypt, Syria, and Morocco.[72] Eventually, a multinational naval force was positioned to implement twelve UN resolutions that called for Iraq to disgorge Kuwait or face economic ruin and catastrophe through an enforced global blockade of all products traveling to Baghdad.[73] The United States added to its military components in the Saudi desert by fielding combined US force strength of nearly half a million men and women by the end of 1990.[74] War fever raced through both US and Iraqi camps whereas diplomacy essentially remained unexplored.[75]

During the initial period of the crisis, Saddam Hussein cleverly manipulated first the internment, and then the release of hundreds of US, French, British, Arab, and other nationals caught unaware in Kuwait and Iraq by the August 2 invasion.[76] He then annexed and looted Kuwait while his military forces ravaged the women of Kuwait City.[77] He even attempted to destroy all known records of the Kuwaitis, thereby erasing their nationality from recorded memory.[78] The thousands of Kuwaitis who fled to nearby Saudi Arabia stood helpless while their rulers in exile pledged billions for assistance as a means of recovering their territory and promised a more democratic and open society upon the ruling family's return to power.[79]

Saddam Hussein also downplayed his secularism as he cynically called upon all Muslims to assert their opposition to US deployments on Saudi soil.[80] The call for a jihad, or holy war, was answered rhetorically but with great enthusiasm and pride by overflowing crowds of fundamentalists in Jordan and Algeria, and among Palestinians on the West Bank and in Gaza.[81] Even those Iraqis who stood against Saddam Hussein and were in self-imposed exile in the West publicly expressed their regret over the US buildup.[82] Perhaps the most opportunistic move was that of Yassir Arafat when he appropriated the holy war summons as a symbolic gesture for Palestinians to reinvest in their intifada.[83] Third World countries in general were encouraged to mount an international campaign against Israel's flouting of the several UN resolutions that spoke for better Palestinian treatment in the occupied territories.[84]

The United States, for its part, was reduced to playing out a tragicomical role by year's end. The world was told to keep itself focused on Iraq's naked aggression. And while the military forces of a slew of countries waited nervously in the desert sands, fundamentalist rage was building to deny the multinational units the fruits of any victory that might be in plain sight. The United States simply had to bear the burden of bringing imperialism back to the Gulf, whatever else might have been engineered in the way of Iraqi withdrawal from Kuwait.[85] Saddam Hussein thereby may have succeeded in ensuring mass Arab and Muslim disapproval for the US military posture in the area, despite more positive signals from their leaders. In any event, the charge that Washington was responsible for all the ills that plagued the Muslim peasant—to live stripped of decency and equity—was now out there for Saddam Hussein falsely to bestow upon George Bush.

Iraq's chilling move against Kuwait also led to a cementing of relations between Saudi Arabia and Iran; glorious foes became brand-new allies.[86] In the words of a timeless Arab proverb, the enemy of one's enemy is a friend. Significantly, at an early point in the crisis, the Saudis offered a way out that might reward Iraqi withdrawal by allowing Saddam Hussein either rights to oil concessions in Kuwait or the ceding of small parcels of land from Kuwaiti territory. And in the first week of 1991, France and Germany proposed a way to avoid the start of war: Iraq should be guaranteed against attack if it totally withdraws from Kuwait and then any unresolved question in the region could be discussed in international meetings.[87]

But within hours after a UN deadline for Iraq to leave Kuwait had expired, in the pre-dawn of January 16, 1991, US, British, and Saudi aircraft began a massive bombardment of Baghdad. A continuous day-and-night air campaign—amounting to over 100,000 sorties—lasted for several weeks before US-led coalition forces struck at Iraqi ground units, already softened up, in the Kuwaiti theater of operations. US, British, French, and Saudi armor as well as infantry conducted large-scale sweeps, and together with total allied mastery of the air, caught escaping Iraqi forces, destroying two-thirds of the divisional strength sent into Kuwait. More than 50,000 Iraqis were taken prisoner during the final hours of the month-long military campaign.[88]

President Bush, on the evening of February 27, announced that a temporary cease-fire was in place, and US and allied forces moved swiftly to retake Kuwait City and carve out a fifteen-mile occupation zone in southern Iraq. Saddam Hussein ordered an acceptance of terms attached to the cease-fire on March 3, and the newest Gulf war came to an end.[89] Principal conditions for the cease-fire included unconditional acceptance of all twelve UN-passed resolutions relating to Iraqi withdrawal from Kuwait, the return of all prisoners of war, and liability for damages suffered by the Kuwaitis. The United States for its part agreed to leave southern Iraq as soon as stability in the area had been achieved. (A small contingent of UN forces in fact replaced US ground units in southern Iraq by the last week in April.)

In the weeks that followed, Saddam Hussein attempted to consolidate a power base badly in need of repair. But the Kurds in the north proclaimed their independence and Shias rebelled to the south. Remnants of Iraq's elite Republican Guard, using helicopter gunships banned to them under terms of the cease-fire, overwhelmed lightly armed Kurdish as well as Shia elements. These Iraqi military successes enabled Saddam Hussein to gather desperately needed internal strength. The Kurds, meanwhile, fled by the thousands to the border areas with Iran and Turkey. As of this writing, they are existing in semisqualid conditions while US military in the area have erected, on presidential orders, a series of refugee encampments; these same allied units moved south from the Turkish border to secure a thirty-five–mile zone in northern Iraq, thereby giving the Kurds force protection.

In any case, when the aftereffects of this new Gulf war are finally understood, the United States may have to pull out of the desert at the request of local parties. The Gulf then could return to a hegemonic struggle of Iran, Saudi Arabia, and Iraq, with the former two states making a try at unity based upon traditional cultural identity patterns. What is crucial for the United States to believe is that its presence, albeit requested, can only be temporary. Even if the United States had suffered heavy casualties in war, its Arab allies would not have wanted a NATO-style military relationship to develop in the Gulf.

5

Crosscurrents of US
Strategy: The Levant

George Bush may have intended only a slight connection between the new Gulf crisis spurred by the Iraqi invasion of Kuwait and resolution of tensions on the West Bank and Gaza when he spoke about the Middle East during a UN speech in October 1990.[1] But the linkage—however finely spun—gives new focus to the Middle East peace process. Israelis object strenuously to even a hint of a tie between Iraqi maltreatment of Kuwaitis and their behavior toward Palestinians. Meanwhile, the killing of seventeen Palestinians on Jerusalem's Temple Mount in early October by an undermanned and panicky Israeli police contingent marked the largest number of deaths on a single day in the three-year-old intifada.[2] And when the hard-line, right-wing Likud government of Yitzhak Shamir, installed at the end of July after breakup of a 1988 coalition, refused a UN investigation of the incident, the most serious rift in US-Israeli history began.[3] Washington reluctantly joined in a UN Security Council vote to censure Jerusalem's handling of the Temple Mount shooting.[4]

ISRAEL AND THE INTIFADA

The character of Israel's response to the intifada in fact has given formal expression to the loss of a democratic will by the Jewish state's leadership. The army was at first ordered to teargas demonstrators, then to club the youthful rock throwers, and finally to wound and kill Palestinians, at close range and with automatic weapons. When the stone throwing showed no signs of tapering off, Israeli authorities began demolishing and sealing off residences belonging to so-called ringleaders; others, more fortunate, were shipped off to Lebanon. Nevertheless, a doubling of incidents was recorded during 1989, as the effort to resist Israel's curbing of the Palestinian revolt gained strength from the outside.[5]

Despite the government's imposing intermittent curfews on those refugee camps thought to be particularly irksome and cutting off electricity to large numbers of villages, and despite the collapse of public services in much of the West Bank—in addition to intimidations, beatings, and mass arrests— the intifada continued.[6] Official figures confirm more than 900 Palestinians dead, many times more wounded, and thousands imprisoned without due process.[7] Yet, Israel's populace has been infrequently critical of the government's countermeasures; only a limited number of prominent individuals or those otherwise involved in the disorders have spoken out.[8] Although some in the officer ranks have grumbled about army ineffectiveness,[9] increases in the number of Palestinian-inflicted stabbings of innocent passersby on Jerusalem's streets or other types of attacks directed at those in Jewish settlements have led to a strengthening of Israeli security measures.[10]

Israel, as it enters its fifth decade, is no longer a "light unto the nations." The Jewish state, in fact, has traded universalistic premises for particularistic ones.[11] Western values, especially enjoyment of decent standards by minorities, are considered inconsequential when opposed by the interests of a growing segment of Israelis already committed to defending the state in nonpluralist terms. The intifada is responsible for bringing Jews into direct confrontation with a democratic process that has seen the state through five wars and countless attacks organized by intractable neighbors. It should not be surprising that ideals built on nostalgia are being abandoned by a Jewish society undergoing simultaneous population changes, ethnic and religious cleavages, international disrespect, and threat of revolution by a subjugated minority.[12]

GEORGE BUSH AND THE PEACE PROCESS

When the Bush administration looked more closely at how to organize and deliver a peace between Israelis and Palestinians, it saw a process stuck on convening an international conference. In the final weeks of the Reagan presidency, former Secretary of State George Shultz tried but failed to get a two-stage negotiation going, based on interim self-rule for Palestinians and an end to Israel military occupation, decided in Geneva-style discussions.[13] Bush's appointee to succeed Shultz—James Baker—was the consummate Washington insider and pragmatist. Baker, a former White House chief of staff, campaign director for both Reagan and Bush, and treasury secretary in the second Reagan cabinet, was determined to take a step-by-step approach to the Middle East peace process, with Israelis engaging Palestinians directly.[14]

Baker and his policy planning director, Dennis Ross, believed that because Jordan was no longer an active negotiating partner for either Palestinians or Israelis, and because the intifada made territorial compromise a more odious task, peace could be brought about only through politicized arrangements.[15] Prime Minister Shamir, much to the surprise of all of the parties, obliged by offering an election plan for the West Bank and Gaza during the middle of May 1989. The Shamir plan was in keeping with proposals made at Camp David in 1978 and called for elected Palestinian representatives to conduct negotiations for self-rule with Israelis at a future unspecified date.[16] Shamir and his advisers hoped by this maneuver to exclude the PLO from participation in subsequent peace talks, as the method by which candidates were to run for office would be a matter for Israeli administration.[17] The United States, nevertheless, was buoyed by the fact there was now a political context to the peace process that would have to include responses to questions about the rights of assembly, speech, and organization.[18]

Meanwhile, the elections themselves became hostage to squabbling among a divided Israeli cabinet—a leftover of the 1988 decision to mount a unity government—and actions and counteractions by those on either side of the intifada. Egyptian President Hosni Mubarak offered a way out of the stalled elections in July through a ten-point plan that specified voting and candidate participation for East Jerusalemites, free campaigning before and during the day of selection, prior Israeli commitment to abide by the results, and international supervision of the entire process. According to the Egyptian proposal, Israel also was to halt further Jewish settlements in the territories and work toward final arrangements in accord with UN Resolutions 242 and 338.[19]

Bickering inside the Israeli cabinet prevented the Jewish leadership from agreeing to Mubarak's plan, so Secretary Baker attempted to clarify matters in October with the addition of several new points. The so-called Baker plan asked for an Israeli-Palestinian dialogue in Cairo to make decisions about how the election process should proceed.[20] Meanwhile, Israel's government was already at odds with itself regarding who should make up the Palestinian delegation, and the Palestinians themselves were split by a fundamentalist-nationalist struggle. The cause of peace atrophied over the first few months of 1990. When the United States publicly objected in March to Jewish émigrés from the Soviet Union settling on the West Bank, and in particular within East Jerusalem, the Shamir government stepped out of the peace process.[21] An embattled Laborite leadership that staked its reputation on a peaceful resolution of the Palestinian issue thereupon withdrew from the unity government and new elections were called.[22]

Israel took three months to form its thirteenth government, and peace efforts were, of course, totally abandoned through this period. In the meantime, a spasm of violence fed the government's repressive tactics throughout the territories. The interim regime of Yitzhak Shamir used the time to add Jewish settlements to those already strung out over much of the West Bank.[23] And a US-PLO dialogue started a year earlier was broken off as a consequence of the umbrella organizaton's failed attempt to breech Israeli defenses along the Tel Aviv beach. Arafat refused to do anything to punish the perpetrators of the raid, so President Bush ordered a suspension of talks.[24]

A US-Egyptian effort to revive the Baker plan was floated for a time in early July.[25] Thereafter, any contribution to peace had to be discarded because a new Israeli cabinet flanked by two hard-line ex–defense ministers took its place under the lead of Yitzhak Shamir.[26] Responsibility for housing in the territories came under the direction of one of the former defense heads, Ariel Sharon.[27] The Arab world looked on these developments as almost amounting to a declaration of war.[28] The United States continued, though, to seek some method for promoting elections in the territories.[29] West Bank and Gaza voting no doubt had fallen victim to prospects for an immediate Gulf conflict until the United Nations and the world could see to it that linkage might open a fruitful way of handling both of these difficult Middle East matters.

When it became clear, though, how grand a military victory the US-led coalition achieved against Saddam Hussein's troops, President Bush decided to use the allied unity as a prod for advancing the peace process. So he ordered Secretary Baker to the Middle East once again and hoped that Israel and its Arab neighbors could be persuaded to find new flexibility for peace.

James Baker's March 11, 1991, visit to Israel—his first to the Jewish state—was followed by travels to Egypt, Saudi Arabia, and Syria. While in Israel, the secretary of state also met with a delegation of Palestinians. In each of these meetings, Baker found willingness to consider new formulas toward making the peace process work. For example, the Israelis presented the secretary with a proposal for starting talks with both Arab state leaders and Palestinians; the dialogue with Arab representatives would not be preceded by meetings with the Palestinians but be held concurrently. Discussions were thereby seen within a regional context instead of operating as an international conference. Syria, however, wanted a UN and European presence. Saudi Arabia felt that only the parties to peace—Israelis, Palestinians, Jordanians and Syrians—should be represented, so they declined to join.[30]

Baker's trips to the area in mid- and late April seemed to accomplish little. The later visit was interrupted by the secretary of state breaking off talks to attend the funeral of his 96-year-old mother. In the meantime, new Jewish settlements sprouted in the West Bank, the Shamir government failed to allow for East Jerusalem Palestinians to attend any negotiation, and the Syrians seemed determined to shift the onus for being the most recalcitrant party onto their Jewish neighbor. A promising sign, however, occurred when Baker journeyed to Moscow and appeared with Foreign Minister Bessmertnykh to announce that the Soviets would indeed cosponsor whatever meeting or conference emerged from the secretary of state's travels. Jordan and PLO roles in any forthcoming discussion remain unclear, although the United States has welcomed back King Hussein into the peace process. Yassir Arafat, on the other hand, has not been accorded a position in the search for peace, according to US spokesmen.[31]

A fifth journey to the Middle East was undertaken by Secretary Baker in the middle of May, but this too proved unsuccessful. The GCC states led by Saudi Arabia now offered to attend a peace conference but only as observers. Israeli officials became offended by the artificial nature of the compromise.

Prime Minister Shamir also refused to grant the United Nations a role in a future meeting or to accept the possibility of additional sessions if the conference should stall. So Baker returned to the United States, since neither Syria nor Jordan would meet Israelis in a regional conference without the provisos that Prime Minister Shamir had just rejected.

Quiet diplomacy, however, seemed to work in July as Soviet Foreign Minister Bessmerthykh joined Secretary Baker in pressuring Syria to change its stance on attending a conference. Assad announced that he could go to a meeting with silent UN presence. Baker flew off to Damascus to personally accept the Syrian leader's change of position and thereby begin his sixth try at cobbling together a regional peace.

Egypt's President Mubarak followed with a suggestion that the Arab states suspend their 43-year old Israeli boycott provided the Jewish state halted construction of its West Bank settlements. Baker received assurances of such a move at stops in Saudi Arabia and Jordan. The Lebanese indicated that they too would attend any forthcoming conference. And with acceptances for direct talks by Egypt, Saudi Arabia, Jordan, and Lebanon in his pocket, Baker journeyed to Jerusalem for Prime Minister Shamir's response.

Shamir, noting the changed circumstances, conditionally accepted the US formula for a meeting; he would go if Palestinian representation could be satisfactorily resolved. A week of discussions at the summit in Moscow between Presidents Bush and Gorbachev to sign a START Treaty intervened. But at the conclusion of their summit, the US and Soviet leaders announced that they would issue invitations for a Middle East peace conference for October. Baker thereupon traveled back to Jerusalem to hear Shamir say that Israel would accept the invitation if neither the PLO nor Palestinians from East Jerusalem would be among the attendees. Baker publicly agreed to the limitation and called upon the Palestinians to be flexible. The US secretary of state then completed his journey by visiting Morocco and Algeria, winning support for the comference idea at each location. Baker even announced that he would not mind Libyan leader Qhadafi's attendance as an observer. As of this writing the United States is left with a host of procedural matters to resolve before a regional peace meeting can get underway. It is also too early to determine how the failed Soviet right-wing coup may affect the timing of a Middle East regional peace meeting, whether in fact Gorbachev will move as swiftly to implement the US formula for resolving tensions in the area.

Bush and Baker, nonetheless, have found a strong desire on the part of Israelis to reach normalization with the Arab states. The Shamir cabinet may also be willing to talk with a new core of Palestinians that are neither activist nor tied to incidents sparked by the PLO or leaders of the intifada. Arab leaders, for their part, have to accept that giving back territory quickly or dealing earnestly with Palestinians is not on the Israeli agenda. Instead, Jerusalem intends the Arab world and the United States to be subjected to a limited version of peace.

EGYPTIAN-ISRAELI RELATIONS AFTER CAMP DAVID

In the meantime, Egyptians and Israelis have felt disappointed and resentful at being unable to arrange even modest improvements in a ten-year relationship noted more for missed opportunities than real accomplishments. In retrospect, the decade since Camp David is devoid of cultural exchanges, loosening of travel or trade barriers, and understanding about political or religious attachments. In fact, suspicions only deepened as experience seemed to confirm that leaders in Cairo and Jerusalem could be misdirected when confronted by history and the priorities of important domestic constituencies.[32]

Enmity, born of many years of fierce struggle and sacrifice in which thousands on both sides have died, could not be easily erased despite the best efforts of Anwar Sadat, Menachem Begin, and their successors in office. Isolated events, such as the shooting of six Sinai-based Israeli tourists by a crazed Egyptian soldier[33] and an anti-Semitic propaganda campaign on the part of Cairo's press,[34] have been annoying reminders of the tenderness of a normalization process made more problematic each day. And beyond the brittleness of security and media performances lay a package of domestic grievances that shadowed the Egyptian government's plans to manage some sort of peace with the Jewish state.

Egypt's President Mubarak has been buffeted by the conflicting demands of a military and bourgeoisie used to benefits from liberalization programs, political oppositionists grown critical of an environment riddled by bribes and corruption, and Islamicists who eagerly look toward removal of secularization in society.[35] Mubarak, in fact, ended decades of mistrust in Muslim groups by approving their participation in parliamentary elections as well as greater association in education, social, and professional organizations. He endorsed Islamic demands to establish Muslim law as a basis for statutory requirements at a time when Muslim extremists accused of Anwar Sadat's murder were standing trial.[36] In addition, elements not yet a part of the group structure, marginalized by their meager share of resources, have been poised to join with those more cynical and radical to overturn the political order.[37]

So far, Hosni Mubarak has outwitted his adversaries and avoided the gathering of opposing forces by taking few risks, responding to the country's pressing economic difficulties cautiously and through nonideological solutions, and instituting divide-and-rule tactics to prevent political confrontation.[38] The tempo of government activity, therefore, came from how artful Mubarak was in masking polarized attitudes among national elites on the one hand and Egypt's underrepresented poor and those comparatively well off on the other hand. However, the scales were tipped against Mubarak whenever the Egyptian president mentioned relations with Israel.

The question of how to deal with the Jewish state troubled a wide spectrum of groups that normally stood apart on most matters. Pressure to dilute Egypt's relationship with Israel came from such diverse sources as lawyers' guilds and Islamic extremists to nationalists and worker-peasants[39]—the last facing grim living conditions despite their newly won enfranchisement. A burgeoning rentier class within the bourgeoisie, however, saw its status helped by Egypt's continued association with Israel, which they saw as improving their chances to capitalize on higher levels of foreign economic support.[40] But, while the military, especially arms procurement officers, received benefits from a US-supplied weaponry program—in part prompted by steady Egyptian-Israeli relations—they were unwilling to be bound by its implications.[41]

Israelis, for their part, fragmented along ideological rather than socioeconomic or sociopolitical lines when ties with Egypt were tested internally. Right-wingers exhibited discomfort at the prospect of a more expansive Egyptian relationship because they were sure that prolonged contacts with Arabs would interfere with their mission to spread Jewish culture and tradition.[42] Leftists, meanwhile, saw relations with Egypt improved by giving way on the overheated Taba dispute.[43]

The contest for Taba—how to resolve title to an 800-meter stretch of beachfront on the Red Sea—dragged on for an interminable period before an arbitration panel awarded the parcel of land to Egypt in late February 1989.[44] Seven years of forbearance to reconcile rival claims and the high visibility given the issue, in spite of its ordinariness, provide some measure of how focused the parties have been on each other. In fact, Taba was merely the latest in a string of encounters that had been made to respond more directly to the bureaucracies, in whose custody the peace machinery resided, than to short-sighted domestic constituencies. Egypt and Israel appeared to be saying that officials who showed great sensitivity in relieving anxieties about war were held in greater esteem. And, in a highly charged atmosphere permeated by both a strong possibility for compromising Egypt's pan-Arab aspiration and the weakening of Jewish solidarity, keeping the relationship to a discrete minimum instead of severing bonds altogether gave to some an impression of enfeeblement if calculated on a strictly cost-benefit basis.

Why, then, have Mubarak and his counterparts in Israel chosen to set aside the preferences of powerful internal groups while preserving an otherwise burdensome and strained relationship? And should ties already pressed beyond normal limits inexorably be dissolved, or can the parties substitute a warming trend as a result of reassessing and US nudging? The United States may soon find itself entering a bargaining period in which the Egyptian and Israeli governments see their future relationship as fanciful, even Kafkaesque. Leaders in Cairo and Jerusalem believe that their nations' flawed performances drew directly upon a decade of unremarkable purposes on the part of each side. Moreover, these same statesmen doubt that change can be made unless the premises under which talks originally surfaced take a radical step away from the "cold peace" lately used to describe their relations.[45]

When Israelis look at the past ten years with Egypt, they come away with a sense of restrictions intentionally placed on the boundaries of association. Jewish officials point to special labeling for Egyptian travelers bound for Israel, a tendency for imported goods licenses and letters of credit to be mysteriously held up in the Egyptian bureaucracy, and a noticeable lack of solicitation by Cairo in the fields of energy and agricultural technology transfer. Egypt's preference for multilateral over bilateral frameworks, its practice of refusing to grant resident visas or work permits to aspiring Israeli soil experts, and its decision to do without long-term, large-scale arrangements—for example, the diversion of Nile waters to Gaza—have further convinced the Jerusalem government that obstructions to normalization were planned all along.[46]

Egypt found Israel's attack on the Iraqi nuclear storage site at Osarik, the Jewish state's invasion of Lebanon, and its maltreatment of West Bank Palestinians embarrassing. The government in Cairo saw the lack of prior notice of these damaging events as proof of Israel's disregard for Arab and Islamic sensitivities, and Egyptian elites concluded—considering the Jewish military's complicity in the 1982 massacres at Sabra and Shatilla refugee camps—that a withdrawal of Cairo's ambassador to Tel Aviv was warranted. The Egyptian public additionally thought poorly of their opposite number's unwillingness to push its government toward compromise in the interval that separated Jewish mishandling of Lebanon and an Israeli cabinet decision to go ahead with arbitration on Taba.[47]

Israeli officials attempted, during the first half of the unity government lasting from 1984 to 1988, to work their way back into Egypt's confidence by ending Israel's occupation of Lebanon as well as slightly improving conditions for Palestinians on the West Bank. An unprecedented July 1986 visit to Morocco's King Hassan helped former Prime Minister Peres pave the way for a resumption of dialogue between Cairo and Jerusalem that September in Alexandria, Egypt. The Mubarak-Peres summit talks were followed by a joint agreement to go to arbitration over Taba, the return of Egypt's ambassador to Tel Aviv, and a set of inconclusive discussions in Cairo, Jerusalem, and elsewhere about the wisdom of convening an international peace conference to settle matters left open by the Camp David Accords.[48]

The United States, meanwhile, was pulled in separate directions by each of the parties, who hoped to recast the intifada and at the same time rescue a moribund Middle East peace process. Israelis tried to show Washington that they could crush the uprising quickly, thereby making it costly for terrorists to attempt to predetermine outcomes.[49] Egyptians signaled their fears that the United States would not take seriously a locally inspired response to years of Palestinian mistreatment by an increasingly stubborn and haughty occupation force.[50] Each party, though, saw the violence of Palestinian youth as a consequence of a peace process fallen into disuse. Egypt and Israel, therefore, in the spring of 1988 concluded that the United States must regain its role in helping to move the region toward a workable peace formula.[51]

Although US Secretary of State Shultz's 1988 Middle East peace mission meant that any settlement was certain to include an international dimension, Palestinian attendance, and security guarantees, it foundered on the dynamics of how and when to accomplish such moves. The Soviet connection to peace, which Egypt seemed so keen to arrange, was made more difficult by Moscow's failure to reestablish ties with Israel in the twenty years since the 1967 war. A Russian consular mission sent to Jerusalem at the end of 1986 did not succeed in moving the Jewish state toward resolution of their inchoate relations.[52] Moreover, with elections in Israel coming up in November, hawkish elements in a unity government now controlled by the Likud party were quite resistant to conference participation by Palestinians separated from Jordan. Mubarak's public patronage of Arafat led many in the Jewish state to wonder whether Egypt's intent was to win for the PLO head a seat at the table, a prospect that remained insupportable to all segments of Israel's vocal population.[53] In any case, the parties may have seen, in the timing of Shultz's trip, the Reagan administration's leaving to its successor a major void in securing a revived Egyptian-Israeli relationship.

Egyptian-US relations benefited in the Bush period by Mubarak's taking the Arab lead in a Palestinian-Israeli dialogue and his furnishing troops for the multinational effort to dislodge Iraq from Kuwait.[54] Egypt's president also showed himself to be an adept peacemaker when he proposed a ten-point plan in the first half of 1989 to get elections on the West Bank moving. He exhibited further flexibility for peace by holding the PLO accountable for terrorism directed against Israel midway in 1990.[55] Nonetheless, Mubarak angrily lashed out at the right wing in Israeli politics for making peace unworkable when Shamir's Likud government insisted on settling Soviet Jewish émigrés in East Jerusalem.[56] And neither the election proposals nor pressure applied to Arafat for disciplining maverick PLO groups who sponsored terror brought Mubarak a successful outcome. His condemning Israel for planning to build more West Bank Jewish settlements also fell on deaf ears both inside the Shamir-led government and among moderates in the PLO.[57] Once a US-Egyptian initiative to establish direct Palestinian-Israeli talks was aborted and a new hard-line Israeli government set up, Arafat shifted the focus of the PLO's peace offensive to Baghdad.[58]

Meanwhile, Mubarak had engineered his way back into the Arab fold. He reestablished ties with Syria's President Assad and coordinated a strategy with him that might lead to improvements in Damascus's view of Washington.[59] In fact, Assad was later persuaded to give additional Arab cover to the 1990 multinational deployment in the Gulf by contributing an armored unit.[60] The Arab League also allowed Cairo to resume its seat in the second half of 1990, after a twelve-year absence.[61]

US-EGYPTIAN TIES

The United States welcomed Mubarak's help in the peace process, especially his interceding with those who felt uneasy about resolution of the conflict with Israel. Baker was openly grateful to the Egyptian president when Mubarak committed the largest Arab force to the defense of Saudi Arabia. Baker publicly consulted with Mubarak about US plans for pushing Iraq out of Kuwait.[62] And the Bush administration made a great show of easing Cairo's financial pain by persuading the US Congress to forgive a $7 billion debt for previous purchases of US military supplies.[63] France followed suit when it canceled a quarter of the monies owed it on similar sales to Egypt.[64]

But US and Egyptian governments were worried most about how Mubarak's efforts to retrieve peace in the West Bank and Gulf may have enflamed fundamentalist passions. Working for an Israeli-Palestinian dialogue always has entailed risks for Mubarak, especially now that the Muslim Brotherhood has been legalized. An outbreak of violence in February against Israeli tourists[65] and the October assassination of the Parliament speaker, killed by mistake instead of the interior minister,[66] showed how important religious extremism had become. Cairo originally blamed the speaker's death on Iraqis smuggled into the Egyptian capital to retaliate against Mubarak's wanting Saddam Hussein removed from Kuwait and from power in Iraq.[67] However, when those arrested for the incident later confessed that their target had been the interior minister, it became clear that the event had religious purposes. The overthrow of Egypt's secularized government and its replacement by a strict Islamic regime was said to be the intended motive.[68]

How deep the fundamentalist appeal runs in Egypt is debatable. But what cannot be questioned is the spread of an ethic that demands religious sanction for programs as well as policies and that legitimates and revives Egyptian cultural tradition. How focused Cairo and Washington are on associating the United States with a sense of realpolitik, or a conventional wisdom approach, could give fundamentalism a real boost not only in Egypt but elsewhere in the Levant.

JORDAN AND THE PEACE PROCESS

In the meantime, King Hussein's march away from the West Bank and Gaza on July 31, 1988, gave little hope to those who espoused a Jordanian option as a legitimate way out of the Palestinian problem. His determination to have Jordan's presence vanish from the territories, especially removing subsidies for school construction and salaries of teachers and other administrative cadres, emerged in part from sheer frustration over Arafat's fickleness on behalf of Palestinians, but also as a consequence of refusal on the part of the inhabitants there to sit for the king's rule.[69] The thirty-nine months since King Hussein's surprise announcement saw Jordan itself gripped by a degree of insecurity it has seldom experienced over its nearly seventy year history. Economic shortfalls, unstable prices, and internal bickering aroused a fundamentalist-sponsored reaction that interfered with the king's governance. Strikes ensued and King Hussein was even called away from a state visit to Washington in order to curb dissidence and bring about necessary changes in the economic and political management of his kingdom.[70] The unrest prompted speculation about the king's intentions concerning Middle East peace and started a round of questions about whether King Hussein could regain his earlier prominence in the bargaining process.

Alluding to a Jordanian option—an elliptical reference to the exercise of Hashemite political control east and west of the River Jordan[71]—has been a game, an essentially unproductive practice enjoyed by left-wing Israeli politicians and some US officials who were prone to thinking of the Palestinian issue in idyllic rather than cold, hard terms. The fact remains that King Hussein at his magnanimous best never conceived of accepting responsibility for any less than the whole of the West Bank and Gaza.[72] Territorial compromise (i.e., slicing up the area between Jordan and Israel) had no serious chance of working despite the approval given it by every US administration since that of President Gerald Ford.[73]

The struggle now occurring within Jordan has much to do with how King Hussein's subjects look at themselves in relation to Palestinians, vis-à-vis Israelis, and in comparison to nearby Islamic-run states. The intifada, therefore, has had a corrosive effect on Jordan's near-term role in Middle East peace but, strangely, has prepared the Hashemite kingdom well for longer-term strategies that may enable it to find better solutions for managing fundamentalism on the East Bank. The intifada closed the door on a perspective that took for granted that the king somehow could adequately represent and bargain for Palestinian rights on the ground.[74] The spectacle of youngsters willing to lay down their lives in defense of their freedoms acted as a spur to King Hussein's own estimate of his irrelevancy and decided him to disengage from the territories. Nevertheless, that understanding may have made the king so sensitive to a fundamentalist dynamic operating in Jordan that the way has now been opened to accept populist indignation at the US military role in the Gulf.[75]

King Hussein's reliance on Iraq for trade is widely understood in the West. And his early equivocation over Jordan's becoming a bridge in the supply of goods entering Aqaba bound for Baghdad was forgiven, so long as Amman continued to adhere to the global economic blockade against Saddam Hussein.[76] The king struck a lonely and pathetic pose when he insisted at the end of 1990 that the United States and its Arab allies cancel their war preparations in the Gulf.[77]

Jordan's real tragedy comes, though, as a consequence of local support deserting moderate solutions on the Gulf and West Bank crises. Jordan's populace has been lately reeling from too much poverty, too much violence, and too much inequity, arising out of a flood of refugees who cannot be dealt with by simply waiting for the monied interests in the Gulf to come to their rescue.[78] Neither can Palestinians, who make up fully 60 percent of the Jordanian population, allow their lives to be subjected any longer to the whims of a quixotic and increasingly immoderate Israeli government. A combination of the Palestinian and Jordanian disaffected—probably a majority in the kingdom—have thus been militating their way toward a fundamentalist perspective that may be seen as legitimate by the royal family or found to be threatening and destablizing. King Hussein and his entourage might find themselves driven from office if they choose to temporize about the pull of fundamentalism or meet the phenomenon head on in an attempt to defeat it.[79] Whatever happens, the Jordanian option has now proved its uselessness as an aspect of conventional wisdom and deserves to be retired from US Middle East policy.

SYRIA AND ISRAEL IN THE LEVANT

Strangely enough, Israel alone among the states in the Levant shares prospective Syrian views on the makeup of the Middle East. Israeli military leaders, politicians, statesmen, and businessmen seem to have converged on the need to favor some sort of future arrangement with Iran.[80] They also see continued Iraqi development of its nuclear weapons program and chemical storage effort as a reminder of the Jewish state's vulnerabilities to attack.[81] A majority of Israel's population believe that a Palestinian state will amount to their elimination.[82] Few regard Jordan as either a proximate or necessary solution to their quandary.[83] But most Israelis would find it extremely difficult, if not impossible, to reach an accommodation, strategic or otherwise, with Syria. Many would certainly remember how Syrian snipers claimed planter-settler lives in the valley below the Golan before Israel's 1967 occupation of the heights. Others, especially those belonging to the religious right, would be eager to point out that the Golan had been annexed according to Israeli law during 1981.[84]

Israeli rancor toward Assad and his regime was reciprocated by Syrians who felt a need to register contempt for Jewish citizens' presence on their land, but the disapproval each side meant to show for the other's actions failed to create in either country a domestic consensus for engaging in another military conflict. In fact, despite public statements to the contrary, neither party made menacing troop movements or participated in breaching their common border.

Although Syria maintains what may be the largest inventory of sophisticated Russian armaments outside the Soviet Union, its projected use of the weapons could be circumscribed by recent attitudes toward Middle East diplomacy agreed to between Damascus and Moscow. Former Soviet Foreign

Minister Edvard Shevardnadze's ten-day journey through the region in February 1989 was noteworthy for winning a commitment from Assad to attend a future international peace conference.[85] At an Arab summit meeting held in Casablanca, Morocco, that May, Syria reiterated its support for internationally supervised peace attempts.[86] But this time Assad—who held reconciliation meetings with PLO Chairman Arafat and Egypt's Mubarak—won important delays in shackling Syria's hand in Lebanon. Compromise wording enabled Syria to overcome an Iraqi challenge to its preferential position in Lebanon, making it easier for Assad to go along with Soviet-inspired peace efforts.[87]

Producing the requisites for peace with Israel has, nonetheless, been a lasting premise of Assad's politicomilitary strategy. His hoped-for lead in the Arab world was enhanced by Syria's outdistancing the pace and performance of rivals—Iran, Iraq, Jordan, and the PLO—in nearby Lebanon. He believed, though, that the only peace worth having was one in which strategic parity was attained. The military buildup inside Syria was intended to enable it to deal from equal or nearly equal strength with Israel.[88] Conversely, should Arafat or King Hussein bargain with Jerusalem lacking a ready-made equivalent to Jewish power, then Assad meant to block the effort.[89] The Syrian president saw his role as that of a master strategist capable of entering into a peace formula based on the balance of power and taking advantage of stable borders with its neighbors—Israel, Lebanon, Iraq, and Jordan—as well as an equilibrium of forces achieved with the strongest regional player—Israel. This arrangement, not unlike one managed historically in the Southeast Asian subsystem between Vietnam and Thailand, would find its momentum in superpower guarantees. Thus, Assad was initially willing to accommodate Soviet entreaties to join in a peace conference provided he was not robbed of either the security of a paramount position in Lebanon or the self-assuredness that goes with military symmetry vis-à-vis Israel.

Assad's complex reasoning was not entirely lost on Israelis. They, too, looked for tranquility on their northern and eastern frontiers. They also benefited from an occasional demonstration of Syrian muscle against Palestinians in southern Lebanon and a more permanent use of border control on the eastern slopes separating their two states; but giving sanction to fixed forces or to a looming Soviet presence in the area was, to most Israelis, a dangerous and unwelcome prospect.

Division in the Israeli electorate otherwise strained talk of a strategic proposition with Syria, about which there was already considerable doubt. The Likud portion of the population, representing slightly more than half of Israel's eligible voters, has continued to lobby for a nationally approved policy that assigns the entire Golan to Israel.[90] Jewish funda-mentalists, who will be certain to expend their major effort and resources on the West Bank and Gaza, may also think of the Golan as a worthy place to become attached. In that case, the argument for advancing a security plan with Syria must be made, if at all, by left-leaning Israeli strategists.[91]

The Syrian-Israeli border has been neglected since a 1974 disengagement agreement separated combatants and established a UN zone at Kuneitra, thirty kilometers west of Damascus.[92] The entire Golan—some seventy-five miles of territory—has been held by Israel from the time the last shot was fired in the October 1973 war, and occupation threatens to ignite a sixth land war between Arabs and Israelis in which the consequences of escalation to nuclear or chemical and biological warfare have grown dramatically. At a minimum, the United States sees an unsettled Golan as a violation of the land-for-peace formula that undergirds the Camp David spirit and offers the parties terms to settle the overall Arab-Israeli conflict. Moreover, Syrian absence from any prospective peace arrangement has tended to impair the value of getting a third-party negotiation under way.[93]

SYRIA AND THE SUPERPOWERS

How can the United States reshape the mix influencing Syrian and Israeli behavior? And will just the attempt cause a reordering of US priorities on Jerusalem as well as Damascus? Crucially, has the time passed in which the United States, together with the Soviet Union, can work for a Syrian-Israeli détente before positions in their capitals totally harden? Both the United States and Israel accuse Syria of participating in as well as promoting terrorism.[94] Syrian misdeeds have been thought of as so heinous and troubling to relations between Washington and Damascus that US officials have not bothered to inquire how improvements could be made in Syrian-Israeli attitudes. The lack of a US discourse with Assad's regime plays heavily into the hands of Israeli's right-wing politicians and their constituencies, who offer no hope of a dialogue with Syria.

Ways of starting a conversation do exist that draw upon earlier experiences of Syrians and Israelis at their common border, and tacit arrangements already a part of mutual efforts to keep the unwanted from trespassing could be broadened. Nevertheless, setting up demilitarized zones, activating early warning systems, or giving approval for UN or multinational monitoring poses unacceptable risks to the Jewish state and its US patron so long as terrorism remains a factor in Syrian policy.

The Soviet Union may be the most suitable party to start redressing a balance that favors conventional standards in the Syrian-Israeli relationship. Gorbachev's eagerness for an international peace conference and his renewed interest in reducing the scale of regional conflict could be reason enough for Assad to disavow terrorist support. But coupling such a Soviet request, for example, with US agreement to give the Golan precedence on the peace agenda, as well as linking the matter to how onerous Soviet terms would be for arms resupply, could greatly influence the outcome. The superpowers acting concertedly then might unlock the way toward the parties' at least talking to each other.

US-SYRIAN RELATIONS AFTER THE KUWAITI INVASION

US-Syrian relations showed some improvement during George Bush's second year in office. Iraq's invasion of Kuwait gave Syria an opportunity to place troops and armored units in the Saudi desert as part of the US-led multinational effort to contain Saddam Hussein. The move may have been prompted in part by a desire to be seen as more agreeable in the West now that Soviet patronage has all but disappeared[95]—a function of the Cold War's ending and Moscow's preoccupation with perestroika. Syria's hostility to Iraq, moreover, was matched only by the distaste Damascus felt for Israel. In addition, Saudi willingness to pay transport costs for airlifting Syrian forces to the Gulf front may have been seen by President Assad as a signal for future financial assistance coming from Riyadh at a time when the Syrian economy is ailing.[96] Finally, a linkage of Gulf matters to longer-term developments in the West Bank and Gaza could mean to Assad that a Golan Heights settlement is nearer.[97]

Nonetheless, the United States kept Syria on its list of states supporting terrorism. Ahmed Jabril, head of a Damascus-based PLO splinter group and still believed to be a key figure in the December 1988 bombing of Pan Am flight 103, remained under the protection of President Assad.[98] Meanwhile, the European Community lifted only part of its antiterrorist sanctions against Syria. Syrians complain that they see no difference between their country and Iran or the People's Republic of China for whom the European Community had terrorist affiliations wiped clean.[99]

A cross section of popular opinion inside Syria did not approve the government's decision to airlift military units to the Gulf. Students, lawyers, engineers, and writers objected to the deployment as fitting within a pro-US, pro-Israeli feeling that sparked immediate and sharp disapprobation from all segments in the country.[100] Although Saddam Hussein gained little sympathy from the Syrian populace for invading Kuwait, sentiment runs even deeper in Damascus that a foreign troop presence is a more disturbing event.[101] A US presence in the Gulf based on a conventional wisdom approach that speaks of Iraq as a persistent threat to stability in the Middle East holds no attraction for Syrians, who continue to think of themselves as a powerful factor in the future politics and strategy of the Levant.[102]

6

Beyond Crisis:
A Policy for the 1990s

Despite the frustrations and setbacks that characterize recent diplomatic efforts to gain favorable outcomes from the newest war in the Gulf, the United States can again be instrumental in achieving a Middle East peace. When the United States successfully arranged a regional peace, it did so within a policy regime that drew upon US pragmatism, notably in the emphasis on equity. Whether US officials can find new ways to enhance the lives of most citizens in the area by offering a value perspective has been a major theme of this book. Moreover, how the United States looks at the Gulf—how it sees the phenomenon of fundamentalism, Israeli occupation of the West Bank and Gaza, tensions in Lebanon and on the Golan Heights, and Egyptian and Jordanian roles in the peace process—may shape US status in other disquieting Third World places during the 1990s.

The Middle East surely has a unique set of problems not easily replicated in other geographic regions. But worry over how properly to deal with religion and politics, how to assure the sanctity of the individual, when to promote standards, where to assign strategy—all of these issues affect half the globe and offer the United States a vitally important way to use its Middle East experience on behalf of the deprived elsewhere in the world. How the United States promotes peace opportunities in the Middle East may provide crucial lessons for the principled and those interested in a safe course.

THE REAGAN WORLDVIEW AND THE GULF

When US strategists look at the possibility of war in the Middle East, it is the Gulf that captures their attention, not only now in the face of obvious threat, but historically. They saw in Ronald Reagan's time a Soviet interest in eroding US power there, in making the United States appear hostile to local aspirations. These analysts believed that Soviet leaders may have sought ways to trivialize US commitments to allies in the area. These same individuals, however, doubted that the Soviet Union would militarily intervene in the life of the Gulf.[1]

US skepticism about a lowered Soviet strategic role typically drew upon signals coming from theater force posture. Troop capability and readiness status were key indicators in deciding the likelihood of Soviet military deployments, but Moscow chose to keep forces normally available for Gulf duty under strength and ill equipped.[2] There was always the possibility of augmenting units from elsewhere in the Soviet inventory, but such a contingency depended on progress made in East-West conventional arms-reduction talks as well as through negotiations leading to decreases in Far East border defense.[3]

In any case, Gorbachev's "new thinking," his drive for reform, and the turn toward glasnost suggested to some US analysts near the end of Reagan's second term that Soviet plans for the Gulf were primarily political and diplomatic.[4] The Soviet leader had already tested out a program of cooperation in the region by attempting formal relations with Oman, the United Arab Emirates, and North Yemen. He sought better ties with Saudi Arabia and seized on the Kuwaiti desire for maritime protection before an unfriendly Iran entirely disabled the Gulf as a commercially viable waterway.[5]

Reagan administration officials, nonetheless, were uneasy with the gentler behavior in the Third World attributed to Soviets, even when Gorbachev spoke without the customary rigidity associated with Communist doctrine. The United States welcomed his soothing remarks concerning cuts in the nuclear arsenal, but a number of Reagan's people still had forebodings about the motives behind Gorbachev's dramatic break with the past as they prepared to leave office.[6]

A legacy of mistrust mixed with fear and anger was bequeathed by the Reagan government's military record in the Gulf. Area residents as well as the Soviet Union could bear witness to a botched US operation until NATO minesweepers rescued an ill-fated escort service.[7] And, although the Iran-Iraq war was brought to an end, the United States continued to be blamed for inept behavior. Meanwhile, Gorbachev's withdrawal of troops from Afghanistan was applauded despite a decade of brutishness on the part of Soviet occupation forces.[8] The United States, nevertheless, stayed involved in a campaign to regain worldwide credibility after having been savaged by exposure of the Iran-Contra scandal.[9]

Although Reaganites came to accept Soviet-US solidarity on nuclear matters, they found it difficult to believe in Kremlin agreeableness as a preeminent feature of Soviet foreign policy. A reversal in Soviet attitudes on constructing weapons of mass destruction was easy to reconcile—the Soviet empire was reeling under economic catastrophe, which could be remedied only by drastically curtailing military expenditures. Maintaining a sensitive security role in the Gulf, however, required the allocation of few Soviet resources. Moreover, the United States remained fearful of a Kremlin positioned to take advantage of turmoil in the area, either as a result of internal unrest among conservative Gulf monarchies or from a new revolutionary situation growing out of Khomeini's death.[10]

Influential US policymakers, therefore, began to promote the use of deterrence theory in nonnuclear issues in which US and Soviet interests were likely to differ. Deterrence meant avoiding attack on one's home territory; extended deterrence argued for preventing another's losses—on land or against holdings—with a minimum degree of effort.[11] The US decision militarily to enter the Gulf in 1987–1988, reflag eleven Kuwaiti tankers, and otherwise perform escort duty for unarmed vessels traveling in the waterway constituted an attempt at extended deterrence.[12]

US officials did not expect the Soviet navy to seek control of the Gulf in the final period of Reagan's presidency, and, in fact, Soviet sea-based strength increased only slightly after Kuwaiti ships were reflagged.[13] Nor was it assumed that Gorbachev would authorize mounting a military expedition in the region. Instead, Reagan's advisers were worried that with the removal of Soviet forces from Afghanistan coming soon after a general warming in Russo-Arab relations, Gulf states might be willing to provide the Kremlin base rights in special circumstances.[14]

In any case, when deterrence was extended to the Gulf, the United States came in for sharp criticism and a severe loss of stature. The expanded US naval presence in the area was intended to deter Iranian small craft from striking unarmed shipping as well as to make help from the Soviets unnecessary. Enhanced US military deployments, however, succeeded neither in preventing any damage to ships plying the Gulf nor in averting Soviet defense for Arab states located astride the waterway. Enlarging the scope of the US military pledge beyond mere escort duty—thereby changing the rules of engagement—simply allowed Iran the opportunity to raise the stakes for conflict without sharing any responsibility for controlling the outcome.[15]

Moreover, because Khomeini's forces had repeatedly sponsored clashes with US combatants as well as forays on US-supervised shipping, the lightly armed Iranians could be thought of as having undermined any plan for extended deterrence. Khomeini had amply demonstrated that if the United States wished to protect Gulf shipping, it would have to increase its forces, thereby violating extended deterrence, which anticipated only limited combat.[16]

GEORGE BUSH AND THE GULF

George Bush began his administration with a tarnished US reputation in the area. The new president tried to rebound by ordering a reassessment of Soviet relations within a context of uncertainty about the suitability of Cold War thinking. Strategic review, for example, found a return to former Soviet conduct unthinkable, even if Gorbachev were driven from power.[17] Moreover, recent political advantages in the Gulf came to the Soviets as a result of their diplomatic triumphs—an outcome many believed would never have been theirs through military means.

When George Bush ordered a massive buildup of US forces in the Gulf during the winter of 1990, hoping to put a brake on Iraqi plundering of

Kuwait,[18] Saddam Hussein had reason to believe that the United States no longer saw extended deterrence as an upper limit on Washington's strategic thinking. The flip-flop in US force structure sent to the Gulf nevertheless produced unease in the US public.[19] Revolutionary regimes such as those of Iran and Iraq are more easily able to absorb military loss es without incurring the depth of criticism the US government has to shoulder.

People throughout the Middle East may still be moved to wonder how Washington can justify the taking of lives when the Cold War and a corresponding Soviet threat to the Gulf have ended and regimes the US military was sent to protect practice little in the way of equity on behalf of their citizenry. Fundamentalists in Iran, for example, charged the United States with imperialism the moment bombs and missiles rained down destruction on innocent and hapless Muslims. Even a bolstering of US troop and equipment strength in the Saudi desert opposite Saddam Hussein's forces gave the fundamentalists a powerful argument for tying George Bush to a realpolitik vision of how to deal with the Middle East.

Because US-Iraqi relations depend on what the postwar period brings, and inasmuch as populism has already proved to be an outcome of Saddam Hussein's crisis manipulation, Washington would be misguided if it subscribed to the belief that conservative religion was a wrongful value to uphold by any Gulf state, especially Iran. When Khomeini took power, most in the Gulf objected to the dogmatic exercise of a spiritual pattern that excludes other Islamic views. The ayatollah's millenarianism and his dedication to the art of replacing regimes that half believed or did not believe at all exceeded the tolerance of the most generous interpretations. The Iran-Iraq war, injuries during the Haj, the undermining of leaders in Kuwait and Bahrain—these were so onerous that the United States and the Soviet Union were approached for aid and comfort, but extraterritorial intervention was never intended to vitiate, compromise, or otherwise tamper with the devotion and salvation adhered to as part of Islam.

When Bush administration officials therefore confront Iran, they should be sensitive to the place that fundamentalism occupies throughout the Gulf region. They would do well to understand that fundamentalism has not assumed a negative identity; only Khomeinism, with its insistence on exporting revolution, or Shiism as an unexceptionable doctrine, has become profane in the eyes of Gulf residents. Iranian fundamentalists who might insist on merely recapturing Islamic orthodoxy, who would inspire the masses to rededicate their souls to Allah, who would call upon citizens of other states to reassess their values, and who were to couch social goals in religious terms would be obeyed and revered throughout the Gulf area.[20] The United States ought to work for the formation of a leadership in Iran that has that peculiar blend of traditionalism and hard-headed political tenacity to make society work again.

Rafsanjani has been touted as a nearly perfect mix of tough, seasoned, expert manager along with loyalty to the principles of a pious life.[21] Should the capable and somewhat enigmatic president of Iran survive his adversaries and stay in front as political successor to Khomeini, the United States could help solidify his position by meeting some of the nation's long-standing demands. For example, Bush could unfreeze Iranian assets in the United States,[22] could make good on a promise to indemnify the families who suffered by the mistaken downing of an Iranian civilian aircraft in 1988,[23] could openly acknowledge that Iraq was the aggressor in the Iran-Iraq war, and could use the occasion of a transfer of power in Iran to end the bitter invective that has characterized discussions at the United Nations and elsewhere. Finally, a new Iranian government might be willing to accept a more influential role in negotiating a release of Lebanese-held hostages as well as give some future guarantees of shunning terrorism in return for gestures of respect.[24]

Bilateral ties with Iran may also be steadied by how the United States sees regional dynamics. The president could choose to isolate Iran from its Gulf neighbors, as Bush's predecessors did. This course of action may serve to make Iran's leaders notice their vulnerability, but it could additionally lead to questions about the wisdom of Washington's contributing to Gulf solidarity. The United States was invited to take part in protecting the Gulf in the face of a common threat to security and stability of the member nations. If the Bush administration persists in treating Iran as a pariah state even in the absence of any proof that Khomeini's successors wish harm to their neighbors, then Washington rather than Tehran would be labeled as interventionist. The United States can expect to be thought of as a genuine and positive force for Gulf stability only if it pursues the objectives of a majority in the region. Associating itself—out of either pique or retribution—with discredited and failed policies of the past will merely ensure that the United States, not Iran, must bow out of area determinations.

President George Bush, therefore, holds in delicate balance the future of the United States and Iran, Iran and the Gulf, and the Gulf and the United States. He can pretend that fundamentalism is inherently incompatible with a prosperous and stable Gulf. He could also believe in an image of sweating torsos, marching feet, menacing fists ready to swing at those unbound to the ritualistic chant of a mosque prayer leader. The president may, instead, desire to rid his countrymen of the mistrust that has characterized feelings between Iran and the United States for more than a decade. The morose quality of the two nations' relations has been for much too long based on a misperception that fundamentalists poison any chance at peace. US citizens have room to accept faiths and peoples that they know little about. Bush must not only endorse that concept, he also needs to demonstrate generosity by embracing the right of a post-Khomeini government to make and correct its own mistakes. How the United States feels about Iran's place in the Gulf may impinge on the way administration officials react to regional dynamics elsewhere in the Middle East.

THE UNITED STATES, EGYPT, AND ISRAEL

Although George Bush has a very different nature and outlook on how to achieve peace than do rivals Hosni Mubarak and Yitzhak Shamir, the three men share a pragmatic vision of the world they inhabit. Mubarak has essentially gone against the grain of domestic advice by keeping a semblance of ties with Israel because he, like predecessor Sadat, believed that peace is preferable to war and that Jews could be steered toward ever more equitable arrangements. But to accomplish such an awesome task, Mubarak has reasoned that he needs to remain tough and even belligerent in the face of known Israeli partiality for the status quo. The Egyptian president has chosen to move back and forth across Israel's dividing line as a way of informing the Jewish state that he is uncomfortable with military expeditions to defeat Arab neighbors or the pursuit of intolerable acts to punish Palestinians for their excessive conduct. These warnings to Israelis serve as a reminder to internal groups as well as other Islamic states that Egyptian-Israeli relations have limits and can be shattered if the consequences to Arabs of maintaining the dialogue are grave.[25]

Yitzhak Shamir has looked at developments and attitudes in Cairo as a worrisome matter. He, too, has prized peace as a better alternative than war. The Jewish prime minister has also distinguished between the appearance of anti-Israeli activities on the part of Egypt and Mubarak's resolve to win his seat back at Arab summits. But the nature of Israel's political system does not permit so easy a midcourse corrective as has seemed possible in Cairo. Shamir has been too much the captive of a shaky Israeli electoral system to move effectively in the direction of satisfying Egyptian appetites. Nevertheless, the Israeli premier would not allow his place in history to be spoiled by avoiding a break with the past should circumstances require it.[26]

Meanwhile, George Bush has understood that neither Mubarak nor Shamir was nearly as dependent on the United States as earlier Egyptian and Israeli leaders have been portrayed. The nations of Europe and Asia are in many respects an easier as well as more lucrative source for Egypt's economic and military well-being, and Israel has learned to be almost entirely self-sufficient in the making and preparing of weapons for use against bitter enemies. The Jewish state has always been a leader in the techniques of scientific advancement. It is for all of these reasons that the United States has thought of Egypt and Israel and their relationships as an appealing example of how cooperation can lead to mutual discovery and benefit.[27]

Nonetheless, there is uncertainty about whether the Bush administration sees closer Egyptian-Israeli ties as a worthy endeavor in itself or merely as a bridge toward more palpable regional peace prospects. A reservoir of goodwill for each other surely exists in some Egyptian and Israeli quarters, but rebuilding a relationship, now largely in disrepair, will demand the full attention of the United States. Reassessments by the parties alone cannot substantially alter shared misconceptions or equip them to implement successfully new peace efforts. Bush's people, therefore, may wish to shelve for the time being recent attempts to work out a final settlement of the Palestinian problem until they are able to help Mubarak and Shamir remove doubts about their relations.

THE UNITED STATES, THE WEST BANK, AND GAZA

The United States could enable a greater degree of equity for West Bank and Gaza residents by more wisely confronting the difficult interplay among faith, power, rights, security, and resource allocation. US officials react to a bewildering assortment of signals in order to factor conflict resolution in the territories. Some of the steps that could be taken to alleviate further trouble are for the United States (1) to convince the Jewish state to give up mass deportations, news censorship, university disruptions, and barring of Palestinians at local, regional, or international meetings, as a way of muting fundamentalist appeal on the West Bank; (2) to deny radical West Bank fundamentalists a loftier platform by continuing to give Arafat entry into peace discussions; (3) to strengthen bonds between lower-level Palestinian officials and Jewish leaders in the absence of a formal Israeli-PLO dialogue; (4) to work toward holding elections in the territories without compromising East Jerusalemite participation; (5) to promote a Jordanian role in the West Bank if the situation there grows uglier as a result of Arafat's isolation and a fundamentalist-inspired revolution; (6) to encourage a spirited public debate inside Israel over the future direction of its society—the legacy that Holocaust survivors in particular wish to leave children and grandchildren—thereby sapping strength from Jewish fundamentalists who wish annexation of the territories; (7) to establish a NATO-style legal defense pact with Israel to permit Jewish moderates an equal voice in the coming internal struggle; and (8) to draw the governments of Israel, Egypt, and Jordan toward water exchanges, agricultural equipment and technology loans, and shared energy and transportation links, thereby producing a tripartite economic union.

An intifada grown more uncompromising with each passing month nonetheless raises questions about whether any style of settlement in the West Bank and Gaza may still be possible. The three-year-old intifada, thus far, has increased suffering for Palestinians and Jews alike, fed their mutual dislike, and made extremist visions of a future stained by blood more likely. However, the intifada has not convinced Israelis to abandon Jewish settlement plans in the territories or change their tactics of suppressing the uprising. In fact, the intifada showed signs of abating[28] until the October 1990 Temple

112 CONVICTION & CREDENCE

Mount incident supplied reasons for Palestinians and Jews to ready themselves for new and more troubling occasions.

Extremists of both sides—Jewish and Palestinian—take advantage of the exploding atmosphere. Fundamentalists have registered gains among a dependent Palestinian citizenry that has seen its 1988 youth-led victories turn to pitiful defeat when many participants in the uprising receive jail sentences or are maimed or deported. Conservative religion has even come to the Israeli Arab towns in the Galilee. The mayor of the largest Arab community in that region recently enforced a fundamentalist-inspired devotion to faith and a show of resistance to his more powerful Israeli Jewish neighbors.[29]

Jewish fundamentalists, seized by a need to demonstrate what they think of a third temple on the present site of the Dome of the Rock, incited a show of defiance by mosque officials at al-Aqsa.[30] The resulting Temple Mount incident was a further reminder of how easily extremists ranged on either side could poison any thought of Palestinians and Jews worshipping simultaneously in peace. Meanwhile, the assassination of Jewish extremist leader Rabbi Meir Kahane, while on a November 1990 New York visit, by an Egyptian-born, ex–West Bank resident,[31] will undoubtedly spur another, even more frightening cycle of terror as Jewish fundamentalists take additional self-righteous acts of retribution.

The PLO, as well as neighboring Arab states, has not seen fit to offer any reasonable suggestion for curbing the violence on the West Bank and Gaza. Instead, Egypt, Syria, and Jordan remain mostly preoccupied by the ill effects of the Gulf crisis. The leaders of these states worry about how to respond to the strong impact of Saddam Hussein's populist rhetoric on increasingly volatile domestic audiences.

Israelis, for their part, can be expected to order more curfews against Palestinians eyed with suspicion. Jewish authorities could engage in a larger number of deportations. Live-bullet displays by nervous occupiers against unruly Palestinian mobs may even help Israelis to complete their garrison state. Desperate Palestinians without enough forethought might deliver their youthful and inspirational intifada to a more permanent fundamentalist control. When Jewish and Arab extremists are able to command the rhythm of the intifada, then the character of the uprising will be transformed from the present cycle of West Bank and Gaza incidents to a more chaotic and less manageable form of revolution.

What can the United States do to prevent such an outcome? US-Israeli relations have already plummeted as a consequence of Jerusalem's refusal to stop settling Jews in the territories and Israel's refusal to allow a proper UN investigation of the Temple Mount incident.[32] George Bush and Yitzhak Shamir, furthermore, have never gotten along.[33] Not unlike Carter and Begin, they publicly dispute almost every statement attributed to conclusions purportedly reached by them in private meetings.

The United States, therefore, might start a successful negotiation with Israel and the Palestinian community by proposing to incur all or part of rebuilding costs involved in a major housing program for Gazans. Model villages for the poorest and neediest in Gaza would be consistent with the US experience of dampening the attraction of violence. The move could expect to gain international relief agency support. And the development of improved living standards for Palestinian residents in Gaza has already earned the approval of Israel's Prime Minister Shamir. US budgeting to operate such a program is obviously straitened by the costs of deployment in Saudi Arabia; it would be further constrained by the financial burden of renewed warfare in the Gulf. Nonetheless, Washington could draw down funds through reallocating current Agency for International Development expenditures earmarked for Israel. This would not only achieve the goal but would also stress US displeasure with how the Shamir government has responded to the intifada. The announcement alone should remove doubt that the United States is indifferent to happenings on the West Bank and Gaza.

Whatever else may be done by US officials to alleviate tensions, the moves would have to stem from whatever level of confidence the parties extend to Washington. For example, tightening US-Israeli security relationships by supplying a NATO- style defense agreement may be the best method for building faith among Jews in the United States. It would also mean that the United States should have more say in how Israelis use their equipment to quell outbreaks on the West Bank and Gaza. Shifting US funds around to erect Palestinian housing in Gaza, or to reconstruct the Mosque for Arab fundamentalists, or to furnish books and materials to Muslim villagers could also add to the trust shown Washington. There are, in short, many ways still open for the United States to recreate community life in the West Bank and Gaza that could put an end to the spiral of violence so viciously portrayed as an inevitable by-product of the Arab-Israeli conflict.

Should negotiation over how to manage creatively the West Bank and Gaza prove successful, a way toward development of an economic union in the area bounded by the Mediterranean, the Gulf of Aqaba, and the River Jordan would be opened. No single one of the three—Israel, Egypt, or Jordan—would enter into a state of economic self-sufficiency, but a pooling of resources and sharing of market advantages would enable each party to gain greater leverage over its finances at a time when its treasuries face uncertainty. Israel's soaring inflationary rate of a few years ago was brought down, but by artificial means. The Jewish state's trend toward deflation, however, started to revert once large, unplanned expenditures resulting from the government's anti-intifada military campaign. Moreover, local measures instituted by Jewish settlers on the West Bank to cope with daily Arab attacks drew upon a financial base already weakened by growing unemployment and sharp reductions in revenue—a consequence of falling tourism, soft currency, and limited support from diaspora Jews.[34]

Egypt's economic maladies are even more troubling and varied. They derive from a performance level that bases improvements on a comparison to the previous year's statistical results: How much were food imports and exports rising or falling; had trade flows steadied; was the schedule of foreign remittances dropping; were domestic subsidies to the poor growing; and had Suez Canal tolls, oil, and tourism revenues tapered off?[35] Serious obstacles to reform presented by a bloated, inefficient, and corrupt bureaucracy add to the woes of a country reeling under the combined weights of overpopulation and underdevelopment. Land is worked at a capacity insufficient to keep even meager resources available for average increases in the birthrate. With Egypt's population growing at a million a year, pressure is severe on a land surface capable of producing only a few crops and acts as a prohibition on thinking about self-nourishment for the more than 55 million Egyptians. Further, industrialization in Egypt has been restricted by a poor agricultural base and the absence of substantial foreign investment.[36]

Jordan is a more promising place in which to live, with far fewer demands from population growth and a strong potential for being able to feed its people during stable times. Jordan's financial independence has been eaten away as a consequence of lower earnings from the sale and transfer of products to the Gulf states, a lessening of worker remittances caused by the drying up of foreign hiring on the part of these same oil-rich countries, and the leveling off of Arab League subsidies intended to benefit West Bank Palestinians no longer cared for by King Hussein.[37] The end of the Iran-Iraq war, furthermore, eroded Baghdad's dependence on Amman for supply of goods and services.[38] The disruption of ties to West Bankers brought additional economic woe to Jordan. In pleasanter times, Palestinians thronged to the Hashemite kingdom, either across the bridges connecting the West Bank to Jordan or by plane to Amman's busy international airport. These special visitors carried Jordanian passports and were an important source of earnings through a variety of services bought and paid for. Revenues from this unique tourist trade helped shore up a currency sometimes in dire need. Banking liquidity was jeopardized once King Hussein opted to pull out of the territories. Agricultural patterns formed decades ago and capable of serving both East and West Bank populations were particularly endangered by the hasty separation from the territories.[39]

Communities in Israel, Egypt, and Jordan have not, therefore, enjoyed the kind of bustling, robust economies their forebears anticipated. Neither have present-day citizens seen an abatement of tensions produced by wobbly finances. The unease of the peoples of these states is made more noticeable by the intifada. Wounds—both physical and spiritual—will be harder to heal as a result of the uprising, and each side can expect suspicions and recriminations to linger. What role and what degree of help can economic union between former and current enemies—Israel and Egypt, Jordan and the Jewish state—have in reducing the level of mistrust, and how can the effort begin?

Economic integration among Israel, Egypt, and Jordan may be looked at in terms of resources, services, and products. What assets can be made available for protecting the interests of the parties, how could services be rendered in order to achieve common results, and when will production increases be seen by the consuming public? The answers to these questions rely first on the judgment and goodwill of each state, second on a buildup of mutual confidence that cooperative efforts have made, and third on how experience in economic sharing is perceived as a basis for future politico-military solutions.[40]

The problems of the Middle East, especially in the Levant, have often been manifest: Who owns the land; how can it best be worked; which fields are the most fertile; where should water flow to more evenly irrigate the soil; and when can bountiful crops be produced? The residents of the area have fought over responses to these questions for centuries, and, aside from their political and social differences, Arabs and Jews remain convinced that these agricultural issues have been at or near the core of present difficulties.

Israelis have long known that their technological and scientific capacities provided them a qualitative edge. Egyptians, meanwhile, relied on a huge manpower base to support them, while Jordanians trusted that success lay in how tractable they were. The West Bank and Gaza offer a landscape largely unsuited to farming, as it is desert mixed mostly with barren plateau; valleys provide better soils here and there but they too suffer from a lack of proper irrigation. A number of alternatives exist to bring larger portions of the territories into cultivation, depending on whether upper or lower elevations receive preferential treatment and how such moves are seen politically as well as economically.[41]

The most available source of water supply for Gaza is the Nile River. Irrigation for the West Bank, though, may be helped as well from the waters of the Yarmouk or Litani rivers. The Nile waters, in certain cases, could be conveyed farther eastward, thereby servicing Israel's Negev, the West Bank, and Jordan. Egypt's costs—about a half a percent of normal consumption—should be minimal, especially because the government has been sitting on water surpluses; Lake Nasser holds several billions of cubic meters beyond Cairo's needs. Diverting the waters of the Nile River to Israel's Negev would be more cost-effective than is the present system of pumping the Sea of Galilee. Moreover, a free exchange of water could allow for conveyance from the Galilee to new destinations along the West Bank and Jordan.[42]

The Yarmouk River, whose waters have been mainly allocated to Jordan, could be another source for making the West Bank more fertile if exploited cooperatively by Amman and Jerusalem. Most of the Yarmouk's flow consists of winter floodwaters and remains unutilized because of the lack of off-season storage. Building upstream dams requires both approval of riparian states for construction and a heavy financial investment in relation to the value of projected agricultural production. Channeling the Yarmouk's excess flow to a natural reservoir, such as the Sea of Galilee, therefore would be the easiest and economically best thing to do. The quantity of water that could be stored in the unused portion of Israel's central lake facility may be sufficient for Jordan's short-term needs. Besides, Israelis themselves could make use of the winter flow, pumping it south for subterranean storage in aquifers. Crucially, the extra amount of stored water might be supplied to the West Bank through existing Israeli and Jordanian pumping stations or might spur the development of new ones. In any case, a hydrographic study of the area would show that common uses for the Yarmouk have not been favorably explored by either Jordan or Israel.[43]

Water is so essential to the economic life of the Middle East because of the arid-semiarid climate that characterizes the region. Improving on the use of common water carriers, such as the Nile or Yarmouk rivers, would enable a higher crop yield on land made more irrigable. Israel possesses the technology to convert desiccated areas into thriving vegetable and flower gardens as well as groves of fruit-bearing trees. The Jewish state has accomplished as much in the short span of a generation, irrigating earth previously left dry. A marvel of modern Jewish history has been the development, manufacture, and marketing of machinery that allows a green revolution to displace barren desert. This technology—drip irrigation—has been exported to Third World nations in Africa, Asia, and Latin America, and sold to Europe, and could be of enormous benefit to Egypt and Jordan as the former goes about reclaiming land and the latter assists West Bank redevelopment.

Water exchanges and equipment loans buttressed by the know-how to broaden agricultural possibilities may provide the groundwork for enhanced cooperation in other fields. A complementarity already exists between Egypt and Israel in agricultural matters—differences in nature (soil, climate), labor costs, availability of capital, and extent and knowledge of technology explain their disparity. Thus, a shopping list of products could be traded by the parties without altering regular patterns of commerce.[44] But in energy matters—power transmission grids, hydroelectric power, natural gas deposits, and oil—joint development inhibits the usual competition and augurs well for closer ties between the parties.[45] Finally, transportation links such as road, rail, and canals go a long way toward bringing people, products, and plans for the future together, thereby transforming what would otherwise pass for simple burden sharing into a grander form of economic union.[46]

Secretary of State Shultz attempted to bring Israel and Egypt out from under their "cold peace" just prior to his retirement from office, but to no avail. The Taba settlement had a salubrious effect for a short time, but the arbitration award to Egypt soon prompted suspicions among Israelis, and Egypt's President Mubarak continued to criticize Jewish handling of the intifada.

Settlement in the West Bank and Gaza, at least for the time being, would offer both states as well as Jordan a way to throw off particularism. Shared economic perspectives and a willingness to tackle the difficult issues of resource allocation, production levels, and consumption needs may help them to see how a political context that has raised such troubling questions could now lead to easing their citizens' pain.

THE UNITED STATES AND LEBANON

Satisfying Israeli security needs through a formal defense treaty and enabling improvements in the condition of Palestinian existence on the West Bank and Gaza might allow the United States much leeway in preparing the Lebanese for alterations in their tangled governing process. Foremost among the changes that US leadership should recommend are alterations to:

- the present system of confessionalism empowering a Christian Maronite president to rule the country
- a Sunni Muslim prime minister with no real power except to preside over cabinet ministries
- lower-ranking positions accorded to Shia personnel with little specification among their sects
- a geographic distribution determined by a 1932 census, confirmed by colonial agreement in 1946

President Bush might amend this outdated spoils system by insisting on a ceremonial role for the Maronite next chosen president by the Lebanese legislature; a prime minister selected from among the Shias; and Sunni responsibility devolving to the third-ranking position, speaker of the Parliament. US economic assistance could be used as a goad to prompt Lebanese agreement to these modifications. The new government would reflect the distribution of power in current demographics, although it should be remembered that relative numbers as understood by the population are unconfirmed by any recent census. There is, nonetheless, no doubt that clear shifts have taken place among major groups since the 1930s. If a UN commission composed of respected and learned international figures could study the available figures and endorse, albeit tentatively, the probable distribution of factions, new political arrangements would have a still greater chance to succeed.

Meanwhile, Nabih Berri, leader of the Shia Amal movement and previously entrusted with control of the important southern and southeastern districts of Lebanon, might be named prime minister. Conferring full authority on Berri to govern the country not only would be consistent with stabilizing Lebanon but also would operate within US pragmatic standards of equality. The Amal head has shown himself to be a steadying influence in

Lebanon, attacking Palestinian guerrillas south of Beirut to prevent the PLO's enforced reappearance, mediating for release of TWA flight 847 passengers, resisting Israeli occupation, and opposing extension of influence by Iranian-supported Shias belonging to the cleric-led Hezbollah organization.

Berri has worked hard to improve the distribution of social justice among the poor of all faiths, and Amal counts itself successful in attracting a wide political and social following. Critically, the Amal group has been especially favored by Syria's President Assad, and a Lebanese government run by Berri would serve as an adequate security buffer if Damascus and Jerusalem were to agree on settling their respective border problems.

These combined moves would be enormously helped by how well the Lebanese implement the charter drawn up in Taif, Saudi Arabia, during November 1989 to help Muslims obtain larger roles in the country's governing structure. The Taif accord promised a presidency in Christian Maronite control but with reduced power. A Shiite head of Parliament, elected on a four-year basis, would obtain a stronger voice in decisionmaking, and the Sunni prime minister would be compensated by receiving additional national security responsibilities. Leadership of the Senate chamber would go to a Druze. And the parliament itself would expand, with increases in seats allocated to the numerically superior Shiites and Druzes.[47]

A new president, René Moawad—a three-time Maronite cabinet minister—upon whom the whole reform was based, was selected on November 5, but he was assassinated seventeen days later in the strife-ridden and wartorn environment of divided Beirut.[48] His Christian successor was ex–Parliament deputy and businessman Elias Hrawi,[49] who managed to prohibit the fiery and defiant militia leader General Michel Aoun from commanding any part of the Christian forces. Nearly a year was spent in consolidating control of Lebanon according to the terms of the Taif document before Syrian forces drove Aoun to defeat and refuge in East Beirut's French embassy.[50] Meanwhile, the troops of nine militias—historical contenders for control of the Lebanese capital—have left Beirut.[51] This may encourage Syria to begin thinning out its own 40,000-man force. Should these encouraging developments result in the withdrawal of all foreign forces, then the Lebanese, for perhaps the first time in fifteen years, might be able to create their own constitutional changes and field an entirely new system of governing.

THE UNITED STATES AND THE
SOVIET UNION IN THE LEVANT

What of the role of the Soviet Union? When the Soviets have confronted their past in the Levant, they have come away dispirited. Their reputation for peacemaking has been sullied as a consequence of choosing to arm the most obstructionist elements in the area instead of offering incentives for moderates seeking compromise solutions. They have played on ways to reduce US power and prestige rather than paying attention to how swiftly local alliances were reforming. The Soviets of the 1970s seemed to show greater interest in benefiting from the turmoil produced by continued Arab dissatisfaction with Israel and its patron, the United States, than in working toward a change in the status quo.

Mikhail Gorbachev meant to correct the mistaken assumptions of the Brezhnev period and eliminate the mistrust and bewilderment that has characterized US official views as well as the feelings of most states in the Middle East. He tried to bring the United Nations into the peace process, proposing a short transitional period during which UN-appointed officials could care for the West Bank and Gaza until suitable and permanent arrangements were made. He consoled Jordan when the king's attempt at reconciliation with the PLO fell apart, and he rebuked Arafat for his unwillingness to accommodate Hussein's wishes. He warmed to the European Community's idea of an international conference to extract concessions from Israel and even sought to reestablish ties with the Jewish state, if the move would coax Israel to be flexible on the start of an international meeting. And he relaxed restraints on Jewish emigration from the Soviet Union as a further inducement for Israeli compliance. Most importantly, in 1989 the Kremlin took on a mediating role, first proposing, in Cairo, to the Egyptians, Jordanians, and the PLO on one side and Israel on the other how to narrow their differences, then persuading Syria to attend an international conference by conditioning additional military aid on President Assad's agreement. Finally, Gorbachev met with France's President François Mitterand to seek ways of resolving the Lebanese matter so as to cool down tensions in the Levant.

Soviet worry about weapons of mass destruction—chemical and biological agents—and their easy availability in the Middle East, as well as a desire to limit regional flashpoints in order to help transform the Cold War, may be at the core of Gorbachev's more reasoned conduct. Whatever caused the Kremlin's newfound cooperative mood, the Bush administration now has sufficient reason to recapture a Middle East peace process gone sour. Experience gained from the way in which former US negotiators conducted their mediation should be central to Bush. How the president sees the parties and what degree of commitment he chooses to display might depend to a large extent on the nature of Bush's worldview.

Syria's President Assad has been an enigma to the United States and a spoiler in the try for comprehensive peace in the Middle East. The United States, however, has noticed that Assad, whose shrewdness is exceeded only by his dexterity, seemed willing to limit terrorist support, reduce opposition to an internationally supervised settlement in the Arab-Israeli quarrel, and show interest in stabilizing Syria's frontiers. Keeping 30,000–40,000 Syrian troops inside Lebanon over a fifteen-year period was a function of Assad's nervousness during an equally unstable period of governing among the

Lebanese. Should Nabih Berri, therefore, emerge in a strong position with unparalleled power—guaranteed by the US president—Assad may have sufficient reason for removing entirely his occupation force from Lebanon and garrisoning the troops nearer to Damascus.

Syrian withdrawal of even a portion of its army from Lebanon might enable favorable action on the Golan. Damascus and Jerusalem share misgivings about the strategic motives of neighboring states, Iraq, Iran, and Jordan. They agree on a need to have reliable borders with Lebanon. Israel, however, sees Amal as unable to prevent PLO reoccupation of southern Lebanon and prefers to rely either on its own forces or a surrogate South Lebanon army that is armed and trained by Israel. Nevertheless, if Nabih Berri emerges in control of a new Lebanese government, Israeli leaders would have a strong incentive to work out a political arrangement with the more powerful and dependable Syrian regime. Assad may welcome an accommodation with Israeli officials that adds to area security. However, he will not be able to strike a bargain until Syrian territory has been released from Israel's military grasp.

The United States and the Soviet Union, by testing out Gorbachev's much-heralded cooperative approach to regional issues, could find a way to resolve the parties' dilemma on the Golan. Moscow has already been convincing in helping Assad think of attending an international peace conference. US and Soviet representatives could give precedence on the peace agenda to settling the Golan matter, but Assad would have to pledge to discontinue his support of terrorists and appear as more pliant in any negotiation. The Soviet Union might remind the Syrian leaders of his vulnerabilities by promising to withhold future arms deliveries should Assad return to a belligerent mood.

The modalities of returning Golan territory would require working out agreements for troop redeployments, gradual reductions in force posture abutting the heights, and the creation of demilitarized zones. Such a package could be tied to normalization procedures between Israel and Syria. The United States might bring some leverage to the negotiation by promising Damascus compensatory damages for two decades of lost territory, and, to allay Israel's anxieties, the United States may be able to commit the Syrian government to repatriate several thousand Jews huddled in a Damascus ghetto. The process of agreeing on even a partial withdrawal of Israeli troops from the Golan will be long and arduous, accompanied by the strain of convincing recalcitrant domestic bodies in both countries, but worth the trouble if a Syrian-Israeli war can be averted in the near term.

THE UNITED STATES AND FUNDAMENTALISM

The essential place that fundamentalism holds in Iran, Israel, and among West Bank and Gaza Palestinians gives evidence that US policymaking in the

Middle East may be impeded unless the United States finds a way to be sympathetic to fundamentalists' goals. Religious revivalists in the Middle East think of the United States as a worldly society in which the desire for wealth and success is paramount. They see the people of the United States as selfish, unreflective, and immoral. But the United States has prospered when its citizens chose to be passionate about a spiritual life. The founders of US society were puritanical: They felt their religion deeply and struggled to make piety a part of governing. Their heritage can be seen in today's conservative agenda—school prayer, the right-to-life platform, recitation of the pledge of allegiance, and the inclusion of references to God in the opening of congressional sessions and in presidential inaugural rituals. Liberals in US politics also insist on ethical norms as true to the country's face in the preservation of human rights, international security, and economic fairness abroad.

The popularity of relativism as a way for youth to deal with inescapable national and global problems, the information explosion, and technological and scientific discoveries have led to the appearance of a value-free environment in the United States. The country has to respond to these issues as well as correct mistaken foreign impressions by promoting abroad the view of a United States more responsive to theological principles.

Fundamentalists in the Middle East would be gratified by a United States that has a stake in the concepts of equity, populism, and spiritualism. They would, however, expect George Bush to give up labeling Middle Eastern leaders, both governmental and religious, as "crazy." The Bush administration would also do well to emphasize anticorruption, humanism, and devotion to God when it meets members of cleric-run movements or governments in the region.

Iran, for its part, will move away from the millenarianism of Khomeini now that the ayatollah's rule may be just a memory. His successors have divided the governing responsibility so that newly elected president Rafsanjani and clerical head Ali Khamenei have different responsibilities. Civil matters such as improving on economic productivity or building a secure military will fall under Rafsanjani's aegis; the need to ensure the populace's commitment to the principles of Islam remains the province of the recently appointed Khamenei.

Khamenei held powerful posts in the revolutionary government of Iran— party and National Guard head, deputy minister of defense, and two-term president of the Republic—before his elevation to succeed Khomeini in religious matters. He urged a tough line on the fundamental unity of religion and state, but he is not a mystic or fanatic given to the otherworldliness of his predecessor. Moreover, Khamenei has on occasion looked to public sector development and the role of regular military forces instead of the more radicalized Pasdaran in national defense, and he can thus be seen as aligned with the views of Rafsanjani. Khamenei also has no special claim to the clerical authority or status that Ayatollah Khomeini enjoyed. He is, therefore, a figure whom neither the West nor Rafsanjani ought to fear or think of as encouraging the rise of radicalist fundamentalism. In fact, the government of Iran should now be seen as caring for a populist image at home while seeking to recover its previous ties with the United States in order to rescue the country from further chaos.

In Israel and in the West Bank and Gaza, the United States will run up against a fundamentalism that is less hospitable to a civil religion. The Jewish messianics have welcomed the intifada and Arafat's unusual gesture of recognizing Israel as symbols of an immanent apocalypse. Whereas the younger generation of Israelis may be drawn to the promise of a more pious and ethically motivated life, they cannot be fulfilled by the prospect of an enduring struggle with Arabs in the territories. These prayerful souls, therefore, might see the US civil religion as a proper holistic response, prodding Jews toward an equitable resolution of the Palestinian issue without harming their religious tradition or identity.

In any case, the fundamentalists in the West Bank and Gaza will be fully engaged trying to wrest control of the Palestinian movement away from the PLO, should success in benefiting the territories continue to elude Arafat. These youthful rock throwers may be able to ignite a revolution against Israel's harsh, repressive rule if they can spur generous support among a rural population energized by religious revival and given to recreating society in their own image. Undoubtedly, the Israelis would be hard-pressed not to launch their considerably stronger military into the melee. The United States and Jordan might then decide to rescue the situation by substituting pragmatic solutions for slaughter of the innocent. Producing a US attitude and viewpoint tied to spiritual values and beliefs—a civil religion—prior to the dreaded alternative of all-out war in the territories might sufficiently ward off fundamentalist temper. In the interim, the United States may fruitfully sharpen its negotiating tools.

THE UNITED STATES, IRAN, AND THE GCC

Whereas the United States may have to wait on implementing its preferences in the Levant, the Gulf region—propelled by swiftly consolidated Iranian leadership in the aftermath of Khomeini's death—will be quicker to respond to Bush administration policy direction. The United States should draw Iran into an overall management plan that looks at ways to enhance the political and economic significance of the GCC, as well as to downgrade any potential for outside military intervention.

And when the Gulf has moved past the Iraqi invasion of Kuwait, the United States may find that Saudi Arabia and the lesser sheikdoms have no further need of a Western military presence in order to project power into the region. The Saudis, for example, can be expected to return to a standard role that assumes protection for Muslim holy places and uses oil and wealth as a lever to achieve a balance of influence in the area. Iraq, even in diplomatic and military defeat, will thereby be viewed in Riyadh as a necessary counterweight, albeit a weakened one, to the growing significance of a pragmatically governed Iran.

In any event, worry about a Gulf vulnerable to renewed conflict has been substantially eased through the Soviet cooperation shown to the United States during the Iraqi-instigated crisis. Mikhail Gorbachev gave ample evidence, by Moscow's UN votes and repeated tactical coordination with Washington, that he stood for order as the best hedge against a future Gulf aggression. But Gorbachev's continued forbearance for democratic movements inside Eastern Europe also demonstrated that close attention needs to be paid to reforms based on the moral rights of individuals as a universally valid premise, instead of to the rulers' desires always to aggrandize.

Saudi Arabia and the exiled rulers of Kuwait announced early in the Gulf crisis that they expected to grant more freedoms to their residents. Plans to attend to the ills of everyday life will no doubt do more to enhance the stability of the region that would a plentitude of US arms given for defense of these moderate regimes.

Perhaps also central to a Gulf more at ease with the West would be an Iran neither in direct conflict with its neighbors nor at loggerheads with the United States. Iran's relations with the Saudis at times have been conciliatory, and its ties to Kuwait, Bahrain, and the United Arab Emirates less marked by cordiality. And, of course, the official attitude toward Iraq remains hostile. But the new government in Tehran under President Rafsanjani can be expected to be more moderate and pragmatic than it was under Khomeini. Previous calls to overthrow governments that did not heed a strict orthodoxy in their approach to Islam will no longer guide Iranian policy in the region. Iran's wrecked economy may now require both the assistance of neighboring states and a waterway available to bring goods and services from foreign ports. A more realistic leadership in Tehran might even be willing to join the GCC should the organization, now under Saudi tutelage, determine that security and stability in the area would be aided by the move. In any case, President Bush will be confronted by a less odious and more responsible government in Iran.

THE UNITED STATES AND NEGOTIATION STRATEGIES

Henry Kissinger found that understanding the limits on a party's capacity to negotiate with honesty and straightforwardness often led to a favorable mediation. Jimmy Carter viewed the Middle East peace process as an appropriate arena in which to promote pragmatism and equality. Ronald Reagan judged that US values might not be compelling enough to bring the sides together, so he eventually came to a multistaged, pragmatic resolution of the conflict.

When any of the three principal US mediating officials confronted the bargaining process, they approached outcomes from the vantage of their own beliefs, origins, and philosophies. Carter and Reagan regarded US pragmatism and values as central factors in their vision of a settlement. Kissinger, given more to a Europeanist training, saw the modalities of peace through incremental adjustments and consideration for the narrow field of operation of each party. The three US statesmen always respected the role that domestic politics played in developing options.

George Bush may wish for more time, greater scope for defining the issues, and further opportunity to reach a perspective on settling the Arab-Israeli contest. He will be frustrated and angered, no doubt, by the parties' dissembling and their vigorous disapproval as well as threats of complete withdrawal from the process. He will come to understand, however, that what the players argue most about and warn against, they often accept with the least anxiety. And he will learn—as most Middle East leaders already have—that the United States must depend on the skill, imagination, detachment, and national value system of its mediator if it intends to deliver a peace capable of withstanding the test of time.

US VALUES AND THE MIDDLE EAST

Any agreement, though, ought to be conceived, considered, and strengthened within a framework that reflects an honest approximation of the parties' national values and objectives. The art of statesmanship may see its finest hour when all players in the negotiations accept universal standards and principles by which peace must be observed. The US creed—at least the part that includes equality and liberty—might offer those in the Middle East a basis for reaching their most cherished goals: equal rights to live free of peril, the freedom to choose, the liberty to say and do whatever one wishes within the limits of law and order. How the peoples and leaders of the region see their problems will in large measure determine the type of solution that lies ahead.

The United States has been saddled with an unholy choice: satisfy the desires of Israel to offer elections in the West Bank without East Jerusalemite participation, thereby violating the will of Arab citizens, or disallow the step and suffer further erosion of chances for peace. Lebanese and Iranians meanwhile have played out the consequences of radicalist fundamentalism left unattended. The Syrians, Egyptians, Jordanians, and others in the Arab world, for their part, stood by to assess the damage from their inadequate response to disturbing events such as the murder of a US hostage in revenge for the Israeli abduction of a militant Hezbolleh leader. George Bush and his capable secretary of state, James Baker, must find a way to silence the terror that has merely promoted vengeance and postponed settlement. Devising an integrated plan based upon analogous beliefs on the part of the United States and the states of the Middle East may yet prove a hopeful start to conflict resolution in this violent region of the world. It is my wish that this book might offer ideas for such a remedy.

Notes

INTRODUCTION

1. For discussions of the conventional wisdom behind US Middle East policy, see Spiegel, "The Philosophy Behind Recent American Policy in the Middle East," pp. 5–8; Spiegel, "Does the United States Have Options in the Middle East?" pp. 395–412; and Garfinkle, "'Common Sense' About Middle East Diplomacy," pp. 24–32.

2. The regional versus global approach is discussed in Garfinkle, "'Common Sense' About Middle East Diplomacy"; see also Spiegel, *The Other Arab-Israeli Conflict*, pp. 1–10; and Tanter, *Who's at the Helm? Lessons of Lebanon*, pp. 19–23.

3. See Spiegel, "America and Israel—How Bad Is It?" pp. 11–22; see also S. E. Eisenstat, *Formalizing the Strategic Partnership*.

4. Kissinger, *Years of Upheaval*, p. 200.

5. See Carter, *Keeping Faith*, pp. 506–522; for an authoritative analysis of the failed mission, see Sick, "Military Options and Constraints," pp. 144–172.

6. Reagan, *An American Life*, pp. 517–520.

7. See Hoffman, "Baker Sets Syria Visit Thursday"; see also Goshko and Lardner, "Bush's Plan to See Assad Controversial," p. A55.

8. For a discussion of the debate on Iran and fundamentalism during the last days of the Reagan administration, see Gigot, "Iraq: An American Screw-Up," pp. 5–7; for an analysis of how Iran was valuable to the United States in strategic terms (one side of the debate offered by a Reagan official at the State Department), see Khalilizad, "The United States and Iran: Beyond Containment," pp. 3–10.

9. Miller and Mylroie, *Saddam Hussein and the Crisis in the Gulf*, pp. 139–147; see also Woodward, *The Commanders*, p. 203.

10. For a discussion of Iranian speedboat attacks and US response, see J. G. Stein, "The Wrong Strategy in the Right Place," pp. 148–156.

11. Reed, "Jordan and the Gulf," pp. 23–24.

12. Randal, "Iranian Advocates Killings," p. A1.

13. For a discussion of the Salman Rushdie matter, see Pipes, *Rushdie Affair*.

14. Kaslow, "Iraq Banks on Its Oil to Fuel Reconstruction," pp. 42–45.

15. Seale, *Asad of Syria: The Struggle for the Middle East*, pp. 332–334.

16. MacDonald, "The Kurds in the 1990's," p. 31.

17. See Schiff and Ya'ari, *Israel's Lebanon War*, pp. 250–285.

18. Brown, *The Last Crusade*, pp. 281–287.

19. Kissinger, "Domestic Structure and Foreign Policy," pp. 503–529.

20. J. G. Stein, "Structures, Strategies, and Tactics of Mediation," pp. 331–347.

21. Ibid., pp. 342–344.

22. See Kissinger, *A World Restored*, p. 326.

23. Brown, *The Last Crusade*, pp. 291–296.

24. Quandt, "Kissinger and the Arab-Israeli Disengagement Negotiations," p. 42.

25. For Arab ways of conducting negotiations, see Brown, *The Last Crusade*, p. 301; for Israeli mannerisms, see p. 302.

26. See Vance, *Hard Choices*, p. 163.

27. Carter, *A Government as Good as Its People*, pp. 166–171.

28. Carter, *Keeping Faith*, pp. 276, 279.

29. Ibid., p. 281.

30. Ibid., p. 274.

31. Ibid., p. 303.

32. Vance, *Hard Choices*, p. 216.

33. Carter, *Keeping Faith*, pp. 356–357.

34. Ibid., pp. 269–403; for the text of the first draft, see Quandt, *Camp David: Peacemaking and Politics*, pp. 362–368.

35. Quandt, *Camp David*, p. 320.

36. See Sadowski, "Egypt's Islamist Movement," p. 42.

37. See Hussein, "The Jordanian-Palestinian Peace Initiative," pp. 15–18.

38. Rubin, "Middle East: Search for Peace," p. 592.

39. See Silk, *Spiritual Politics*, p. 17.

40. Ibid., p. 18. Silk points out that religion remains an integral part of the US cultural system; for good or ill, it is one of the principal means by which the US populace conducts their cultural business.

41. See Anthony and Robbins, "Culture Crisis and Contemporary Religion," pp. 9–29.

42. See Bellah, "Religion and Legitimation in the American Republic," pp. 42–44; see also Vetterli and Bryner, *In Search of the Republic*, pp. 89–120; and Semmel, "Democracy, Virtue and Religion," pp. 43–52.

43. See Wuthnow, *The Restructuring of American Religion*, pp. 244–250.

44. Ibid., pp. 250–255.

45. Ibid., pp. 264–265.

46. Ibid., pp. 241–244; also, Vetterli and Bryner, *In Search of the Republic*, pp. 89–120.

47. This version of "civil religion" has been drawn from Liebman and Don-Yehiya, *Civil Religion in Israel*, pp. 4–12. The concept of "civil religion" was popularized by Robert Bellah in his pioneering study, "Civil Religion in America," pp. 1–21. Bellah's ideas on "civil religion" were elaborated in his book, *The Broken Covenant*. In his essay, he stressed transcendence as a crucial element in US civil religion. For another reference in the growing literature that followed Bellah's works, see Wilson, "The Status of 'Civil Religion' in America," pp. 1–21.

48. Woocher, "Civil Religion and the Modern Jewish Challenge," pp. 157–162.

49. Ibid.

50. Ibid.

51. For a discussion of the founding fathers' (Franklin, Adams, and Madison) attitudes toward religion and state, see Vetterli and Bryner, *In Search of the Republic*, pp. 101–108; Botein, "Religious Dimensions of the Early American State," pp. 315–330; McLoughlin, "The Role of Religion in the Revolution," pp. 197–255; and Reichley, *Religion in American Public Life*, pp. 53–114. For an analysis of Tocqueville and religion, see Boesche, *The Strange Liberalism of Alexis de Tocqueville*, pp. 185–189; Vetterli and Bryner, *In Search*

of the Republic, pp. 108–115; Diggins, *The Lost Soul of American Politics*, pp. 244–252; and Bellah, "Religion and Legitimation in the American Republic," p. 45. For Jefferson's views, see Vetterli and Bryner, *In Search of the Republic*, pp. 143–146.

52. Boesche, *The Strange Liberalism of Alexis de Tocqueville*, pp. 185–189; Vetterli and Bryner, *In Search of the Republic*, pp. 110–113.

53. Vetterli and Bryner, *In Search of the Republic*, p. 105.

54. Ibid., p. 106.

55. For Madison's views on religion, see ibid., pp. 107, 139–143.

56. Ibid., p. 107.

57. Ibid., pp. 107–108.

58. Boesche, *The Strange Liberalism of Alexis de Tocqueville*, pp. 27–41.

59. Vetterli and Bryner, *In Search of the Republic*, pp. 124–130; see also Shi, *The Simple Life*, pp. 8–27.

60. Vetterli and Bryner, *In Search of the Republic*, p. 132.

61. Ibid., pp. 121–127.

62. Ibid., pp. 139–145.

63. Ibid., pp. 140, 145.

64. Ibid., p. 146.

65. Ibid., p. 140.

66. Huntington, *American Politics*, pp. 33–39.

67. Ibid., pp. 34–37. See also Reck, "The Philosophical Background of the American Constitution(s)," pp. 273–293. Reck argued against an interpretation that places the foundation of the Republic solely within "classical republicanism," with its stress on a blend of aristocracy and democracy—a focus central to John Adams and the notion of virtue and the public good. Instead, Reck stated that balancing competing interests was an essential characteristic that animated the founding fathers' understanding of their mission, along with classical republican concepts. He concluded that a continuum exists along the often contradictory views. For the most complete and persuasive discussion of public virtue, see Vetterli and Bryner, *In Search of the Republic*, pp. 1–88; and Kramnick, "Republican Revisionism Revisited," pp. 629–664.

68. Huntington, *American Politics*, p. 36. For a discussion of the relationship of religion to republican government, as well as separation of church and state and factionalism, see Vetterli and Bryner, *In Search of the Republic*, pp. 89–199; for a slightly different interpretation, see Price, *America's Unwritten Constitution*; see also Shi, *The Simple Life*.

69. Huntington, *American Politics*, p. 36. For an interesting but unconventional interpretation of Hobbesian theory as it applies to a liberal state and a reconciliation of the rights and interests of individuals with their obligations, see Kavka, *Hobbesian Moral and Political Theory*. For a recent, intelligent discussion of a Lockean concept of nature as the founding spirit behind the vision of the United States, see Thomas L. Pangle, *The Spirit of Modern Republicanism*, pp. 129–275.

70. Huntington, *American Politics*, p. 37. See also Hoffmann, *Janus and Minerva*, especially "Rousseau on War and Peace," pp. 25–49; and Yack, *The Longing for Total Revolution*, pp. 35–88.

71. Huntington, *American Politics*, p. 37.

72. Ibid., p. 39.

73. Ibid., pp. 39–40. For an excellent discussion of the rise of the West and the factors that led to the development of liberalism in its societies, see Hall, *Power and Liberties*, esp. pp. 111–188; see also Barrington Moore, Jr.'s classic *Social Origins of Dictatorship and Democracy*.

74. Huntington, *American Politics*, p. 40; see also Quester, "Consensus Lost," pp. 18–32.
75. Huntington, *American Politics*, pp. 40–41.
76. Bill and Leiden, *Politics in the Middle East*, pp. 74–98.
77. Arian, *Politics in Israel*, pp. 7–8; see also Gutmann and Landau, "The Political Elite and National Leadership in Israel," pp. 163–200.
78. Arian, *Politics in Israel*, p. 8; and Aronoff, *Israeli Visions and Divisions*, pp. 1–19.
79. For a general discussion of the application of democracy to other nations, see Barzun, "Is Democratic Theory for Export?" pp. 53–72. For Tocqueville's impact, see Joffe, "Tocqueville Revisited," pp. 161–172; and Clinton, "Tocqueville's Challenge," pp. 173–189. An excellent discussion of democratic theory can be found in Dunn, *Western Political Theory in the Face of the Future*, pp. 1–28; on democracy and leadership, see Schlesinger, *The Cycles of American History*, pp. 419–438; for democracy in comparative perspective, see Lipset, *The First New Nation*, pp. 205–348.
80. Max Weber characterizes patrimonial systems as consisting of an elaborate administrative organization, spreading throughout society and taking on specialized and technocratic tasks. The relationship between ruler and ruled is filtered through a huge network of administrative officers and officials chosen for their loyalty, dependence, and kinship status, or on the basis of cronyism instead of experience or expertise. See the classical typologies of political authority in Max Weber, *The Theory of Social and Economic Organization*, pp. 341–392.
81. For a discussion of Muhammad's political and personal characteristics, see Bill and Leiden, *Politics in the Middle East*, pp. 134–176; see also Watt, *Muhammad: Prophet and Statesman*.
82. See Bill and Leiden, *Politics in the Middle East*, pp. 9–15. For a novel discussion of the dialectic between liberalism and traditionalism within Arab states and, in particular, the prospects for liberalism in Egypt and Iran, see Binder, *Islamic Liberalism*, esp. pp. 336–360. Also see Bill, "Populist Islam and U.S. Foreign Policy," pp. 125–128.
83. See Bill, "Populist Islam and U.S. Foreign Policy," pp. 130–133.
84. Bill and Leiden, *Politics in the Middle East*, pp. 61–69; see also Binder, *Islamic Liberalism*, pp. 357–359.
85. Bill, "Populist Islam and U.S. Foreign Policy," pp. 130, 132. For a discussion of Islam and capitalism, see Binder, *Islamic Liberalism*, pp. 206–242; and Rauf, *A Muslim's Reflections on Democratic Capitalism*, pp. 1–69.
86. Bill and Leiden, *Politics in the Middle East*, pp. 134–148.
87. See Khaldun, *The Muqaddimah;* Lacoste, *Ibn Khaldun;* Majid Khadduri, *The Islamic Conception of Justice*, pp. 182–189; and Baali, *Society, State and Urbanism*.
88. See Shimshoni, *Israel Democracy*, pp. 408–409; and Cohen, "Ethnicity and Legitimation in Contemporary Israel," p. 113.
89. The intifada, an Arabic term meaning "throwing off," grew from a single incident on December 8–9, 1987, in which a fatal traffic collision in Gaza sparked rumors that Israeli military occupation authorities were retaliating for the stabbing of a Jew the previous week. Youthful Palestinians, who felt the years of repression by Israeli security authorities and were protesting their squalid conditions, responded to curfews and other measures by hurling stones at the occupying soldiers. The ensuing disturbances were joined in by the PLO and received worldwide attention as the months of attack and counterattack dragged on. See Elon, "Letter from Israel," p. 74; and Peretz, "Intifadeh: The Palestinian Uprising," p. 964.

90. See Lissak, "Ideological and Social Conflicts in Israel," pp. 20–37; and Eisenstadt, *The Transformation of Israeli Society*, pp. 343–442.

91. See Shipler, *Arab and Jew;* Lustick, *Arabs in the Jewish State;* and Benevinisti, *The West Bank Data Project.*

92. See Avishai, *The Tragedy of Zionism*, pp. 298–307.

93. Ibid., pp. 307–325; see also Avineri, "Ideology and Israel's Foreign Policy," pp. 3–13. For a discussion of public attitudes toward the land and its protection, see Yishai, *Land or Peace*, pp. 173–193.

94. For a discussion of growing militarism and its impact on democratic procedures, see Peri, *Between Battles and Ballots*, pp. 281–287.

95. See Y. Shamir, "Israel at 40," pp. 581–582, 586–588; Arens, "Israel's Approach to the Peace Process," pp. 4–5; Amram Mitzna (Israeli army general in command of central front), "The Uprising in the West Bank and Gaza Strip," pp. 13–15; and Fuller et al., *The Impact of the Uprising*, pp. 6–11.

96. See three works by Seliktar: "Israel: The New Zionism," pp. 118–138; "Ethnic Stratification and Foreign Policy in Israel," pp. 34–50; and *New Zionism and the Foreign Policy System of Israel*, pp. 169–182. See also Yishai, *Land or Peace*, pp. 100–173; Lissak, "Ideological and Social Conflicts in Israel," pp. 20–37; Cohen, "Ethnicity and Legitimation in Contemporary Israel," pp. 115–124; Avruch, "The Emergence of Ethnicity in Israel," pp. 327–339; Lustick, "Israel's Dangerous Fundamentalists," pp. 118–139; Beilin, "Inter-Generational Friction in Three Parties in Israel," pp. 18–39; and Shapiro, "Generational Units and Inter-Generational Relations in Israeli Politics," pp. 161–180.

97. See Swirski, "The Oriental Jews in Israel," pp. 77–91.

98. See Lustick, *For the Land and the Lord*, pp. 1–71, 153–176; Avruch, "Gush Emunim," pp. 27–28; Newman, "Gush Emunim Between Fundamentalism and Pragmatism," pp. 36–39; Don-Yehiya, "Jewish Messianism, Religious Zionism and Israeli Politics," pp. 215–219, 228–233; Sprinzak, "The Politics of Zionist Fundamentalism in Israel"; Aronoff, *Israeli Visions and Divisions*, pp. 69–92.

99. For background, see Aronoff, *Israeli Visions and Divisions*, pp. 19–68; also see Avishai, "Israel's Divided Unity," pp. 40–47; Reich, "Israel Faces the Future," pp. 22–23; and Friedman, "The Israeli Elections," pp. 1–20.

100. For a discussion of the press in war and peace, see Schiff, "Security vs. Democracy in Israel," pp. 3–9.

101. See Arian, *Politics in Israel*, pp. 120–132.

CHAPTER 1

1. See Hoffmann, *Janus and Minerva*, p. 55.
2. Kissinger, "The Meaning of History."
3. Ibid., pp. 115–117.
4. Ibid., p. 22.
5. Ibid., p. 258.
6. See Reiss, *Kant's Political Writings*, pp. 16–21.
7. Ibid., pp. 18–19.
8. Dickson, *Kissinger and the Meaning of History*, p. 74.
9. Ibid., p. 75.
10. Ibid., p. 76.
11. Ibid., p. 90.
12. Ibid., pp. 80–82; see also Kissinger, *White House Years*, p. 70.
13. M. J. Smith, *Realist Thought from Weber to Kissinger*, pp. 197–199.

14. Kissinger, "The Meaning of History," p. 325.
15. Kissinger, *A World Restored*, p. 325.
16. Ibid., p. 326.
17. Ibid., pp. 327–328.
18. Ibid., p. 329.
19. Ibid.
20. Dickson, *Kissinger and the Meaning of History*, p. 43.
21. Ibid., pp. 6–7.
22. Ibid., p. 76.
23. See Crabb, *American Diplomacy and the Pragmatic Tradition*, pp. 87–91.
24. Ibid., pp. 91–95.
25. Ibid., p. 95.
26. See Barzun, *A Stroll with William James*, p. 83.
27. Carter, *Why Not the Best*, pp. 13–60.
28. Barzun, *A Stroll with William James*, pp. 83–103.
29. Carter, *Why Not the Best*, pp. 77–86.
30. Ibid., pp. 31–32.
31. Kucharsky, *The Man From Plains*, pp. 16–17.
32. Barzun, *A Stroll with William James*, pp. 109–127.
33. See Crabb, *The American Approach to Foreign Policy*, p. 27.
34. Ibid., p. 30.
35. Carter, *Why Not the Best*, p. 110.
36. M. J. Smith, *Realist Thought from Weber to Kissinger*, p. 102.
37. Kucharsky, *The Man From Plains*, pp. 19–20.
38. Ibid., pp. 21–23.
39. Ibid., pp. 21–22.
40. M. J. Smith, *Realist Thought from Weber to Kissinger*, pp. 112–113.
41. Ibid., pp. 113–115.
42. Ibid., pp. 115–116.
43. Dallek, *Ronald Reagan: The Politics of Symbolism*, p. 7.
44. Ibid., pp. 7–8.
45. Wills, *Reagan's America: Innocents at Home*, p. 2.
46. Ibid., p. 353.
47. Dallek, *Ronald Reagan: The Politics of Symbolism*, p. 163.
48. Wills, *Reagan's America: Innocents at Home*, pp. 93–94.
49. Dallek, *Ronald Reagan: The Politics of Symbolism*, p. 129.
50. Wills, *Reagan's America: Innocents at Home*, p. 381.
51. See Kissinger, "What a Mideast Peace Could Look Like."
52. Ibid.
53. Ibid.
54. Ibid.; see also Kissinger, "Israel and the PLO—Wishes and Reality."
55. Carter, "Interview with Jimmy Carter," pp. 24–37; Carter, "The Middle East Consultation," pp. 187–192.
56. Carter, "The U.S. Need to Lead in Israel"; see also Carter, "A US Role in Middle East Peace."
57. Carter, "The U.S. Need to Lead in Israel."
58. Ibid.
59. Ibid.
60. Carter, "Interview with Jimmy Carter," pp. 27–29.
61. Dayan, *Breakthrough*, pp. 66–72.
62. Carter, "Interview with Jimmy Carter," p. 30.
63. Carter, "The U.S. Need to Lead in Israel."

64. Peres, "Peace as an Alternative Strategy," pp. 116–117; Y. Shamir, "Israel at 40," p. 578.

65. Fuller et al., *The Impact of the Uprising*, pp. 3–4.

66. Ibid., pp. 6–8.

67. See Wuthnow, *The Restructuring of American Religion*, pp. 134–138; see also J. D. Hunter, *Evangelicalism: The Coming Generation*, pp. 116–125; Lawrence, *Defenders of God*, pp. 153–188.

68. Wuthnow, *The Restructuring of American Religion*, pp. 177–181.

69. Ibid., p. 181.

70. Ibid., pp. 182–183; for an interesting discussion of Billy Graham's impact on the evangelical movement, see Silk, *Spiritual Politics*, pp. 54–69.

71. For a discussion of televangelism and its impact on society, see Wuthnow, *The Restructuring of American Religion*, pp. 197–207.

72. See Hunter, *Evangelicalism: The Coming Generation*, pp. 19–50.

73. Ibid., pp. 51–115.

74. For a discussion of how evangelicals are redefining their orthodoxy, see ibid., pp. 13–141.

75. Ibid., pp. 141–147.

76. Ibid., pp. 148–151.

77. Ibid., p. 152.

78. Ibid., p. 153; see also Wuthnow, *The Restructuring of American Religion*, pp. 211–214.

79. Hunter, *Evangelicalism: The Coming Generation*, pp. 153–154.

80. Frykenberg, "On the Comparative Study of Fundamentalist Movements."

81. Ibid.

82. Ibid.

CHAPTER 2

1. Khomeini died at age eighty-six on June 3, 1989, after suffering five heart attacks following surgery for stomach cancer on May 23. His attempted recovery had been supervised by forty Iranian physicians at a small clinic near his home in North Tehran. Over the past several years, Khomeini has been occasionally reported near death, and his daughter confirmed in an interview with *The Washington Post* that he had been hospitalized three times since 1986 with heart ailments. An attack in the spring of 1986 was so serious that he was given little chance to survive. For a discussion of these facts, see Tyler, "Kin Says Khomeini Had Cancer," pp. A1, A24. For details of Khomeini's death and burial, see also Tyler, "Thousands Mourn Khomeini"; and Tyler, "Khomeini Buried in Chaotic Scene."

2. See Zonis and Brumberg, "Shi'ism as Interpreted by Khomeini," pp. 47–64; Fischer, "Repetitions in the Iranian Revolution," pp. 117–131; Bakhash, *The Reign of the Ayatollahs*, pp. 217–239; Fischer, "Imam Khomeini: Four Levels of Understanding," pp. 150–174; and Zonis and Brumberg, *Khomeini, the Islamic Republic of Iran and the Arab World*, pp. 1–79.

3. See Bill, "Populist Islam and U.S. Foreign Policy," pp. 129–134; see also Arjomand, *The Turban for the Crown*, pp. 147–174; Bakhash, "Islam and Social Justice in Iran," pp. 95-113; Milani, *The Making of Iran's Islamic Revolution*, pp. 304–310; and Cottam, "Inside Revolutionary Iran," pp. 172–178.

4. For details of how Khomeini governed and consolidated his control, see

Arjomand, *The Turban for the Crown*, pp. 91–176; Milani, *The Making of Iran's Islamic Revolution*, pp. 239–309; Bill, "Power and Religion in Revolutionary Iran," pp. 27–45; and Bakhash, *The Reign of the Ayatollahs*, passim. For a discussion of Khomeini's use of the jurisconsult role (the *velayat-e faqih*), see Rose, "Velayat-e Faqih and the Recovery of Islamic Identity," pp. 166–190; see also Shahrough Akhavi, "Islam, Politics and Society," pp. 420–421, 424–426; Arjomand, *The Turban for the Crown*, pp. 147–154; and Sivan, "Islamic Radicalism: Sunni and Shiite." For matters pertaining to Khomeini's appointment of Ayatollah Montazari as his successor, see Akhavi, "Elite Factionalism in the Islamic Republic of Iran," pp. 194–198.

5. See Bakhash, "Islam and Social Justice in Iran," pp. 95–113; for a discussion of how successful the Iranian government had been in achieving justice for its populace, see also Bakhash, "The Politics of Land, Law and Social Justice in Iran," p. 201; and Bakhash, *The Reign of the Ayatollahs*, pp. 247–249.

6. See Mottahedeh, *The Mantle of the Prophet*, pp. 187–194; see also Akhavi, "Islam, Politics in Society," pp. 406–407; Arjomand, *The Turban for the Crown*, p. 100; and Sivan, "Islamic Radicalism: Sunni and Shiite."

7. Mottahedeh, *The Mantle of the Prophet*, pp. 138–144, 179–185.

8. Ibid., pp. 183–185.

9. Ibid., pp. 190–191; for a discussion of anti-US themes, see Beeman, "Images of the Great Satan," pp. 191–217; and Fischer, "Imam Khomeini: Four Levels of Understanding," pp. 150–171.

10. Mottahedeh, *The Mantle of the Prophet*, pp. 287–315.

11. Fischer, "Imam Khomeini: Four Levels of Understanding," pp. 160–162; for a general discussion of the power of language in Iran, see Beeman, *Language, Status and Power in Iran*.

12. See Arjomand, *The Turban for the Crown*, pp. 134–188; and Fischer, "Imam Khomeini: Four Levels of Understanding," pp. 160–166.

13. Arjomand, *The Turban for the Crown*, pp. 134–174; Bakhash, *The Reign of the Ayatollahs*, pp. 71–91, 240–250.

14. For the most complete discussion of the doctrine and Khomeini's interpretation, see Rose, "Velayat-e Faqih and the Recovery of Islamic Identity," pp. 166–190. Other important sources for the interpretation of jurisconsult include Akhavi, "Islam, Politics and Society," pp. 413–414; Sivan, "Islamic Radicalism: Sunni and Shiite"; Arjomand, *The Turban for the Crown*, pp. 148–159; and Bayat, "The Iranian Revolution of 1978–79," pp. 34–42. For ideological differences between Khomeini and the leading thinkers of the fundamentalist revolution in Iran, see Akhavi, "Islam, Politics and Society," pp. 404–429; Akhavi, "Shariati's Social Thought," pp. 125–144; Abrahamian, "Ali Shariati: Ideologue of the Iranian Revolution," pp. 25–28; Ajami, "The Impossible Life of Moslem Liberalism," pp. 26–32; Sachedina, "Ali Shariati: Ideologue of the Iranian Revolution," pp. 191–212; and Bayat, "Mahmud Taleqani and the Iranian Revolution," pp. 67–94.

15. See Bill, "Power and Religion in Revolutionary Iran," pp. 41–45; Akhavi, "Elite Factionalism in the Islamic Republic of Iran," pp. 181–194; Cottam, "Inside Revolutionary Iran," pp. 168–181; Fischer, "Becoming Mullah: Reflections on Iranian Clerics," pp. 83–117; Fischer, "Imam Khomeini: Four Levels of Understanding," pp. 160–162; and Bakhash, *The Reign of the Ayatollahs*, pp. 241–242.

16. For themes relating to the martyodom of Ali and Husayn, see Fischer, "Becoming Mullah: Reflections on Iranian Clerics," pp. 104–110. For a general discussion on these themes, see Fischer, *Iran from Religious Dispute to Revolution*, pp. 12–27. For a discussion relating to unmet domestic matters as

well as foreign relations, see Bakhash, *The Reign of the Ayatollahs*, pp. 251–266; and Bakhash, "The Politics of Land, Law and Social Justice in Iran," pp. 186–201. For foreign relations in particular, see R. K. Ramazani, *Revolutionary Iran*, pp. 86–146.

17. For Montezari positions, see Akhavi, "Elite Factionalism in the Islamic Republic of Iran," pp. 194–198; Milani, *The Making of Iran's Islamic Revolution*, pp. 311–312; and Hiro, "Iran: Constitutional Reform and Future Leadership," pp. 12–14; reasons for his ouster have been advanced in pp. 13–14; see also Ottaway, "Khomeini's Designated Heir Resigns Amid Purge in Iran"; and Sciolino, "Khomeini Purifies, and Confuses, Iran's Future," p. 2.

18. Cottam, *Khomeini, the Future and US Options*, pp. 18–20. A spate of newspaper reports in the period immediately before and after Khomeini's death suggests that the regime will pursue a more pragmatic course; see Tyler's articles in *The Washington Post:* "Iran Has New Revolutionary Goal: Cash," "Rebuilding Plan to Cost 15 Billion, Tehran Says," "Iran Elects Rafsanjani President," and "Pragmatists Emerging in Iran."

19. Although Khomeini's successors may be divided into "hard-liners" and "soft-liners," pragmatists, moderates, and other designations, none of those elected or appointed have subscribed to mysticism or Erfan. On the contrary, each of these leaders—Rafsanjani, Khamenei, Karrubi—has been known as energetic, experienced, "this-worldly" figures who can be expected to move swiftly toward improving Iran's position at home and abroad. For a discussion, see Cottam, "Inside Revolutionary Iran," pp. 181–185; Akhavi, "Elite Factionalism in the Islamic Republic of Iran," pp. 194–201; Milani, *The Making of Iran's Islamic Revolution*, pp. 310–317; and Cottam, *Khomeini, the Future, and US Options*, pp. 17–30.

20. For Rafsanjani's positions, see Cottam, *Khomeini, the Future and US Options*, pp. 18–30; Akhavi, "Elite Factionalism in the Islamic Republic of Iran," pp. 181–201; Bakhash, "The Politics of Land, Law, and Social Justice in Iran," p. 199; Bill, "Power and Religion in Revolutionary Iran," pp. 36–37; Bakhash, "Islam and Social Justice in Iran," pp. 103–113; Tyler, "Rafsanjani Sweeps out Hard-Liners"; see also Tyler, "Rafsanjani Takes Oath to Lead Iran."

21. Former Iranian President Ali Khamenei was chosen by a two-thirds vote of the Assembly of Experts on June 4, 1989, to succeed Khomeini as spiritual leader. There was no mention of his assuming the role of jurisconsult. See Tyler, "Khamenei Succeeds Khomeini"; see also Tyler, "Iranian (Rafsanjani) Says Khamenei Appointment May Not Be Permanent," and "Clerics Ordered to Obey New Iranian Leader." For background on Khamenei and his positions, see Bill, "Power and Religion in Revolutionary Iran," pp. 38–39; and Akhavi, "Elite Factionalism in the Islamic Republic of Iran," pp. 183–201.

22. For an assessment of Khomeini as a political leader in addition to his anti-US bias, see Cottam, *Khomeini, the Future and US Options*, pp. 11–16. See Tyler articles cited in notes 18 and 20 for comments on the pragmatic approach of the new Iranian government; for a more recent examination of the government's economic problems, see J. Miller, "Iran's Economic Changes Cause Pain."

23. For thoughts on various scenerios, see Cottam, *Khomeini, the Future and US Options*, pp. 21–30. Cottam cites the government under Rafsanjani as the most likely but without liberalization; although he does not totally discount the probability of a more moderate outcome. For a more optimistic forecast of reform measures taking place in the way that a new leadership would govern, see Hiro, "Iran: Constitutional Reform and Future Leadership," pp. 11–15.

24. For a discussion concerning the prospects for a liberalizing trend emerging as the focal point of government in Iran after Khomeini, see Binder,

Islamic Liberalism, pp. 355–359; for a more recent discussion of the Rafsanjani government and its successors in this area, see J. Miller, "Islamic Radicals Lose Their Tight Grip."

25. Lustick, *For the Land and the Lord*, pp. 10–12; for a discussion of the origins of Gush Emunim, see Avruch, "Traditionalizing Israeli Nationalism," pp. 47–56; see also Sprinzak, "The Politics of Zionist Fundamentalism in Israel," pp. 3–7; Aronoff, *Israeli Visions and Divisions*, pp. 70–71; Rubinstein, *The Zionist Dream Revisited*, pp. 99–126; and Aran, "Redemption as a Catastrophe."

26. Lustick, *For the Land and the Lord*, pp. 29–30, 34; also Don-Yehiya, "Jewish Messianism, Religious Zionism and Israeli Politics," p. 225.

27. See the excellent study by Idel, *Kaballah: New Perspectives*, p. xi; also Idel, "Mysticism," p. 650.

28. Idel, *Kaballah: New Perspectives*, pp. xii–xvi, 74–111; Idel, "Mysticism," pp. 651–655.

29. Idel, *Kaballah: New Perspectives*, pp. 112–155.

30. Don-Yehiya, "Jewish Messianism, Religious Zionism and Israeli Politics," pp. 225–227; also Lustick, *For the Land and the Lord*, pp. 29–34.

31. Lustick, *For the Land and the Lord*, p. 34.

32. Ibid., p. 34–35.

33. Don-Yehiya, "Jewish Messianism, Religious Zionism and Israeli Politics," pp. 226–227.

34. As told in Lustick, *For the Land and the Lord*, pp. 36–37.

35. See Avruch, "Gush Emunim: The 'Iceberg Model' of Extremism Reconsidered," pp. 31–32.

36. For details surrounding the evacuation of these settlements, see Lustick, *For the Land and the Lord*, pp. 48–53, 59–61.

37. Ibid., p. 58.

38. Ibid.

39. For an analysis of Tehiya's success in 1984, see M. A. Friedlander, "The Impact of Arab-Israeli Relations on the 1984 Elections," pp. 55–56.

40. See election tally, *The Washington Post*, November 5, 1988.

41. See M. A. Friedlander, "The Impact of Arab-Israeli Relations on the 1984 Elections," p. 59.

42. Lustick, *For the Land and the Lord*, pp. 68–69.

43. Ibid., pp. 70–71.

44. As quoted in ibid., p. 83.

45. Ibid., pp. 84–85.

46. For a discussion of borders and territory, see ibid., pp. 104–110.

47. For Begin's worldview, including his concept of the land and his effort to achieve victory against the Palestinians in Lebanon, see Sofer, *Begin: An Anatomy of Leadership*, pp. 97–137, 201–215; see also Perlmutter, *The Life and Times of Menachem Begin*, pp. 372–396; and Perlmutter, *Israel the Partitioned State*, pp. 309–340.

48. Lustick, *For the Land and the Lord*, pp. 141–152.

49. Ibid., pp. 148–149.

50. Ibid., p. 151.

51. Ibid., pp. 151–152.

52. Ibid., pp. 131–141.

53. Ibid., pp. 134–135.

54. For details of Kahane's ineligibility, see Yaniv, "Israel Comes of Age," p. 102.

55. Lustick, *For the Land and the Lord*, pp. 125–126.

56. Ibid., pp. 126–127.

57. Ibid., pp. 127–128.

58. See Frankel, "Israeli Settlers Striking Back with Vigilante Action Groups"; Cody, "Jewish Settlers, West Bank Arabs Live and Die in Cycles of Revenge"; and other Frankel articles: "Crackdown on Intifada Demanded," "Angry Jewish Settlers Try to Attack Shamir," and "Protesting Jewish Settlers Clash with Israeli Army in West Bank."

59. See Brinkley, "The Soldiers: Anger and Frustration," pp. 3–32, 46–50.

60. Walzer, *Exodus and Revolution*, p. 139.

61. Ibid., pp. 139–141.

62. See Frankel, "Results of Israeli Election Mirror Nation at War with Itself." For background on Shamir and his hopes for Israel prior to election, see Brinkley, "The Stubborn Strength of Yitzhak Shamir."

63. See Lustick, *For the Land and the Lord*, pp. 165–168.

64. Ibid., pp. 168–176; also Cody, "Feud over Temple Mount Resurfaces."

65. For a discussion of the clash between redemptionism and liberalism, see Walzer, "What Kind of a Jewish State?" pp. 126–128.

66. See Sahliyeh, *In Search of Leadership*, pp. 2–9, 42–86; see also Sahliyeh, "Political Trends Among the West Bank Urban Elite"; and Lederman, "Dateline West Bank: Interpreting the Intifada," pp. 230–234.

67. Sahliyeh, *In Search of Leadership*, pp. 182–185; also Peretz, "Intifadeh: The Palestinian Uprising," pp. 965–966; Lederman, "Dateline West Bank: Interpreting the Intifada," pp. 234–239.

68. Sahliyeh, *In Search of Leadership*, p. 182; Lederman, "Dateline West Bank: Interpreting the Intifada," p. 235; Peretz, "Intifadeh: The Palestinian Uprising," pp. 966–967; R. Wright, "Three New Dimensions of Palestinian Politics," pp. 20–23.

69. Lederman, "Dateline West Bank: Interpreting the Intifada," pp. 232–233.

70. Ibid., p. 233; also Elpeleg, "West Bank Story," pp. 9–10.

71. Lederman, "Dateline West Bank: Interpreting the Intifada," p. 234.

72. Ibid.

73. Ibid., pp. 235–237.

74. Sahliyeh, *In Search of Leadership*, p. 183; also, A. D. Miller, "Palestinians and the Intifada: One Year Later," pp. 74–75.

75. A. D. Miller, "Palestinians and the Intifada: One Year Later," p. 76; Sahliyeh, *In Search of Leadership*, pp. 183–184.

76. For a discussion of the relative popularity of the PLO on the West Bank, see Shadid and Seltzer, "Political Attitudes of Palestinians in the West Bank and Gaza," pp. 16–32; for a discussion of the broader context in which PLO leadership has been viewed, see Nakhleh, "The West Bank and Gaza: Twenty Years Later," pp. 213–226; see also Sahliyeh, *In Search of Leadership*, p. 184; Miller, "Palestinians and the Intifada: One Year Later," pp. 106–107; and Wright, "Three New Dimensions of Palestinian Politics," pp. 27–29.

77. Although there have been sharp divisions between the government in Israel and residents within the Jewish settlements over the army's use of stronger measures to protect their security, the general populace has been comforted by the use of force to repel the intifada. See the results of a poll taken on the eve of Shamir's April 1989 visit to Washington: Brinkley, "Majority in Israel Oppose PLO Talks Now, a Poll Shows."

78. See Lederman, "Dateline West Bank: Interpreting the Intifada," pp. 238–239.

79. Ibid., p. 239. This perception more than any other may have provided sufficient rationale for Arafat and the Fatah leadership to move in the direction of

accommodating itself to a strategy of diplomatic solution in the territories, such as recognition of UN Resolution 242 and the State of Israel as well as foreswearing terrorism. See Abu-Amr, "The Debate Within the Palestinian Camp," pp. 40–49; see also Rubin, *The PLO's New Policy: Evolution Until Victory?* pp. 14–22.

80. Sahliyeh, *In Search of Leadership*, pp. 139–147; for a general discussion of Islamic organizations and their formation, see Satloff, "Islam in the Palestinian Uprising."

81. Sahliyeh, *In Search of Leadership*, pp. 140–141; Satloff, *Islam in the Palestinian Uprising*, p. 8. For an elaboration on the theme of Iranian and Lebanese influences, see Wright, "Three New Dimensions of Palestinian Politics," pp. 23–24.

82. Sahliyeh, *In Search of Leadership*, p. 143.

83. Ibid., pp. 143–144.

84. Ibid., pp. 144–147.

85. Ibid., p. 147.

86. Ibid., p. 148–150; also Satloff, *Islam in the Palestinian Uprising*, p. 2.

87. Sahliyeh, *In Search of Leadership*, p. 151.

88. As quoted in Wright, "Three New Dimensions of Palestinian Politics," p. 27.

89. See Lederman, "Dateline West Bank: Interpreting the Intifada," p. 244.

90. See A. D. Miller, "Palestinians and the Intifada: One Year Later," p. 76.

91. Sahliyeh, *In Search of Leadership*, pp. 158–160.

92. For background leading to Arafat's December 1988 announcement, see Green, "U.S.-PLO Talks: Just a First Step," pp. 51–57; see also A. D. Miller, "Palestinians and the Intifada: One Year Later," pp. 106–107.

93. For background on the Arafat-Assad hostility, see Sahliyeh, *In Search of Leadership*, p. 155; see also R. Wright, "Three New Dimensions of Palestinian Politics," pp. 27–28; and Rubin, *The PLO's Intractable Foreign Policy*, pp. 8–11.

CHAPTER 3

1. See Carter, *Keeping Faith*, pp. 273–277.

2. Brzezinski, *Power and Principle*, p. 91.

3. Carter, *Keeping Faith*, pp. 294–295; also Vance, *Hard Choices*, pp. 191–194.

4. Carter, *Keeping Faith*, p. 296.

5. M. A. Friedlander, *Sadat and Begin: The Domestic Politics of Peacemaking*, pp. 107–108.

6. Brzezinski, *Power and Principle*, pp. 115–120.

7. Carter, *Keeping Faith*, p. 303.

8. Brzezinski, *Power and Principle*, pp. 239–244.

9. Quandt, *Camp David*, pp. 171–172.

10. Ibid., pp. 194–195.

11. Ibid., pp. 220–257.

12. Ibid., pp. 245–249.

13. Carter, *Keeping Faith*, p. 402.

14. Quandt, *Camp David*, pp. 272–281.

15. Ibid., pp. 314–319.

16. See Linowitz, "The Prospects for the Camp David Peace Process," pp. 92–100.

17. Carter, *Keeping Faith*, pp. 440–458.

18. See Haig, *Caveat*, pp. 180, 186; see also Schiff and Ya'ari, *Israel's Lebanon War*, pp. 35–37, 75–76, 90, 146, 151–154, 193.

19. Schiff and Ya'ari, *Israel's Lebanon War*, pp. 32–37. For a discussion of the Syrian purpose behind missile emplacement, see Harris, "The View from Zahle," p. 276.

20. For a discussion about whether the United States gave tacit permission to the Israeli plan for invasion, see Schiff, "Green Light Lebanon," pp. 73–85; for an analysis from Haig's point of view, see Haig, *Caveat*, p. 335. In personal interviews in Jerusalem during July and December 1987, Minister Ariel Sharon confirmed Haig's account, which underscores that the United States objected most strenuously to any thought of an Israeli invasion of Lebanon.

21. For a discussion of the assassination as well as likely causes for the act, see Schiff and Ya'ari, *Israel's Lebanon War*, pp. 246–249.

22. For the most compelling account of the massacres, see ibid., pp. 250–285.

23. Ibid., pp. 208–209, 224–225.

24. See Kemp, "Lessons of Lebanon," p. 58.

25. Ibid.

26. Schiff and Ya'ari, *Israel's Lebanon War*, pp. 230–233.

27. Ibid., pp. 288–292.

28. See Quandt, "Reagan's Lebanon Policy," p. 244.

29. Ibid.; also, Kemp, "Lessons of Lebanon," p. 61; for an excellent discussion about Syria's interests in opposing the May 17 agreement, see Dawisha, "The Motives of Syria's Involvement in Lebanon," pp. 228–236; for agreement itself as well as the differing motives of the participants and negotiating tactics, see Rubin and Blum, *The May 1983 Agreement over Lebanon*; for an Israeli view by a participant, see Tamir, *A Soldier in Search of Peace*, pp. 147–153.

30. For an analysis of Syrian-PLO relations, see Dawisha, "The Motives of Syria's Involvement in Lebanon," p. 235; for details on the various factions in Lebanon and their preferences for attaining strategic positions against one another, see Deeb, "Lebanon: Prospects for National Reconciliation in the Mid-1980's," pp. 267–283, and pp. 276–278 especially regarding Druzes.

31. See Tamir, *A Soldier in Search of Peace*, p. 157; see also Lubrani, "The Israeli Operative Aspect," pp. 37–39.

32. Kemp, "Lessons of Lebanon," pp. 62–63; Quandt, "Reagan's Lebanon Policy: Trial and Error," pp. 246–247.

33. Kemp, "Lessons of Lebanon," p. 63.

34. Ibid., pp. 63–64; Quandt, "Reagan's Lebanon Policy: Trial and Error," p. 248.

35. Quandt, "Reagan's Lebanon Policy: Trial and Error," p. 248.

36. Ibid., pp. 248–249.

37. Ibid., p. 249.

38. Ibid., pp. 253–254; also, Cobban, "Thinking About Lebanon," pp. 69–70.

39. Oakley, "International Terrorism," pp. 621–628.

40. See Cobban, "Thinking About Lebanon," p. 64.

41. Ibid., p. 62.

42. See Cobban, "Lebanon's Chinese Puzzle"; also, Cobban, *The Shia Community and the Future of Lebanon*, p. 3.

43. See Ajami, *The Vanished Imam*, pp. 123–158.

44. Ibid., pp. 182–190.

45. See A. R. Norton, *AMAL and the Shi'a*, pp. 89–91.

46. Khalaf, *Lebanon's Predicament*, pp. 239–260.
47. Cobban, *The Shia Community and the Future of Lebanon*, pp. 6–8.
48. Ibid.
49. A. R. Norton, *AMAL and the Shi'a*, pp. 101–106.
50. See Jureidini, "Lebanon: The Consuming Conflict, The Elusive Consensus," pp. 23–28.
51. For the virtues of the Reagan plan, see Kreczko, "Support Reagan's Initiative," pp. 140–153.
52. Novik, *Encounter with Reality*, p. 60.
53. For text of Israel's communiqué on the Reagan plan, see *The New York Times*, September 3, 1982.
54. Interview with Yehiel Kadishai (chief of cabinet to Menachem Begin), Jerusalem, December 1983.
55. Bailey, *Jordan's Palestinian Challenge, 1948–1983*, pp. 127–128.
56. Ibid., p. 113; also, Rentz, "The Fahd Peace Plan," pp. 21–24.
57. Novik, *Encounter with Reality*, p. 105.
58. Bailey, *Jordan's Palestinian Challenge*, p. 114.
59. Ibid., p. 118.
60. See Rubin, "The Reagan Administration and the Middle East," p. 445.
61. Talal, "Return to Geneva," p. 12.
62. Pollock, "Jordan: Option or Optical Illusion," pp. 22–26.
63. Aruri, "The PLO and the Jordan Option," p. 8.
64. Susser, *Double Jeopardy*, p. 41–46.
65. Ibid., p. 55.
66. Rubin, "Middle East: Search for Peace," pp. 596–597.
67. Oakley, "International Terrorism," pp. 616–620.
68. See the Tower Report; see also Babcock and Oberdorfer, "The NSC Cabal."
69. Robertson, "Chronology, 1986," p. 673.
70. Ibid., p. 674.
71. Susser, *Double Jeopardy*, p. 55.
72. See Eilts, "Reviving the Middle East Peace Process," pp. 4, 7, 9, 12; Y. Shamir, "Israel at 40," pp. 577–578; Carter, "Middle East Peace: New Opportunities," p. 6.
73. Lustick, "Israel's Dangerous Fundamentalists," pp. 136–139.
74. Indyk, "Glasnost and the Middle East," pp. 14–21.

CHAPTER 4

1. For an excellent discussion of the claimed and real purpose behind the Iraqi invasion, see Sick, "Trial by Error: Reflections on the Iran-Iraq War," pp. 233–234; for an opposite view, see Renfrew, "Who Started the War," pp. 98–108; for an analysis of the character of the Saddam Hussein regime and its domestic situation at the time of the invasion, see C. Wright, "Iraq: New Power in the Middle East," pp. 257–277; and Dawisha, "Iraq: The West's Opportunity," pp. 134–153; for an assessment of Iran during the same period, see Rouleau, "Khomeini's Iran," pp. 1–20.
2. See Segal, "The Iran-Iraq War: A Military Analysis," p. 958; Stauffer, "Economic Warfare in the Gulf," pp. 112–114; Maull, "Containment, Competition and Cooperation," pp. 114–115; McNaugher, "The Iran-Iraq War: Slouching Toward Catastrophe?" pp. 5–15.
3. See Heller, "The War Strategy of Iran," pp. 22–23.

4. See Engleberg and Trainor, "Behind the Gulf Buildup"; see also US Department of State, "U.S. Policy in the Persian Gulf," p. 11.

5. See J. G. Stein, "The Wrong Strategy in the Right Place," p. 148; see also, US Congress, House of Representatives "National Security Implications of United States Operations in the Persian Gulf"; and "U.S. Backed Gulf Convoys to Limit Soviet Union, Report Says," *The New York Times*, August 23, 1987.

6. For a discussion of President Reagan's decision to notify the public of the Iran initiative after the secret arms deal had been disclosed in a Beirut newspaper, see US Government, *Report of the President's Special Review Board* (otherwise known as the Tower Report), pp. D11–14.

7. Engelberg and Trainor, "Behind the Gulf Buildup," p. 1.

8. See Lieber, "Middle East Oil and the Industrial Democracies," pp. 228–232; see also Parsons, "Iran and Western Europe," pp. 227–229; and US Department of State, "U.S. Policy in the Persian Gulf," p. 2.

9. See Engelberg and Trainor, "Behind the Gulf Buildup"; see also US Department of State, "U.S. Policy in the Persian Gulf," pp. 11–12.

10. See Engelbert and Trainor, "Behind the Gulf Buildup"; for a discussion of Gorbachev's policy in the Gulf, see Katz, "The Soviet Challenge in the Gulf," pp. 24–27; and Golan, "Gorbachev's Middle East Strategy," pp. 48–49, 52–54. For a Soviet point of view, see Derkovsky, "The Soviet Union and the Middle East," pp. 11–13.

11. Engelberg and Trainor, "Behind the Gulf Buildup."

12. J. G. Stein, "The Wrong Strategy in the Right Place," p. 149.

13. See Engelberg and Trainor, "Behind the Gulf Buildup."

14. Sick, "Trial by Error: Reflections on the Iran-Iraq War," p. 240.

15. See Sick, "What Do We Think We're Doing in the Gulf War."

16. Ibid.

17. Cody, "Chain of Events in Persian Gulf."

18. Ibid.

19. Ibid.; also J. G. Stein, "The Wrong Strategy in the Right Place," p. 150.

20. Cody, "Chain of Events in Persion Gulf."

21. J. G. Stein, "The Wrong Strategy in the Right Place," p. 154.

22. See Moore and Ottaway, "Iran Said to Obtain U.S.-Made Stingers."

23. J. G. Stein, "The Wrong Strategy in the Right Place," p. 156.

24. See Kemp, "Middle East Opportunities," p. 144; see also Sick, "Trial by Error: Reflections on the Iran-Iraq War," pp. 242–243.

25. See Segal, "The Iran-Iraq War: A Military Analysis," pp. 958–959; Ramazani, "Iran's Foreign Policy: Contending Orientations," pp. 211–215; and McNaugher, "The Iran-Iraq War: Slouching Toward Catastrophe?" pp. 9–10.

26. Sick, "Trial by Error: Reflections on the Iran-Iraq War," pp. 241–242; Fuller, "War and Revolution in Iran," pp. 80–82.

27. See Akhavi, "Elite Factionalism in the Islamic Republic of Iran," pp. 192–201; Sick, "Trial by Error: Reflections on the Iran-Iraq War," pp. 237–239.

28. See Sick, "What Do We Think We're Doing in the Gulf War"; see also J. G. Stein, "The Wrong Strategy in the Right Place," p. 153.

29. See Precht, "Ayatollah Realpolitik," pp. 113–114; and Sick, "Trial by Error: Reflections on the Iran-Iraq War," pp. 239–243.

30. See McCartney, "Iran Declares Era of Hostage-Taking Over, W. Germans Say"; see also Bakhash, "What's Khomeini Up To?"

31. Bakhash, "What's Khomeini Up To?"

32. Ibid. For a representative discussion of the broader issues in the furor over Rushdie's novel, see Easterbrook and Freund, "Death and Dogma." For details on Rushdie, see Marzorati, "Salman Rushdie: Fiction's Embattled Infidel,"

pp. 24–27, 44, 47–49, 100.

33. See Ottaway, "Khomeini's Designated Heir Resigns Amid Purge in Iran."

34. Sciolino, "Khomeini Purifies, and Confuses, Iran's Future."

35. See Ottaway, "Iran Says It Arrested US. Spies"; Tyler, "Rafsanjani Touted as Khomeini's Successor"; Randal, "Iranian Advocates Killings"; and Tyler, "Iran Retracts Urging Death of Westerners."

36. For details, see Ramazani, *Revolutionary Iran: Challenge and Response in the Middle East*, pp. 114–116.

37. Ibid., p. 117; see also Faksh, "Saudi Arabia and the Gulf Crisis," pp. 47–48.

38. Ramazani, *Revolutionary Iran*, pp. 116–118.

39. Ibid., pp. 86–90, 96–100.

40. Ibid., pp. 101–111.

41. Ibid., pp. 111–113.

42. Ibid., pp. 93–96; see also Hameed, "After Mecca; Saudi Arabia Is More Stable Than It Looks."

43. See Kemp, "Middle East Opportunities," p. 151.

44. Ibid., p. 152; see also Ottaway, "Middle East Weapons Proliferate"; and Carus, *Chemical Weapons in the Middle East*.

45. Ramazani, *Revolutionary Iran*, pp. 137–143.

46. See Hoffman, "Bush Looking Anew for Ways to Assert U.S. Leadership"; also, Oberdorfer, "Bush Finds Theme of Foreign Policy: 'Beyond Containment.'"

47. Oberdorfer, "Bush Finds Theme of Foreign Policy: 'Beyond Containment.'"

48. See Ottaway, "U.S. Still Ready for Iran 'Dialogue.'"

49. See Tyler, "Iraq Pursues Politics of Pragmatism."

50. Ibid.

51. The Reagan administration took action to end the convoy of Kuwaiti tankers in September 1988; Bush merely continued the downgrading. See Tyler, "U.S. to End 'Convoy' Role in the Gulf"; see also Halloran, "U.S. Altering Strategy for Defense of Arabian Oilfields."

52. See Green, "U.S.-PLO Talks: Just a First Step," pp. 51–57.

53. Nakhleh, "Political Stability in the Gulf Cooperation Council States," pp. 40–43.

54. For the Gulf states' reaction to the Iran arms sale, see Hamdoon, "The U.S-Iran Arms Deal," pp. 35–40; and Kostiner, "Counter-productive Mediation," pp. 41–46.

55. Miller and Mylroie, *Saddam Hussein and the Crisis in the Gulf*, p. 150; see also Oberdorfer, "Mixed Signals in the Middle East," p. 21; and Woodward, *The Commanders*, p. 203.

56. Miller and Mylroie, *Saddam Hussein and the Crisis in the Gulf*, pp. 150–151; Oberdorfer, "Mixed Signals in the Middle East," p. 21; see also Kaslow, "Iraq Banks on Its Oil to Fuel Reconstruction," pp. 42–43.

57. Gigot, "Iraq: An American Screw-Up," p. 7; Oberdorfer, "Mixed Signals in the Middle East," p. 21; also, Frankel, "Iraq Said Developing A-Weapons."

58. Oberdorfer, "Mixed Signals in the Middle East," p. 21.

59. Miller and Mylroie, *Saddam Hussein and the Crisis in the Gulf*, pp. 148–150; for a discussion of biological weapons in Iraq as well as the nature of threat, see Carus, "The Poor Man's Atomic Bomb?"

60. See M. Eisenstadt, "The Sword of the Arabs."

61. Murphy, "Iraq Accuses Kuwait of Plot to Steal Oil, Depress Prices."

62. Ajami, "The Summer of Arab Discontent," pp. 1–20.

63. Miller and Mylroie, *Saddam Hussein and the Crisis in the Gulf*, pp. 177–192.

64. See Karsh and Rautsi, *Saddam Hussein: A Political Biography*, pp. 204–207.

65. Ibid., pp. 211–214.

66. Ibid., pp. 212–213.

67. Murphy, "Mubarak Says Iraq, Kuwait Will Begin Talks This Weekend."

68. Gigot, "Iraq: An American Screw-Up," pp. 9–10; see also Oberdorfer, "Mixed Signals in the Middle East," p. 39; and Karsh and Rautsi, *Saddam Hussein: A Political Biography*, p. 215.

69. Miller and Mylroie, *Saddam Hussein and the Crisis in the Gulf*, pp. 211–213; Karsh and Rautsi, *Saddam Hussein: A Political Biography*, pp. 217–219.

70. Miller and Mylroie, *Saddam Hussein and the Crisis in the Gulf*, pp. 211–213.

71. Ibid, p. 4; for reporting of US-Saudi discussions, see Woodward, *The Commanders*, pp. 240–246.

72. Miller and Mylroie, *Saddam Hussein and the Crisis in the Gulf*, p. 4.

73. Ibid.; for a discussion of the blockade and Iraqi vulnerabilities, see Clawson, "How Vulnerable Is Iraq's Economy," pp. 1–7.

74. Devroy, "Bush Orders 200,000 More Troops to Gulf."

75. Ibid.; for counterarguments about the force of diplomacy, see R. Fisher, "Getting to 'Yes' with Saddam"; and Ball, "The Gulf Crisis."

76. Priest, "Saddam Orders the Release of All Hostages"; also Karsh and Rautsi, *Saddam Hussein: A Political Biography*, pp. 233–235.

77. Miller and Mylroie, *Saddam Hussein and the Crisis in the Gulf*, p. 212.

78. Ibid., pp. 212–213.

79. Y. M. Ibrahim, "Impatiently, Arabs Await 'New Order' in the Gulf."

80. Y. M. Ibrahim, "A Time of Confusion."

81. Ibid.

82. Ibid.

83. Ajami, "The Summer of Arab Discontent," pp. 4–5.

84. Ibid.

85. For a discussion of what other choices the Bush administration had instead of going to war, see US Congress, House of Representatives, "Crisis in the Persian Gulf"

86. Sterner, "Navigating the Gulf," pp. 39–52.

87. M. Fisher, "Europeans Invite Iraq's Aziz for Talks."

88. For a discussion of war, see Vuono (US Army chief of staff), "Desert Storm and Conventional Forces," pp. 49–68; see also Karsh and Rautsi, *Saddam Hussein: A Political Biography*, pp. 244–265.

89. Karsh and Rautsi, *Saddam Hussein: A Political Biography*, pp. 265–266.

CHAPTER 5

1. See Spiegel, "America and Israel—How Bad Is It?" p. 22.

2. Hadar, "Reforming Israel—Before It's Too Late," p. 116.

3. Spiegel, "America and Israel—How Bad It Is?" pp. 11–22.

4. Hadar, "Reforming Israel—Before It's Too Late," p. 116.

5. Elon, "Letter from Israel," pp. 74–75.

6. Ibid., p. 76.

7. Ibid.

8. Ibid.; also Peretz, "Intifadeh," pp. 973–974.

9. Elon, "Letter from Israel," p. 77.

10. Ibid., pp. 77–78.

11. See Cohen, "Ethnicity and Legitimation in Contemporary Israel," pp. 113–115; for a discerning understanding of present-day Israel, see Walzer, "What Kind of a Jewish State?" pp. 34–37, 126–128.

12. Walzer, "What Kind of a Jewish State?" pp. 127–128.

13. See Ross, "The Peace Process—A Status Report," p. 10.

14. Ibid., p. 11.

15. Ibid., p. 10.

16. Ibid., p. 12.

17. Ibid.

18. Ibid.

19. Ibid., p. 14.

20. Spiegel, "America and Israel—How Bad Is It," p. 20.

21. Ibid.

22. Ibid.

23. Ibid.

24. Ibid.

25. Ibid.

26. Hadar, "Reforming Israel—Before It's Too Late," pp. 106–107.

27. Ibid.

28. Sterner, "Navigating the Gulf," pp. 48–52.

29. Spiegel, "America and Israel—How Bad Is It?" pp. 20–21.

30. For Baker's March 1991 trip to the Middle East, see Hoffman and Diehl, "Baker Asks Israel for Peace Moves"; and Hoffman, "Baker Finds Window of Opportunity for Peace." For Saudi rejections of the peace role, see Goshko, "Saudis Reject Role in Talks"; and Elon, "Report From Jerusalem," pp. 80–88.

31. For Baker discussions during his April Middle East visit, see Goshko and Diehl, "Baker, in Israel, Renews Mideast Quest"; Diehl and Goshko, "Baker Presses Israel to Make Concessions"; and Goshko, "Fallacy Might Underlie Baker's Latest Effort."

32. See Dessouki, "Egyptian Foreign Policy Since Camp David," pp. 94–110; also, S. Shamir, "Israeli Views of Egypt and the Peace Process," pp. 187–216; Yaari, *Peace By Piece*, pp. 1–4.

33. Dessouki, "Egyptian Foreign Policy Since Camp David," pp. 99–100.

34. Yaari, *Peace by Piece*, p. 9; also, Mansour, "An Egyptian View of Recent Events," in *Proceedings of the Washington Institute Policy Forum, 1988*, p. 46.

35. See Springborg, *Mubarak's Egypt*, pp. 45–245; see also S. E. Ibrahim, "Domestic Developments in Egypt," pp. 38–59; Aly, "Egypt: A Decade After Camp David," pp. 70–84; and Bianchi, "Islam and Democracy in Egypt," pp. 93–95, 104.

36. Springborg, *Mubarak's Egypt*, pp. 240.

37. Ibid.

38. Ibid., pp. 37–41, 85–87, 244–245; also, Aly, "Egypt: A Decade After Camp David," pp. 91–93; and Bianchi, "Islam and Democracy in Egypt," p. 94.

39. S. E. Ibrahim, "Domestic Developments in Egypt," pp. 26–37; also, Cowell, "To Egypt, Peace Pact Is a Stigma."

40. Springborg, *Mubarak's Egypt*, pp. 69–78, examines the impact and interests of the *Infitah* bourgeoisie.

41. For a discussion of the military under Mubarak, its roles and likely status, see Springborg, *Mubarak's Egypt*, pp. 95–125; see also Springborg, "The President and the Field Marshall," pp. 5–16; and Satloff, *Army and Politics in Mubarak's Egypt*, pp. 8–18. For details on the removal of Defense Minister Abu Ghazala by Mubarak, see Tyler, "Mubarak Reassigns Key Deputy." Mubarak re-assigned Abu Ghazala as a presidential assistant without portfolio, thereby preserving his control over the military, which the former defense chief threatened.

42. For a discussion on how domestic developments interfered with normalization with Egypt, see Chazan, "Domestic Developments in Israel," pp. 150–186; see also S. Shamir, "Israeli Views of Egypt and the Peace Process," pp. 187–216.

43. For a discussion of the Taba issue, see Lesch, "Egyptian-Israeli Boundary Disputes," pp. 43–58; for Peres's efforts to compromise on Taba, see pp. 50–54.

44. See Frankel, "Israel, Egypt Sign Accord on Return of Taba Resort"; for background by a participant, see Tamir, *A Soldier in Search of Peace*, pp. 76–91; also, on turnover of Taba, see Sammakia, "Jublant Egyptians Take Control of Taba Resort from Israel."

45. For mention of the "cold peace," which characterized relations, see Benin, "The Cold Peace," pp. 3–9; see also Quandt, *The Middle East: Ten Years After Camp David*, pp. 1–10; Friedman, "Why Camp David Turned Bitter: The Carter View"; and Tamir, *A Soldier in Search of Peace*, pp. 52–66.

46. Yaari, *Peace by Piece*, pp. 11–16.

47. Lesch, "Egyptian-Israeli Relations," pp. 61–64; Dessouki, "Egyptian Foreign Policy Since Camp David," pp. 96–102.

48. Lesch, "Egyptian-Israeli Relations," p. 64; Dessouki, "Egyptian Foreign Policy Since Camp David," pp. 101–102; S. Lewis, "Israel: The Peres Era," pp. 595–597.

49. For details, see Elon, "Letter from Israel," pp. 74–80.

50. For a discussion of the Mubarak peace initiative at the beginning of 1988, see S. E. Ibrahim, "Domestic Developments in Egypt," p. 37.

51. For a discussion of Shultz's visit to the area to revive the peace process in response to Israeli and Egyptian requests, see Pear, "Shultz Tries Again"; for an Israeli analysis of the Shultz plan, see Tamir, "Israel, The Intifada and the Peace Process," pp. 22–23; for an analysis of the failure of the Shultz plan to unlock the impasse in negotiations, see Hannah and Indyk, "Beyond the Shultz Initiative," pp. 87–106.

52. See Golan, "Gorbachev's Middle East Strategy," pp. 41–43.

53. See Yaari, *Peace by Piece*, pp. 29–32.

54. Quandt, *The United States and Egypt*, pp. 67–72.

55. Springborg, "Egypt: Successes and Uncertainties," pp. 85–86.

56. Quandt, *The United States and Egypt*, pp. 68–72.

57. Ibid.

58. Ajami, "The Summer of Arab Discontent," pp. 4–5.

59. Springborg, "Egypt: Successes and Uncertainties," p. 78.

60. Miller and Mylroie, *Saddam Hussein and the Crisis in the Gulf*, p. 5.

61. Quandt, *The United States and Egypt*, p. 67.

62. Miller and Mylroie, *Saddam Hussein and the Crisis in the Gulf*, pp. 216–230.

63. Ibid.

64. Ibid.

65. Springborg, "Egypt: Success and Uncertainties," pp. 89–90.

66. For a discussion of Islamic fundamentalism in Egypt, see Ayalon, "Fundamentalism in Egypt," pp. 17–20.

67. Ibid.

68. Ibid.

69. See Satloff, "Jordan and Reverberations of the Uprising," Current History, 88, no. 535, pp. 104–105; for the text of Hussein's speech, see Quandt, *The Middle East: Ten Years After Camp David*, pp. 494–498.

70. Satloff, "Jordan and Reverberations of the Uprising," pp. 105–106; see also Andoni, "Jordan's Riots Spread; King Cancels Visit."

71. For arguments against the policy, see Nisan, "The Jordanian Option," pp. 30–35. Nissan has been identified as on the right wing of Israel's academic community; see Lustick, *For the Land and the Lord*, p. 130.

72. See M. A. Friedlander, *Sadat and Begin*, pp. 154–155.

73. The Camp David Accords call for Jordanian association, Reagan's plan looks to King Hussein's participation, and the 1988 Shultz initiative envisages a Jordanian-Palestinian delegation to the negotiations. For texts of all three, see Quandt, *The Middle East: Ten Years After Camp David*, Appendixes C, D, and K, pp. 449–470, 488–489.

74. Satloff, "Jordan and Reverberations of the Uprising," pp. 88, 104.

75. Reed, "Jordan and the Gulf," pp. 21–35.

76. Ibid.

77. Ibid.

78. Ibid.

79. Ibid.

80. From interviews with Ariel Sharon, Jerusalem, July and December 1987; New York, May 1987. The intensity and scope of the Israeli involvement with the United States in devising a strategy for the sale of arms to Iran is persuasive evidence of the motives of Israeli decisionmakers. See Woodward and Pincus, "U.S.-Israeli Accord Said to Authorize North-Nir Operations." For the depth of the Israeli-Iranian relationship during the shah's reign, see Lubrani, "The Iranian-Israeli Relationship," pp. 342–348. Lubrani was the Israeli ambassador to Tehran during the period of the relationship.

81. See Goodman, *Israel's Strategic Reality: The Impact of the Arms Race;* see also Carus, *Missiles in the Middle East;* Carus, *Chemical Weapons in the Middle East;* Ottaway, "Strike on Iraq No Longer an Easy Option"; and Tyler, "Iraq Nuclear Program Stirs Debate."

82. See Alpher and Feldman, *The West Bank and Gaza*, p. 106; see also Brinkley, "Majority in Israel Oppose PLO Talks Now," pp. 1, 18.

83. Alpher and Feldman, *The West Bank and Gaza*, pp. 146–147.

84. For a discussion of the Golan Heights annexation and the pressures that led to it, see Yishai, "Israeli Annexation of East Jerusalem and Golan Heights," pp. 45–60. For the religious commitment to Golan, see Yaniv, "A Syrian-Israeli Detente?" p. 28.

85. See Tyler, "Syria Reported Prepared to Join Peace Discussion."

86. See Tyler and Boustany, "Solution in Lebanon Eludes Arab Summit."

87. Ibid.

88. See Olmert, "Syria-Policy Developments"; Levran, "Syria's Military Strength and Capability," pp. 9–10; Yaniv, "A Syrian-Israeli Detente?" p. 29; and Maoz, *Asad: The Sphinx of Damascus*, p. 184.

89. See Tyler and Boustany, "Assad: Diplomacy by Obstruction"; and Seale, "Assad: Holding the Hardest Line." For details and an analysis of Assad's efforts to block initiatives by Hussein and Arafat, see Seale, *The Struggle for the Middle East*, pp. 461–491.

90. Yaniv, "A Syrian-Israeli Detente?" p. 28.
91. Yaniv could certainly be cited as on the Left of the Israeli political spectrum. See Rabinovich, "Political Aspects of Syrian Strategy," p. 68.
92. For details of the Syrian-Israeli disengagement, see Kissinger, *Years of Upheaval*, pp. 1032–1110.
93. See Eagleburger and Mondale, *Building for Peace*, pp. 50–53; Eilts and Lewis, *Toward Arab-Israeli Peace: Report of a Study Group*, pp. 27–28.
94. For a discussion of the Syrian role in terrorism, see Pipes, "Terrorism: The Syrian Connection," pp. 15–28; Maoz, "State-Run Terrorism in the Middle East," pp. 11–15; and Seale, *Asad: The Struggle for the Middle East*, pp. 466–473.
95. For a discussion of a more constructive Soviet role vis-à-vis Syria and in the Middle East generally, see Yaniv, "A Syrian-Israeli Detente?" pp. 31–32; and Eagleburger and Mondale, *Building for Peace*, pp. 65–70.
96. Boustany, "Second Thoughts in Syria."
97. Ibid.
98. Ibid.
99. Ibid.
100. Ibid.
101. Ibid.
102. Ibid.

CHAPTER 6

1. See US Department of State, "U.S. Policy in the Persian Gulf," p. 5; see also Fukuyama, "Growth and Decline of Soviet Activism," pp. 24–32; Fuller, "The United States and the Soviet Union in the Middle East," p. 7; Ross, "Soviet Decisionmaking for the Middle East," pp. 236–251; and Chubin, "Soviet Policy in the Middle East," pp. 254–261. Fukuyama, Ross, and Fuller have been high government officials in the Reagan administration either at the Department of State or the Central Intelligence Agency.
2. See McGwire, "The Middle East and Soviet Military Strategy," pp. 11–17.
3. For a discussion of why and how tensions in East-West relations have been recently thought about in less confrontational ways, see Shullman, "The Superpowers: Dance of the Dinosaurs," pp. 494–515; Kaiser, "The U.S.S.R. in Decline," pp. 97–113; d'Estaing, Nakasone, and Kissinger, "East-West Relations," pp. 1–21; Holloway, "Gorbachev's New Thinking," pp. 66–81; and Levgold, "The Revolution in Soviet Foreign Policy," pp. 82–98. In 1989 Gorbachev visited China as the People's Republic was in the throes of its own revolutionary student uprising. The visit, although marred by the student event, was supposed to have begun a rapprochement leading, perhaps, to a lessening of Soviet military strength on China's Far Eastern border. For a discussion of the events surrounding the Chinese revolution and Gorbachev's mid-May 1989 visit, see Kristof, "China Erupts," p. 90.
4. See Golan, "Gorbachev's Middle East Strategy," pp. 52–54; Fuller, "The United States and the Soviet Union in the Middle East," p. 7; Indyk, "Glasnost and the Middle East," pp. 14–15; Katz, "The Soviet Challenge in the Gulf," pp. 24–27.
5. Katz, "The Soviet Challenge in the Gulf," pp. 24–25.
6. See Weinberger, "Arms Reductions and Deterrence," pp. 700–719; see also J. G. Stein, "The Wrong Strategy in the Right Place," pp. 148–149.

7. J. G. Stein, "The Wrong Strategy in the Right Place," p. 159; also, Cody, "Chain of Events in Persian Gulf."

8. See Harrison, "Afghanistan: The Geneva Accords and After," pp. 34–39; Klass, "Afghanistan: The Accords," pp. 922–945; and Harrison, "Inside the Afghan Talks," pp. 31–60.

9. See Parry and Kornbluh, "Iran-Contra's Untold Story," pp. 3–30.

10. For a discussion relating to the changes in Soviet strategic thinking, see Holloway, "Gorbachev's New Thinking," pp. 66–81; Levgold, "The Revolution in Soviet Foreign Policy," pp. 82–98; Larrabee, "Gorbachev and the Soviet Military," pp. 1002–1026; and Drell and Johnson, "Managing Strategic Weapons," pp. 1027–1043. US fears of an adventuresome Kremlin in the Gulf are covered in Rubin, "Drowning in the Gulf," pp. 120–134; and Twinam, "U.S. Interests in the Arabian Gulf," pp. 13–14.

11. See J. G. Stein, "The Wrong Strategy in the Right Place," pp. 143–145. The literature on deterrence theory has a rich place in national security studies. For a discussion, see George and Smoke, *Deterrence in American Foreign Policy;* Mearsheimer, *Conventional Deterrence;* Jervis, "Deterrence Theory Revisited," pp. 284–324; Lebow and Stein, "Beyond Deterrence," pp. 3–71; and Jervis, Lebow, and Stein, *Psychology and Deterrence.* For the issue of extended deterrence, see J. G. Stein, "Extended Deterrence in the Middle East," pp. 326–352; Huth, *Extended Deterrence and the Prevention of War;* Huth, "Extended Deterrence and the Outbreak of War," pp. 423–444; Huth and Russett, "Deterrence Failure and Crisis Escalation," pp. 29–46; and Huth and Russett, "What Makes Deterrence Work?" pp. 496–526.

12. J. G. Stein, "The Wrong Strategy in the Right Place," p. 148.

13. Although Soviet naval presence increased, it remained below the level of 1980 when Moscow poured forces into Afghanistan. See US Department of State, "U.S. Policy in the Persian Gulf," pp. 5–6; see also Katz, "The Soviet Challenge in the Gulf," p. 25.

14. J. G. Stein, "The Wrong Strategy in the Right Place," pp. 148–149; Indyk, "Glasnost and the Middle East," pp. 15–16; Katz, "The Soviet Challenge in the Gulf," pp. 24–25; and US Department of State, "U.S. Policy in the Persian Gulf," pp. 1–5.

15. J. G. Stein, "The Wrong Strategy in the Right Place," pp. 149–151.

16. Ibid., pp. 150–154.

17. See Gordon, "Bush Urged to Find a Middle Course on Soviet Changes"; Friedman, "Bush Policy Makers Reach Uneasy Balance."

18. Miller and Mylorie, *Saddam Hussein and the Crisis in the Gulf,* pp. 216–230.

19. Ibid.

20. See Bill, "Populist Islam and U.S. Foreign Policy," pp. 133–134.

21. Cottam, *Khomeini, the Future, and US Options,* pp. 18–30.

22. For Bush's refusal to take this action, see Devroy and Oberdorfer, "U.S. Rules Out Deal on Iranian Funds."

23. For details of Bush's offer on indemnification, see Goshko, "U.S. Offers Amends in Iran Jet Deaths."

24. Iran for a time was said to be agreeable toward arranging for a release of US hostages, but the offer was soon withdrawn as domestic forces intervened following the Israeli abduction of Hezbollah figure, Sheikh Obeid. See Tyler, "Iran Offers, Bush Welcomes Help on Hostages."

25. S. E. Ibrahim, "Domestic Developments in Egypt," pp. 29–37.

26. See Brinkley, "The Stubborn Strength of Yitzhak Shamir," pp. 70–77.

27. For an examination of US thinking toward Egypt and Israel, see Shultz, "The Reagan Administration's Approach to Middle East Peacemaking," pp. 3–9; Eilts, "The United States and Egypt," pp. 111–149; Lewis, "The United States and Israel," pp. 217–257; Quandt, "U.S. Policy Toward the Arab-Israeli Conflict," pp. 357–386; and Atherton, *Egypt and U.S. Interests*.

28. S. E. Eisenstat, "Loving Israel—Warts and All," pp. 87–105.

29. Ibid.; also, E. Friedlander, "'The Green Line' Blurred by Emerging Arab Solidarity," pp. 8–10.

30. Hadar, "Reforming Israel—Before It's Too Late," p. 116. For a discussion of how the Temple Mount incident was seen by Muslim caretakers of the mosque, see E. Friedlander, "The WAKF and Palestinian Nationalism," pp. 7–8.

31. Hadar, "Reforming Israel—Before It's Too Late," p. 116.

32. Ibid.

33. Spiegel, "America and Israel—How Bad Is It?" p. 21.

34. See Diehl, "Israel Plagued by Recession"; for a discussion of Israel's soaring unemployment rate, now at 11 percent and expected to go to between 13 and 18 percent, see Brinkley, "Israeli Economy Is Keeping Many Jews in U.S.S.R."

35. See Sadowski, "The Sphinx's New Riddle," pp. 28–40.

36. Springborg, *Mubarak's Egypt*, pp. 266–272; Atherton, *Egypt and U.S. Interests*, pp. 12–16.

37. Satloff, "Jordan and Reverberations of the Uprising," p. 105.

38. Ibid.

39. Day, *East Bank/West Bank: Jordan and the Prospects for Peace*, pp. 94–116.

40. See Fishelson, "Key Findings of the Middle East Economic Cooperation Projects," pp. 249–257.

41. See Kally, "The Potential for Cooperation in Water Projects," pp. 223–224.

42. Ibid., pp. 224–227.

43. Ibid., pp. 227–230.

44. Fishelson, "Key Findings of the Middle East Economic Cooperation Projects," pp. 252–253.

45. Ibid., p. 253.

46. Ibid., pp. 253–254.

47. Nader, "The Politics of the Future in Lebanon," pp. 10–16.

48. Ibid.

49. Ibid.

50. Ibid.

51. Ibid.

Bibliography

Abrahamian, Ervand. "Ali Shariati: Ideologue of the Iranian Revolution." *MERIP Reports* (January 1982).

Abu-Amr, Ziad. "The Debate Within the Palestinian Camp." *American-Arab Affairs* 26 (Fall 1988).

Ajami, Fouad. "The Impossible Life of Moslem Liberalism." *The New Republic* (June 2, 1986).

———. "Iran: The Impossible Revolution." *Foreign Affairs* 67, no. 2.

———. "The Summer of Arab Discontent." *Foreign Affairs* 69, no. 5 (Winter 1990–91).

———. *The Vanished Imam: Musa al Sadr and the Shia of Lebanon.* Ithaca, N.Y.: Cornell University Press, 1986.

Akhavi, Shahrough. "Elite Factionalism in the Islamic Republic of Iran." *Middle East Journal* 41, no. 2 (Spring 1987).

———. "Islam, Politics and Society in the Thought of Ayatullah Khomeini, Ayatullah Taliqani and Ali Shariati." *Middle Eastern Studies* 24, no. 4 (October 1988).

———. "Shariati's Social Thought." In *Religion and Politics in Iran: Shi'ism from Quietism to Revolution,* edited by Nikki R. Keddie. New Haven, Conn.: Yale University Press, 1983.

Alpher, Joseph, and Shai Feldman, eds. *The West Bank and Gaza: Israel's Options for Peace.* Report of a Jaffee Center for Strategic Studies Study Group, Jaffee Center for Strategic Studies, Tel Aviv University, 1989.

Aly, Abdel Monem Said. "Democratization in Egypt." *American Arab Affairs* 22 (Fall 1987).

———. "Egypt: A Decade After Camp David." In *The Middle East: Ten Years After Camp David,* edited by William B. Quandt. Washington, D.C.: Brookings Institution, 1988.

Andoni, Lamis. "Jordan's Riots Spread; King Cancels Visit." *The Washington Post,* April 22, 1989, pp. A1, A20.

Anthony, Dick, and Thomas Robbins. "Culture Crisis and Contemporary Religion." In *In Gods We Trust: New Patterns of Religious Pluralism in America,* edited by Thomas Robbins and Dick Anthony. New Brunswick, N.J.: Transaction Books, 1981.

Aran, Gideon. "Redemption as a Catastrophe: The Gospel of Gush Emunim." In *Religious Extremism and Politics in the Middle East,* edited by Emmanuel Sivan and Menachem Friedman. Albany: State University of New York Press, 1990.

Arens, Moshe. "Israel's Approach to the Peace Process." Luncheon address to the Washington Institute for Near East Policy, Washington, D.C., March 14, 1989.

Arian, Asher. *Politics in Israel: The Second Generation*. Chatham, N.J.: Chatham House Publishers, 1985.

Arjomand, Said Amir. *The Turban for the Crown: The Islamic Revolution in Iran*. New York: Oxford University Press, 1988.

Aronoff, Myron. *Israeli Visions and Divisions: Cultural Change and Political Conflict*. New Brunswick, N.J.: Transaction Publishers, 1989.

Aruri, Nasser. "The PLO and the Jordan Option." *MERIP Reports* 131 (March–April 1985).

Ashcraft, Richard. *Revolutionary Politics and Locke's Two Treatises of Government*. Princeton, N.J.: Princeton University Press, 1986.

Atherton, Alfred Leroy. *Egypt and U.S. Interests*. Foreign Policy Institute, School of Advanced International Studies, Johns Hopkins University, Washington, D.C., March 1988.

Avineri, Shlomo. "Ideology and Israel's Foreign Policy." *The Jerusalem Quarterly* 37 (1986).

Avishai, Bernard. "Israel's Divided Unity." *New York Review of Books* 31, no. 19 (December 6, 1984).

———. *The Tragedy of Zionism: Revolution and Democracy in the Land of Israel*. New York: Farrar, Straus, Giroux, 1985.

Avruch, Kevin. "The Emergence of Ethnicity in Israel." *American Ethnologist*. 14, no. 2 (May 1987).

———. "Gush Emunim: The 'Iceberg Model' of Extremism Reconsidered." *Middle East Review* 21, no. 1 (Fall 1988).

———. "Traditionalizing Israeli Nationalism: The Development of Gush Emunim." *Political Psychology* 1, no. 1 (Spring 1979).

Ayalon, Ami. "Fundamentalism in Egypt." In *Islamic Fundamentalism in the Levant*. Washington, D.C.: Washington Institute for Near East Policy, June 26, 1990.

Baali, Fuad. *Society, State and Urbanism: Ibn Khaldun's Sociological Thought*. Albany: State University of New York Press, 1988.

Babcock, Charles R., and Don Oberdorfer. "The NSC Cabal: How Arrogance and Secrecy Brought on a Scandal." *The Washington Post*, Outlook Section, January 25, 1987, pp. B1–B2.

Bailey, Clinton. *Jordan's Palestinian Challenge, 1948–1983*. Boulder, Colo.: Westview Press, 1984.

Bailyn, Bernard. "The Central Themes of the American Revolution: An Interpretation." In *Essays on the American Revolution*, edited by Stephen G. Kurtz and James H. Hutson. Chapel Hill: University of North Carolina Press, 1973.

Bakhash, Shaul. "Islam and Social Justice in Iran." In *Shi'ism and Revolution*, edited by Martin Kramer. Boulder, Colo: Westview Press, 1987.

———. "The Politics of Land, Law and Social Justice in Iran." *The Middle East Journal* 43, no. 2 (Spring 1989).

———. *The Reign of the Ayatollahs*. New York: Basic Books, 1986.

———. "What's Khomeini Up To?" *The Washington Post*, op. ed., February 17, 1989.

Ball, George. "The Gulf Crisis." *The New York Review of Books* (December 6, 1990), 8–17.

Barzun, Jacques. "Is Democratic Theory for Export?" *Ethics and International Affairs* 1 (1987).

———. *A Stroll with William James*. New York: Harper and Row, 1983.

Bayat, Mangol. "The Iranian Revolution of 1978–79: Fundamentalist or Modern?" *The Middle East Journal* 37, no. 1 (Winter 1983).

———. "Mahmud Taleqani and the Iranian Revolution." In *Shi'ism Resistance and Revolution*, edited by Martin Kramer. Boulder, Colo.: Westview Press, 1987.

Beeman, William O. "Images of the Great Satan: Representations of the United States in the Iranian Revolution." In *Religion and Politics in Iran: Shi-ism from Quietism to Revolution*, edited by Nikki R. Keddie. New Haven, Conn.: Yale University Press, 1983.

———. *Language, Status and Power in Iran.* Bloomington: Indiana University Press, 1986.

Beilin, Yossi. "Inter-Generational Friction in Three Parties in Israel." *International Journal of Group Tensions* 13, nos. 1–4 (1983).

Bellah, Robert. *The Broken Covenant.* New York: Seabury Press, 1975.

———. "Civil Religion in America." *Daedalus* 96 (Winter 1967).

———. "Religion and Legitimation in the American Republic." In *In Gods We Trust*, edited by Thomas Robbins and Dick Anthony. New Brunswick, N.J.: Transaction Books, 1981.

Ben-Dor, Gabriel. *State and Conflict in the Middle East: Emergence of the Postcolonial State.* New York: Praeger Publishers, 1983.

Benard, Cheryl, and Zalmay Khalilzad. *"The Government of God"—Iran's Islamic Republic.* New York: Columbia University Press, 1984.

Benevinisti, Meron. *The West Bank Data Project: A Survey of Israel's Policies.* Washington, D.C.: American Enterprise Institute for Public Policy Research, 1984.

Benin, Joel. "The Cold Peace." *MERIP Reports* 14 (January 1985).

Benziman, Uzi. *Sharon: An Israeli Caesar.* New York: Adama Publishing, 1985.

Biale, David. *Power and Powerlessness in Jewish History.* New York: Schocken Books, 1986.

Bianchi, Robert. "Islam and Democracy in Egypt." *Current History* 88, no. 535 (Feburary 1989).

Bill, James A. "The Plasticity of Informal Politics: The Case of Iran." *Middle East Journal* 27, no. 3 (Spring 1973).

———. "Populist Islam and U.S. Foreign Policy." *SAIS Review* 9, no. 1 (Winter–Spring 1989).

———. "Power and Religion in Revolutionary Iran." *Middle East Journal* 36, no. 1 (Winter 1982)

Bill, James, and Carl Leiden. *Politics in the Middle East*, 2d ed. Boston: Little, Brown and Company, 1984.

Billington, James H. "Realism and Vision in American Foreign Policy." *Foreign Affairs, America and the World, 1986* 65, no. 3 (1987).

Binder, Leonard. *Islamic Liberalism: A Critique of Development Ideologies.* Chicago: University of Chicago Press, 1988.

Boesche, Roger. *The Strange Liberalism of Alexis de Tocqueville.* Ithaca, N.Y.: Cornell University Press, 1987.

Botein, Stephen. "Religious Dimensions of the Early American State." In *Beyond Confederation: Origins of the Constitution and American National Identity*, edited by Richard Beeman, Stephen Botein, and Edward C. Carter II. Chapel Hill: University of North Carolina Press, 1987.

Boustany, Nora. "Iraq, Syria Increase Tensions." *The Washington Post*, July 9, 1989.

———. "Second Thoughts in Syria." *The Washington Post*, November 1, 1990, pp. A1, A31.

Braibanti, Ralph. "A Rational Context for Analysis of Arab Politics." *American-Arab Affairs* 21 (Summer 1987).

Brinkley, Joel. "Israeli Economy Is Keeping Many Jews in U.S.S.R." *The New York Times*, May 5, 1991, pp. 1, 26.

———. "Majority in Israel Oppose PLO Talks Now, a Poll Shows." *The New York Times*, April 2, 1989, pp. 1, 18.

———. "The Soldiers: Anger and Frustration: Israel Mired in the West Bank." *The New York Times Magazine*, May 7, 1989, pp. 3–32, 46–50.

———. "The Stubborn Strength of Yitzhak Shamir." *The New York Times Magazine*, August 21, 1988, pp. 27–29, 68, 70, 72, 74, 77.

Brown, William R. *The Last Crusade: A Negotiator's Middle East Handbook.* Chicago: Nelson Hall, 1980.

Bryce, James. *The American Commonwealth.* London: Macmillan, 1891.

Brzezinski, Zbigniew. *Power and Principle: Memoirs of the National Security Adviser, 1977–1981.* New York: Farrar, Straus, Giroux, 1983.

Carter, Jimmy. *A Government as Good as Its People.* New York: Simon and Schuster, 1977.

———. "Interview with Jimmy Carter." *American-Arab Affairs* 23 (1987–1988).

———. *Keeping Faith: Memoirs of a President.* New York: Bantam Books, 1982.

———. "The Middle East Consultation: A Look to the Future." *The Middle East Journal* 42 (1988).

———. "Middle East Peace: New Opportunities." *The Washington Quarterly* 10, no. 3 (Summer 1987).

———. "The U.S. Need to Lead in Israel." *The New York Times*, op. ed., February 14, 1988.

———. "A US Role in Middle East Peace." *The Washington Post*, op. ed., April 7, 1991.

———. *Why Not the Best.* Nashville, Tenn.: Broadman Press, 1975.

Carus, W. Seth. *Chemical Weapons in the Middle East.* Research Memorandum Number 9, December 1988, Washington Institute for Near East Policy, Washington, D.C.

———. *Missiles in the Middle East: A New Threat to Stability.* Research Memorandum Number 6, June 1988, Washington Institute for Near East Policy, Washington, D.C.

———. *NATO, Israel and the Tactical Missile Challenge.* Research Memorandum Number 4, May 1987, Washington Institute for Near East Policy, Washington, D.C.

———. "The Poor Man's Atomic Bomb?" In *Biological Weapons in the Middle East*, Policy Paper Number 23. Washington, D.C.: Institute for Near East Policy, 1991.

Chazan, Naomi. "Domestic Developments in Israel." In *The Middle East: Ten Years After Camp David*, edited by William B. Quandt. Washington, D.C.: Brookings Institution, 1988.

Chubin, Shahram. "Soviet Policy in the Middle East." In *Security in the Middle East: Regional Change and Great Power Strategies*, edited by Samuel F. Wells, Jr., and Mark Bruzonsky. Boulder, Colo.: Westview Press, 1987.

Clawson, Patrick. "How Vulnerable Is Iraq's Economy." *Policy Focus*, no. 14 (October 1990).

Clinton, David. "Tocqueville's Challenge." *Washington Quarterly* 11, no. 1 (Winter 1988).

Cobban, Helena. "Lebanon's Chinese Puzzle." *Foreign Policy* 53 (Winter 1983–1984).

———. *The Shia Community and the Future of Lebanon (The Muslim World Today)*, Occasional Paper Number 2. Washington, D.C.: American Institute for Islamic Affairs, 1985.

————. "Thinking About Lebanon." *American-Arab Affairs* 12 (Spring 1985).

Cody, Edward. "Chain of Events in Persian Gulf Led Reluctant Allies to Join U.S." *The Washington Post*, September 20, 1987, pp. A25, A30.

————. "Feud over Temple Mount Resurfaces." *The Washington Post*, April 18, 1989, pp. A18, A21.

————. "Jewish Settlers, West Bank Arabs Live and Die in Cycles of Revenge." *The Washington Post*, May 5, 1989, p. A24.

Cohen, Erik. "Ethnicity and Legitimation in Contemporary Israel." *Jerusalem Quarterly* 28 (Summer 1983).

Cottam, Richard W. "Inside Revolutionary Iran." *Middle East Journal* 43, no. 2 (Spring 1989).

————. *Khomeini, the Future, and US Options*, Policy Paper 38. Muscatine, Iowa: The Stanley Foundation, December 1987.

Cowell, Alan. "To Egypt, Peace Pact Is a Stigma on its Arab Soul." *The New York Times*, March 19, 1989, p. 14.

————. "Syria and U.S. Seek a Wider Dialogue." *The New York Times*, July 11, 1989.

Crabb, Cecil V., Jr. *American Diplomacy and the Pragmatic Tradition*. Baton Rouge: Louisiana State University Press, 1989.

————. *The American Approach to Foreign Policy: A Pragmatic Perspective*. Lanham, Md.: University Press of America, 1985.

Dallek, Robert. *Ronald Reagan: The Politics of Symbolism*. Cambridge, Mass.: Harvard University Press, 1984.

Davis, Tami R., and Sean M. Lynn-Jones. "Citty Upon a Hill." *Foreign Policy* 66 (Spring 1987).

Dawisha, Adeed. "Iraq: The West's Opportunity." *Foreign Policy* 41 (Winter 1980–81).

————. "The Motives of Syria's Involvement in Lebanon." *The Middle East Journal* 38, no. 2 (Spring 1984).

————. "Syria Under Assad, 1970–78: The Centers of Power." *Government and Opposition* 13, no. 31 (Summer 1978).

Day, Arthur R. *East Bank/West Bank: Jordan and the Prospects for Peace*. New York: Council on Foreign Relations, 1986.

Dayan, Moshe. *Breakthrough*. London: Weidenfeld and Nicholson, 1981.

Deeb, Marius K. "Lebanon: Prospects for National Reconciliation in the Mid-1980's." *The Middle East Journal* 38, no. 2 (Spring 1984).

Derkovsky, Oleg M. "The Soviet Union and the Middle East: The Soviet Perspective." *Middle East Insights* 5, no. 4 (November–December 1987).

Dessouki, Ali E. Hillal. "Egyptian Foreign Policy Since Camp David." In *The Middle East: Ten Years After Camp David*, edited by William B. Quandt. Washington, D.C.: Brookings Institution, 1988.

d'Estaing, Giscard Valery, Yasahiro Nakasone, and Henry Kissinger. "East-West Relations." *Foreign Affairs* 68, no. 3 (Summer 1989).

Devroy, Ann. "Bush Orders 200,000 More Troops to Gulf." *The Washington Post*, November 9, 1990, pp. A1, A32.

Devroy, Ann, and Don Oberdorfer. "U.S. Rules Out Deal on Iranian Funds." *The Washington Post*, August 9, 1989, p. A16.

Dickey, Christopher. "Assad and His Allies; Irreconcilable Differences?" *Foreign Affairs* 66, no. 1 (Fall 1987).

Dickson, Peter W. *Kissinger and the Meaning of History*. Cambridge: Cambridge University Press, 1978.

Diehl, Jackson. "Israel Plagued by Recession." *The Washington Post*, July 24, 1989, pp. A13, A16.

Diehl, Jackson, and John Goshko. "Baker Presses Israel to Make Concessions." *The Washington Post*, April 20, 1991, p. A14.

Diggins, John P. *The Lost Soul of American Politics: Virtue, Self Interest and the Foundation of Liberalism.* Chicago: University of Chicago Press, 1984.

Don-Yehiya, Eliezer. "Jewish Messianism, Religious Zionism and Israeli Politics: The Impact and Origins of Gush Emunim." *Middle Eastern Studies* 23, no. 2 (April 1987).

Douglas, Mary. *Cultural Bias.* Occasional Paper 34, Royal Anthropological Institute of Great Britain and Ireland (1978).

Drell, Sidney D., and Thomas H. Johnson. "Managing Strategic Weapons," *Foreign Affairs* 66, no. 5 (Summer 1988).

Dunn, John. *Western Political Theory in the Face of the Future.* Cambridge: Cambridge University Press, 1979; reprinted 1986.

Eagleburger, Lawrence, and Walter Mondale. *Building for Peace: An American Strategy for the Middle East.* Washington, D.C.: The Washington Institute's Presidential Study Group, Washington Institute for Near East Policy, 1988.

Easterbrook, Gregg, and Charles Paul Freund. "Death and Dogma." *The Washington Post*, Outlook Section, February 19, 1989, pp. D1, D4.

Eilts, Herman Frederick. "Reviving the Middle East Peace Process: An International Conference." *Middle East Insight* 5, no. 3 (August–September 1987).

———. "The United States and Egypt." In *The Middle East: Ten Years After Camp David*, edited by William B. Quandt. Washington, D.C.: Brookings Institution, 1988.

Eilts, Herman Frederick, and Samuel W. Lewis. *Toward Arab-Israeli Peace: Report of a Study Group.* Washington, D.C.: Brookings Institution, 1988.

Eisenstadt, Mike. *"The Sword of the Arabs": Iraq's Strategic Weapons*, Policy Paper No. 21. Washington, D.C.: Washington Institute for Near East Policy, 1990.

Eisenstat, Stuart E. *Formalizing the Strategic Partnership: The Next Step in U.S.-Israel Relations*, Policy Paper Number 9. Washington, D.C.: Washington Institute for Near East Policy, 1988.

———. "Loving Israel—Warts and All." *Foreign Policy* 81 (Winter 1990–91).

Eisenstadt, S. N. *The Transformation of Israeli Society: An Essay in Interpretation.* Boulder, Colo.: Westview Press, 1985.

el-Khazen, Farid. "Lebanon's Unfinished Wars: Gods in Politics; Men in Religion." *Middle East Insight* 6, nos. 1 and 2 (Summer 1988).

Elon, Amos. "Letter from Israel." *New Yorker*, February 13, 1989.

———. "Report from Jerusalem." *New Yorker*, April 1, 1991.

Elpeleg, Zvi. "West Bank Story." *Middle East Review* 18, no. 4 (Summer 1986).

Engelberg, Stephen, and Bernard E. Trainor. "Behind the Gulf Buildup: The Unforeseen Occurs." *The New York Times*, August 23, 1987.

Epstein, Joshua. "Soviet Vulnerabilities in Iran and the RDF Deterrent." *International Security* 6, no. 2 (Fall 1981).

———. *Strategy and Force Planning: The Case of the Persian Gulf.* Washington, D.C.: Brookings Institution, 1987.

Fadl Allah, Ayatollah Al-Sayed Muhammed Hussein. "An Islamic Perspective on the Lebanese Experience." *Middle East Insight* 6, nos. 1 and 2 (Summer 1988).

Faksh, Mahmud. "Saudi Arabia and the Gulf Crisis: Foreign and Security Policy Dilemma." *Middle East Review* 19, no. 4 (Summer 1987).

Fischer, Michael M. J. "Becoming Mullah: Reflections on Iranian Clerics in a Revolutionary Age." *Iranian Studies* 13, nos. 1–4 (1980).

————. *Iran from Religious Dispute to Revolution*. Cambridge, Mass.: Harvard University Press, 1980.

————. "Imam Khomeini: Four Levels of Understanding." In *Voices of Resurgent Islam*, edited by John L. Esposito. New York: Oxford University Press, 1983.

————. "Repetitions in the Iranian Revolution." In *Shi'ism, Resistance, and Revolution*, edited by Martin Kramer. Boulder, Colo.: Westview Press, 1987.

Fishelson, Gideon. "Key Findings of the Middle East Economic Cooperation Projects." In *Economic Cooperation in the Middle East*, edited by Gideon Fishelson. Boulder, Colo.: Westview Press, 1989.

Fisher, Marc. "Europeans Invite Iraq's Aziz for Talks." *The Washington Post*, January 5, 1991, p. A17.

Fisher, Roger. "Getting to 'Yes' with Saddam: How Words Can Win." *The Washington Post*, Outlook Section, December 9, 1990, pp. K1–K2.

Frankel, Glenn. "Angry Jewish Settlers Try to Attack Shamir." *The Washington Post*, June 21, 1989.

————. "Crackdown on Intifada Demanded." *The Washington Post*, June 20, 1989.

————. "14 Die as Arab Steers Israeli Bus Off Road." *The Washington Post*, July 7, 1989.

————. "Iraq Said Developing A-Weapons." *The Washington Post*, March 31, 1989, pp. A1, A32.

————. "Israel, Egypt Sign Accord on Return of Taba Resort." *The Washington Post*, February 27, 1989.

————. "Israeli Settlers Striking Back with Vigilante Action Groups." *The Washington Post*, May 1989, pp. A1, A30.

————. "Likud, Labor Agree to New Coalition But Face Same Problems." *The Washington Post*, December 22, 1988, pp. A27, A29.

————. "Protesting Jewish Settlers Clash with Israeli Army in West Bank." *The Washington Post*, January 13, 1989, pp. A23, A26.

————. "Results of Israeli Election Mirror Nation at War with Itself." *The Washington Post*, November 5, 1988, pp. A14, A20, A24, A25.

————. "The Talmudic Ties That Bind." *The Washington Post*, March 11, 1989.

Friedlander, Ellen. "'The Green Line' Blurred by Emerging Arab Solidarity." *Survey of Arab Affairs* 21 (August 1, 1990).

————. "The WAKF and Palestinian Nationalism: Links in the Chain of Political Violence." *Survey of Arab Affairs* 22 (November 15, 1990).

Friedlander, Melvin A. "The Impact of Arab-Israeli Relations on the 1984 Elections." *Middle East Review* 17, no. 4 (Summer 1985).

————. "The Israeli-Egyptian-US Relationship: Policy Implications." Unpublished paper.

————. *Sadat and Begin: The Domestic Politics of Peacemaking*. Boulder, Colo.: Westview Press, 1983.

Friedman, Thomas L. "Bush Policy Makers Reach Uneasy Balance on an Approach to the Soviets." *The New York Times*, July 2, 1989, p. 8.

————. "The Israeli Elections: An Analysis of the Results." Paper presented at the Wilson Center Seminar, Washington, D.C., November 18, 1988, and summarized in *The Wilson Center Reports* (December 1988).

————. "Why Camp David Turned Bitter: The Carter View." *The New York Times*, March 26, 1989.

Frykenberg, Robert E. "On the Comparative Study of Fundamentalist Movements: An Approach to Conceptual Clarity and Definition." Unpublished paper, April 20, 1986.

Fukuyama, Francis. "Growth and Decline of Soviet Activism." In *Strategy and Defense in the Eastern Mediterranean: An American-Israeli Dialogue, Proceedings of a Conference* (Jerusalem, Israel, July 7–9, 1986), edited by Robert Satloff. Washington, D.C.: Washington Institute for Near East Policy, 1987.

Fuller, Graham. "The United States and the Soviet Union in the Middle East: Prospect for Cooperation." *Middle East Insight* 6, no. 4 (Winter 1989).

———. "War and Revolution in Iran." *Current History* 88, no. 535 (February 1989).

Fuller, Graham, et al. *The Impact of the Uprising: Report of a Fact-Finding Mission to Israel, Jordan, Egypt and the West Bank.* Paper presented to the Washington Institute's Presidential Study Group on U.S. Policy in the Middle East, Washington Institute for Near East Policy, Washington, D.C., May 1988.

Galston, William. "Equality of Opportunity and Liberal Theory." In *Justice and Equality Here and Now*, edited by Frank S. Lucash. Ithaca, N.Y.: Cornell University Press, 1986.

Garfinkle, Adam. "'Common Sense' about Middle East Diplomacy: Implications for U.S. Policy in the Near Term." *Middle East Review* 17, no. 2 (Winter 1984–85).

Geertz, Clifford. *The Interpretation of Cultures.* New York: Basic Books, 1973.

———. *Local Knowledge: Further Essays in Interpretative Anthropology.* New York: Basic Books, 1985.

Gellner, Ernest, and John Waterbury, eds. *Patrons and Clients in Mediterranean Societies.* London: Duckworth, 1977.

George, Alexander L., and Richard Smoke. *Deterrence in American Foreign Policy.* New York: Columbia University Press, 1973.

Gigot, Paul. "Iraq: An American Screw-Up." *National Interest* 22 (Winter, 1990–91).

Gillespie, Kate, and Gwenn Okruhlik. "Cleaning Up Corruption in the Middle East." *Middle East Journal* 42, no. 1 (Winter 1988).

Golan, Galia. "Gorbachev's Middle East Strategy." *Foreign Affairs* 66, no. 1 (Fall 1987).

Gold, Dore. *America, the Gulf and Israel: Centcom (Central Command) and Emerging U.S. Regional Security Policies in the Middle East*, Study Number 11, Jaffee Center for Strategic Studies, Tel Aviv University. Boulder, Colo.: Westview Press, 1988.

Goodman, Hirsh. *Israel's Strategic Reality: The Impact of the Arms Race*, Policy Paper Number 4. Washington, D.C.: Washington Institute for Near East Policy, 1985.

Gordon, Michael R. "Bush Urged to Find a Middle Course on Soviet Changes." *The New York Times*, April 9, 1989, pp. 1, 20.

Goshko, John. "Fallacy Might Underlie Baker's Latest Effort." *The Washington Post*, April 28, 1991.

———. "Saudis Reject Role in Talks." *The Washington Post*, April 22, 1991, pp. A1, A13.

———. "U.S. Faults Israel on Territories." *The Washington Post*, 1989.

———. "U.S. Offers Amends in Iran Jet Deaths." *The Washington Post*, 1989, pp. A14, A17.

Goshko, John, and Jackson Diehl. "Baker, in Israel, Renews Mideast Quest." *The Washington Post*, April 19, 1991, p. A18.

Goshko, John, and George Lardner. "Bush's Plan to See Assad Controversial." *The Washington Post*, November 22, 1990, p. A55.

Green, Stephen. "U.S.-PLO Talks: Just a First Step." *American-Arab Affairs* 27 (Winter 1988–89).

Gutmann, Emanuel, and Jacob M. Landau. "The Political Elite and National Leadership in Israel." In *Political Elites in the Middle East,* edited by George Lenczowski. Washington, D.C.: American Enterprise Institute for Public Policy Research, 1975.

Hadar, Leon T. "Reforming Israel—Before It's Too Late." *Foreign Policy* 81 (Winter 1990–91).

Haig, Alexander M., Jr. *Caveat: Realism, Reagan and Foreign Policy.* New York: Macmillan Publishing Co., 1984.

Hall, John A. *Power and Liberties: The Causes and Consequences of the Rise of the West.* Oxford: Basil Blackwell, 1985.

Halloran, Richard. "U.S. Altering Strategy for Defense of Arabian Oilfields." *The New York Times,* December 4, 1988

Hamdoon, Nizar. "The U.S.-Iran Arms Deal: An Iraqi Critique." *Middle East Review* 19, no. 4 (Summer 1987).

Hameed, Mazher A. "After Mecca; Saudi Arabia Is More Stable Than It Looks." *The Washington Post,* Outlook Section, August 9, 1987, pp. C1, C4.

Hannah, John P., and Martin Indyk. "Beyond the Shultz Initiative in the Middle East." *SAIS Review* 9, no. 1 (Winter–Spring 1989).

Harris, William. "The View from Zahle: Security and Economic Conditions in the Central Bekaa, 1980–1985." *The Middle East Journal* 39, no. 3 (1985).

Harrison, Selig S. "Inside the Afghan Talks." *Foreign Policy Number* 72, Fall 1988.

———. "Afghanistan: The Geneva Accords and After." *Middle East Insight* 6, no. 4 (Winter 1989).

Hassan Bin Talal. "Return to Geneva." *Foreign Policy* 57 (Winter 1984–1985).

Heller, Mark A. "The War Strategy of Iran." *Middle East Review* 19, no. 4 (Summer 1987).

Hinnebusch, Raymond A., Jr. *Egyptian Politics Under Sadat: The Post-Populist Development of an Authoritarian-Modernizing State.* Cambridge: Cambridge University Press, 1985.

———. *The Transformation of Leadership in Weber and the Egyptian Presidency.* Paper presented at the Middle East Studies Association, 19th meeting, New Orleans, La., November 1985.

Hiro, Dilip. "Iran: Constitutional Reform and Future Leadership." *Middle East Insight* 6, no. 5 (Spring 1989).

Hoffman, David. "Baker Finds Window of Opportunity for Peace." *The Washington Post,* March 15, 1991, pp. A1, A36.

———. "Baker Sets Syria Visit Thursday." *The Washington Post,* September 11, 1990, pp. A1, A8.

———. "Bush Looking Anew for Ways to Assert U.S. Leadership." *The Washington Post,* May 26, 1989, pp. A1, A34.

Hoffman, David, and Jackson Diehl, "Baker Asks Israel for Peace Moves." *The Washington Post,* March 13, 1991, pp. A1, A24.

Hoffmann, Stanley. *Janus and Minerva: Essays in the Theory and Practice of International Politics.* Boulder, Colo.: Westview Press, 1987.

Holloway, David. "Gorbachev's New Thinking." *Foreign Affairs, America and the World, 1988/89* 68, no. 1 (1989).

Hunt, Michael H. *Ideology and U.S. Foreign Policy.* New Haven, Conn.: Yale University Press, 1987.

Hunter, James Davison. *Evangelicalism: The Coming Generation.* Chicago: University of Chicago Press, 1987.

Hunter, Robert A. "Seeking Middle East Peace." *Foreign Policy* 73 (Winter 1988/1989).

Huntington, Samuel P. *American Politics: The Promise of Disharmony.* Cambridge, Mass.: Harvard University Press, 1981.

Hussein. "The Jordanian-Palestinian Peace Initiative: Mutual Recognition and Territory for Peace." *Journal of Palestine Studies* 56 (1985).

Huth, Paul. "Extended Deterrence and the Outbreak of War." *American Political Science Review* 82, no. 2 (June 1988).

———. *Extended Deterrence and the Prevention of War.* New Haven, Conn.: Yale University Press, 1988.

Huth, Paul, and Bruce Russett. "Deterrence Failure and Crisis Escalation." *International Studies Quarterly* 32, no. 1 (March 1988).

———. "What Makes Deterrence Work? Cases from 1900–1980." *World Politics* 36, no. 4 (July 1984).

Ibrahim, Saad Eddin. "Domestic Developments in Egypt." In *The Middle East: Ten Years After Camp David,* edited by William B. Quandt. Washington, D.C.: Brookings Institution, 1988.

Ibrahim, Youssef M. "Impatiently, Arabs Await 'New Order' in the Gulf." *The New York Times,* October 7, 1990, Section 4, p. 3.

———. "A Time of Confusion Draws the Arab World Into a Troubled Search of Its Own Soul." *The New York Times,* October 14, 1990, Section 4, p. 2.

Idel, Moshe. *Kaballah: New Perspectives.* New Haven, Conn.: Yale University Press, 1988.

———. "Mysticism." In *Contemporary Jewish Religious Thought,* edited by Arthur A. Cohen and Paul Mender-Flohr. New York: Charles Scribner's Sons, 1987.

Indyk, Martin. "Glasnost and the Middle East—How Should the U.S. Respond?" *Middle East Insight* 5, no. 4 (November–December 1987).

Israeli, Raphael. *Man of Defiance: A Political Biography of Anwar Sadat.* Totowa, N.J.: Barnes and Noble, 1985.

Jabber, Paul. "Forces of Change in the Middle East." *Middle East Journal* 42, no. 1 (Winter 1988).

Jervis, Robert. "Deterrence Theory Revisited." *World Politics* 31, no. 2 (January 1979).

Jervis, Robert, Richard Ned Lebow, and Janice Gross Stein. *Psychology and Deterrence.* Baltimore, Md.: Johns Hopkins University Press, 1985.

Joffe, Josef. "Tocqueville Revisited: Are Good Democracies Bad Players in the Game of Nations?" *Washington Quarterly* 11, no. 1 (Winter 1988).

Jureidini, Paul. "Lebanon: The Consuming Conflict, The Elusive Consensus." *Middle East Insight* 6, no. 5 (Spring 1989).

Kadishai, Yehiel, chief of cabinet to Menachem Begin. Interview, Jerusalem, December 1983.

Kaiser, Robert G. "The U.S.S.R. in Decline." *Foreign Affairs* 67, no. 2 (Winter 1988/1989).

Kally, Elisha. "The Potential for Cooperation in Water Projects in the Middle East at Peace." In *Economic Cooperation in the Middle East,* edited by Gideon Fishelson. Boulder, Colo.: Westview Press, 1989.

Kammen, Michael. *Sphere of Liberty: Changing Perceptions of Liberty in American Culture.* Madison: University of Wisconsin Press, 1986.

Kanovsky, Eliyahu. *Another Oil Shock in the 1990's? A Dissenting View.* Policy Paper Number 6. Washington, D.C.: Washington Institute for Near East Policy, 1987.

————. "The Rise and Fall of Arab Oil Power." *Middle East Review* 18, no. 1 (Fall 1985).

Karsh, Efraim, and Inari Rautsi. *Saddam Hussein: A Political Biography*. New York: Free Press, 1991.

Kaslow, Amy. "Iraq Banks on Its Oil to Fuel Reconstruction." *Middle East Insight* 7, no. 1 (January–February 1990).

Katz, Mark. "The Soviet Challenge in the Gulf." *Middle East Insight* 5, no. 4 (November–December 1987).

Kavka, Gregory S. *Hobbesian Moral and Political Theory*. Princeton, N.J.: Princeton University Press, 1986.

Kemp, Geoffrey. "Lessons of Lebanon: A Guideline for Future U.S. Policy." *Middle East Insight* 6, no. 1 and 2 (Summer 1988).

————. "Middle East Opportunities." *Foreign Affairs, America and the World, 1988/89* 68, no. 1 (1989).

Khadduri, Majid. *The Islamic Conception of Justice*. Baltimore, Md: Johns Hopkins University Press, 1984.

Khalaf, Samir. "Entrapment and Escalation of Violence." *American-Arab Affairs* 24 (Spring 1988).

————. *Lebanon's Predicament*. New York: Columbia University Press, 1987.

Khaldun, Ibn. *The Muqaddimah: An Introduction to History*, translated by Franz Rosenthal, edited by N. J. Dawood. Princeton, N.J.: Princeton University Press, Bollingen Series, 1969.

Khalilizad, Zalmay. "The United States and Iran: Beyond Containment." *Middle East Insight* 6, no. 6 (November–December 1989).

Kissinger, Henry. "Domestic Structure and Foreign Policy." *Daedalus* 95, no. 2 (1966).

————. "Israel and the PLO—Wishes and Reality." *The Washington Post*, op. ed., March 21, 1989.

————. "The Meaning of History: Reflections on Spengler, Toynbee and Kant." Undergraduate Honors Thesis, Harvard University, Cambridge, Mass., 1950.

————. "A Pause That Could Lead to Peace." *The Washington Post*, May 15, 1988.

————. "What a Mideast Peace Could Look Like." *The Washington Post*, op. ed., February 21, 1988.

————. *White House Years*. Boston: Little, Brown and Company, 1979.

————. *A World Restored: Matternich, Castlereagh and the Problems of Peace, 1812–1822*. Boston: Houghton Mifflin, Sentry Edition, 1951.

————. *Years of Upheaval*. Boston: Little, Brown and Company, 1982.

Klass, Rosanne. "Afghanistan: The Accords." *Foreign Affairs* 66, no. 5 (Summer 1988).

Kostiner, Joseph. "Counter-productive Mediation: Saudia Arabia and the Iran Arms Deal." *Middle East Review* 19, no. 4 (Summer 1987).

Kramnick, Isaac. "Republican Revisionism Revisited." *American Historical Review* 87, no. 3 (June 1982).

Kreczko, Alan J. "Support Reagan's Initiative." *Foreign Policy* 49 (Winter 1982–1983).

Kristof, Nicholas D. "China Erupts." *The New York Times Magazine*, June 4, 1989.

Kucharsky, David. *The Man from Plains: The Mind and Spirit of Jimmy Carter*. New York: Harper and Row, 1976.

Lacoste, Yves. *Ibn Khaldun: The Birth of History and the Past of the Third World*. London: Verso, 1984.

Larrabee, F. Stephen. "Gorbachev and the Soviet Military." *Foreign Affairs* 66, no. 5 (Summer 1988).

Lawrence, Bruce B. *Defenders of God: The Fundamentalist Revolt Against the Modern Age.* San Francisco, Calif.: Harper and Row, 1989.

Lebow, Richard Ned, and Janice Gross Stein. "Beyond Deterrence." *Journal of Social Issues* 43, no. 4 (Winter 1987).

Lederman, Jim. "Dateline West Bank: Interpreting the Intifada." *Foreign Policy* 72 (Fall 1988).

Leiber, Robert J. "Middle East Oil and the Industrial Democracies: Conflict and Cooperation in the Aftermath of the Oil Shocks." In *Security in the Middle East: Regional Change and Great Power Strategies,* edited by Samuel Wells, Jr., and Mark Bruzonsky. Boulder, Colo.: Westview Press, 1987.

Lesch, Ann Mosely. "Egyptian-Israeli Boundary Disputes: The Problem of Taba." In *Israel, Egypt and the Palestinians from Camp David to Intifada,* by Ann Mosely Lesch and Mark Tessler. Bloomington: Indiana University Press, 1989.

———. "Egyptian Israeli Relations: Normalization or Special Ties?" In *Israel, Egypt and the Palestinians from Camp David to Intifada,* by Ann Mosely Lesch and Mark Tessler. Bloomington: Indiana University Press, 1989.

Levgold, Robert. "The Revolution in Soviet Foreign Policy." *Foreign Affairs, America and the World, 1988/89* 68, no. 1 (1989).

Levran, Aharon. "Syria's Military Strength and Capability." *Middle East Review* 19, no. 3 (Spring 1987).

Lewis, Bernard. *The Political Language of Islam.* Chicago: University of Chicago Press, 1988.

Lewis, Samuel. "Israel: The Peres Era." *Foreign Affairs, America and the World, 1986* 65, no. 3 (1987).

———. "Israel Political Reality and the Search for Middle East Peace." *SAIS Review* 7, no. 1 (Winter–Spring 1987).

———. "The United States and Israel: Constancy and Change." In *The Middle East: Ten Years After Camp David,* edited by William B. Quandt. Washington, D.C.: Brookings Institution, 1988.

Liebman, Charles S., and Eliezer Don-Yehiya. *Civil Religion in Israel: Traditional Judaism and Political Culture in the Jewish State.* Berkeley: University of California Press, 1983.

Linowitz, Sol. "The Prospects for the Camp David Peace Process." *SAIS Review* 2, no. 2 (Summer 1981).

Lipset, Seymour Martin. *The First New Nation: The United States in Historical and Comparative Perspective.* New York: W. W. Norton, 1979.

Lissak, Moshe. "Ideological and Social Conflicts in Israel." *Jerusalem Quarterly* 29 (Fall 1983).

Lubrani, Uri. "The Iranian-Israeli Relationship." In *Israel in the Middle East,* by Itamar Rabinovich and Jehuda Reinharz.

———. "The Israeli Operative Aspect." In *Israel's Lebanon Policy: Where To?* edited by Joseph Alpher. Memorandum Number 12, Tel Aviv University, Jaffee Center for Strategic Studies, August 1984.

Lustick, Ian. *Arabs in the Jewish State: Israel's Control of a National Minority.* Austin: University of Texas Press, 1980.

———. *For the Land and the Lord: Jewish Fundamentalism in Israel.* New York: Council on Foreign Relations, 1988.

———. "Israel's Dangerous Fundamentalists." *Foreign Policy* 68 (Fall 1987).

MacDonald, Scott B. "The Kurds in the 1990's." *Middle East Insight* 7, no. 1 (January–February 1990).

Mansour, Anis. "An Egyptian View of Recent Events." In *Proceedings of the Washington Institute Policy Forum, 1988.* Washington, D.C.: Washington Institute for Near East Policy.

Maoz, Moshe. *Assad: The Sphinx of Damascus.* New York: Weidenfeld and Nicholson, 1988.

———. "Hafiz al-Asad: A Political Profile." *The Jerusalem Quarterly* 8 (Summer 1978).

———. *Palestinian Leadership on the West Bank: The Changing Role of the Mayors Under Jordan and Israel.* London: Frank Cass, 1984.

———. "State-Run Terrorism in the Middle East: The Case of Syria." *Middle East Review* 19, no. 3 (Spring 1987).

Marzorati, Gerald. "Salman Rushdie: Fiction's Embattled Infidel." *The New York Times Magazine,* January 29, 1989.

Maull, Hanns. "Containment, Competition and Cooperation: Superpower Strategies in the Persian Gulf." *SAIS Review* 8, no. 2 (Summer/Fall 1988).

Mazrui, Ali A. "Superpower Ethics: A Third World Perspective." *Ethics and International Affairs* 1 (1987).

McCartney, Robert J. "Iran Declares Era of Hostage-Taking Over, W. Germans Say." *The Washington Post,* October 12, 1988.

McGwire, Michael. "The Middle East and Soviet Military Strategy." *Middle East Report* 18, no. 2 (March–April 1988).

McLoughlin, William G. "The Role of Religion in the Revolution: Liberty of Conscience and Cultural Cohesion in the New Nation." In *Essays on the American Revolution,* edited by Stephen G. Kurtz and James H. Hutson. Chapel Hill: University of North Carolina Press, 1973.

McNaugher, Thomas L. "The Iran-Iraq War: Slouching Toward Catastrophe?" *Middle East Review* 19, no. 4 (Summer 1987).

Mearsheimer, John. *Conventional Deterrence.* Ithaca, N.Y.: Cornell University Press, 1983.

Medcalf, Linda J., and Kenneth M. Dolbeare. *Neopolitics: American Political Ideas in the 1980's.* New York: Random House, 1985.

Medoff, Rafael. "Gush Emunim and the Question of Jewish Counterterror." *Middle East Review* 18, no. 4 (Summer 1986).

Milani, Mohsen M. *The Making of Iran's Islamic Revolution: From Monarchy to Islamic Republic.* Boulder, Colo.: Westview Press, 1988.

Miller, Aaron David. "Palestinians and the Intifada: One Year Later." *Current History* 88, no. 535 (February 1989).

Miller, Judith. "Iran's Economic Changes Cause Pain." *The New York Times,* April 9, 1991, p. A6.

———. "Islamic Radicals Lose Their Tight Grip." *The New York Times,* April 8, 1991, p. A1.

Miller, Judith, and Laurie Mylroie. *Saddam Hussein and the Crisis in the Gulf.* New York: Times Books, 1990.

Mitzna, Amram. "The Uprising in the West Bank and Gaza Strip." In *Proceedings of the Washington Institute Policy Forum, 1988.* Washington, D.C.: Washington Institute for Near East Policy (1988).

Moore, Barrington, Jr. *Social Origins of Dictatorship and Democracy: Lord and Peasant in the Making of the Modern World.* Boston: Beacon Press, 1966.

Moore, Molly, and David B. Ottaway. "Iran Said to Obtain U.S.-Made Stingers." *The Washington Post,* October 10, 1987, p. A1.

Mottahedeh, Roy. *The Mantle of the Prophet: Religion and Politics in Iran.* New York: Simon and Schuster, 1985.

Mrydal, Gunnar. *An American Dilemma.* New York: Harper and Brothers, 1944.

Murphy, Caryle. "Iraq Accuses Kuwait of Plot to Steal Oil, Depress Prices." *The Washington Post*, July 19, 1990, p. A25.

———. "Mubarek Says Iraq, Kuwait Will Begin Talks This Weekend." *The Washington Post*, July 26, 1990, p. A34.

Nader, George. "Interview—General Michel Aoun of Lebanon." *Middle East Insight* 6, no. 5 (Spring 1989).

———. "The Politics of the Future in Lebanon." *Middle East Insight* 7, no. 1 (January–February 1990).

Najmabadi, Afsaneh. "Iran's Turn to Islam: From Modernism to a Moral Order." *Middle East Journal* 41, no. 2 (Spring 1987).

Nakhleh, Emile A. "Political Stability in the Gulf Cooperation Council States: Challenges and Prospects." *Middle East Insight* 6, no. 4 (Winter 1989).

———. "The West Bank and Gaza: Twenty Years Later." *The Middle East Journal* 42, no. 2 (Spring 1988).

Neumann, Robert G. "The Middle East—Challenges, Opportunities and Pitfalls for the Bush Administration." *Middle East Insight* 6, no. 4 (Winter 1989).

Newman, David. "Gush Emunim Between Fundamentalism and Pragmatism." *Jerusalem Quarterly* 39 (1986).

Nisan, Mordechai. "The Jordanian Option: Is it Politically Feasible?" *Middle East Insight* 5, no. 6 (March/April 1988).

Norton, Augustus Richard. *AMAL and the Shi'a: Struggle for the Soul of Lebanon*. Austin: University of Texas Press, 1987.

Norton, David L. "The Moral Individualism of Henry David Thoreau." In *American Philosophy*, edited by Marcus G. Singer, Royal Institute of Philosophy Lecture Series 19. Cambridge: Cambridge University Press, 1985.

Novik, Nimrod. *Encounter with Reality: Reagan and the Middle East (The First Term)*. Boulder, Colo.: Westview Press (for the Jaffee Center for Strategic Studies, Tel Aviv University), 1986.

Oakley, Robert. "International Terrorism." *Foreign Affairs, America and the World, 1986* 65, no. 3 (1987).

Oberdorfer, Don. "Bush Finds Theme of Foreign Policy: 'Beyond Containment.'" *The Washington Post*, May 28, 1989, p. A30.

———. "Mixed Signals in the Middle East." *The Washington Post Magazine*, March 17, 1991.

Olmert, Yosef. "Syria-Policy Developments." Policy Forum Report 1, no. 5, July 1989, Washington Institute for Near East Policy.

Ottaway, David B. "Iran Says It Arrested US. Spies." *The Washington Post*, April 22, 1989, pp. A11, A20.

———. "Israel Reported to Test Controversial Missile." *The Washington Post*, September 16, 1989.

———. "Khomeini's Designated Heir Resigns Amid Purge in Iran." *The Washington Post*, March 27, 1989, pp. A1, A20.

———. "Middle East Weapons Proliferate." *The Washington Post*, December 19, 1988, pp. A1, A4.

———. "Strike on Iraq No Longer an Easy Option for Israel, Analysts Say." *The Washington Post*, March 31, 1989, p. A32.

———. "U.S. Still Ready for Iran 'Dialogue.'" *The Washington Post*, January 31, 1989, p. A24.

Pangle, Thomas L. *The Spirit of Modern Republicanism: The Moral Vision of the American Founders and the Philosophy of Locke*. Chicago: University of Chicago Press, 1988.

Parry, Robert, and Peter Kornbluh. "Iran-Contra's Untold Story." *Foreign Policy* 72 (Fall 1988).

Parsons, Anthony. "Iran and Western Europe." *Middle East Journal* 43, no. 2 (Spring 1989).

Pear, Robert. "Shultz Tries Again, But Peace Seems as Elusive—and Complex—as Ever." *The New York Times*, June 12, 1988.

Peres, Shimon. "Peace as an Alternative Strategy." In *Strategy and Defense in the Eastern Mediterranean: An American-Israeli Dialogue, Proceedings of a Conference*, edited by Robert Satloff, Jerusalem, Israel, July 7–9, 1986. Washington, D.C.: Washington Institute for Near East Policy, 1987.

Peretz, Don. "Intifadeh: The Palestinian Uprising." *Foreign Affairs* 66, no. 5 (Summer 1988).

Peri, Yoram. *Between Battles and Ballots*. Cambridge: Cambridge University Press, 1983.

Perlmutter, Amos. *Israel the Partitioned State: A Political History Since 1900*. New York: Charles Scribner's Sons, 1985.

———. *The Life and Times of Menachem Begin*. Garden City, N.Y.: Doubleday and Company, 1987.

Peterson, J. E. "The GCC States After the Iran-Iraq War." *American-Arab Affairs* 26 (Fall 1988).

Pipes, Daniel. "Terrorism: The Syrian Connection." *The National Interest* 15 (Spring 1989).

———. "Lebanon: The Real Problem." *Foreign Policy* 51 (Summer 1983).

———. *Rushdie Affair*. New York: Carol Publishers, 1990.

Pollock, David. "Jordan: Option or Optical Illusion." *Middle East Insight* 4, no. 1 (March–April 1985).

Precht, Henry. "Ayatollah Realpolitik." *Foreign Policy* 70 (Spring 1988).

Price, Don K. *America's Unwritten Constitution: Science, Religion and Political Responsibility*. Cambridge, Mass.: Harvard University Press, 1985.

Priest, Dana. "Saddam Orders the Release of All Hostages." *The Washington Post*, November 19, 1990, pp. A1, A56.

Quandt, William B. *Camp David: Peacemaking and Politics*. Washington, D.C.: Brookings Institution, 1986.

——— "Kissinger and the Arab-Israeli Disengagement Negotiations." *Journal of International Affairs* 9, no. 1 (1976): 42.

——— "Reagan's Lebanon Policy: Trial and Error." *The Middle East Journal* 38, no. 2 (Spring 1984).

——— *The United States and Egypt*. Washington, D.C.: Brookings Institution, 1990.

——— "U.S. Policy Toward the Arab-Israeli Conflict." In *The Middle East: Ten Years After Camp David*, edited by William B. Quandt. Washington, D.C.: Brookings Institution, 1988.

Quandt, William B., ed. *The Middle East Ten Years After Camp David*. Washington, D.C.: Brookings Institution, 1988.

Quester, George. "Consensus Lost." *Foreign Policy* 40 (Fall 1980).

Rabinovich, Itamar. "Political Aspects of Syrian Strategy." In *Strategy and Defense in the Eastern Mediterranean: An American-Israeli Dialogue*, edited by Robert Satloff, Proceedings of a Conference, Jerusalem, Israel, July 7–9, 1986. Washington, D.C.: Washington Institute for Near East Policy, 1987.

———. "Syria and Lebanon in 1988." *Current History* 88, no. 535 (February 1989).

Ramazani, R. K. "Iran's Foreign Policy: Contending Orientations." *The Middle East Journal* 43, no. 2 (Spring 1989).

———. *Revolutionary Iran: Challenge and Response in the Middle East*. Baltimore, Md.: The Johns Hopkins University, 1988.

Randal, Jonathan. "Iranian Advocates Killings." *The Washington Post*, May 6, 1989, pp. A1, A18.

―――. "Iraq Seen Bolstering Role in Lebanon." *The Washington Post*, June 6, 1989.

Rauf, Muhammad Abdul. *A Muslim's Reflections on Democratic Capitalism*. Washington, D.C.: American Enterprise Institute for Public Policy Research, 1984.

Rawls, John. *A Theory of Justice*. Cambridge, Mass.: Harvard University Press, 1971.

Reagan, Ronald. *An American Life*. New York: Simon and Schuster, 1990.

―――. "The Time Has Come for a New Realism on the Part of All . . ." *The Washington Post*, September 2, 1982.

Reck, Andrew J. "The Philosophical Background of the American Constitution(s)." In *American Philosophy*, Royal Institute of Philosophy Lecture Series 19, Supplement to Philosophy. Cambridge: Cambridge University Press, 1985.

Reed, Stanley. "Jordan and the Gulf." *Foreign Affairs* 69, no. 5 (Winter 1990–91).

Reich, Bernard. "Israel Faces the Future: The 1988 Elections." *Middle East Insight* 6, no. 3 (Fall 1988).

Reichley, A. James. *Religion in American Public Life*. Washington, D.C.: Brookings Institution, 1985.

Reiss, Hans. *Kant's Political Writings*. Cambridge: Cambridge University Press, 1970.

Renfrew, Rita. "Who Started the War." *Foreign Policy* 66 (Spring 1987).

Rentz, George. "The Fahd Peace Plan." *Middle East Tonight* 2, no. 2 (January–February 1982).

Robertson, Sara, ed. "Chronology, 1986." *Foreign Affairs, America and the World, 1986* 65, no. 3 (1987).

Rose, Gregory. "Velayat-e Faqih and the Recovery of Islamic Identity in the Thought of Ayatollah Khomeini." In *Religion and Politics in Iran: Shi'ism from Quietism to Revolution*, edited by Nikki R. Keddie. New Haven, Conn.: Yale University Press, 1983.

Rosen, Lawrence. *Bargaining for Reality: The Construction of Social Relations in a Muslim Community*. Chicago: University of Chicago Press, 1984.

Rosenthal, Erwin I. J. *Political Thought in Medieval Islam*. Cambridge: Cambridge University Press, 1958.

Ross, Dennis. "Considering Soviet Threat to the Persian Gulf." *International Security* 6, no. 2 (Fall 1981).

―――. "The Peace Process—A Status Report." In *Policy and the Middle East Peace Process*, Fourth Annual Policy Conference, September 15–17, 1989. Washington, D.C.: Washington Institute for Near East Policy (1989).

―――. "Soviet Decisionmaking for the Middle East." In *Security in the Middle East: Regional Change and Great Power Strategies*, edited by Samuel F. Wells, Jr., and Mark Bruzonsky. Boulder, Colo.: Westview Press, 1987.

Rouleau, Eric. "Khomeini's Iran." *Foreign Affairs* 59, no. 1 (Fall 1980).

Rubin, Barry. "Drowning in the Gulf." *Foreign Policy* 69 (Winter 1987/1988).

―――. "Middle East: Search for Peace." *Foreign Affairs, America and the World*, 64, no. 3 (1985).

―――. *The PLO's Intractable Foreign Policy*, Policy Paper Number 3. Washington, D.C.: Washington Institute for Near East Policy, 1985.

―――. The PLO's New Policy: Evolution Until Victory? Policy Paper Number 13. Washington, D.C.: Washington Institute for Near East Policy, 1989.

―――――. "The Reagan Administration and the Middle East." In *Eagle Resurgent? The Reagan Era in American Foreign Policy*, edited by Kenneth Oye, Robert Lieber, and Donald Rothchild. Boston: Little, Brown, and Company, 1987.

Rubin, Barry, and Laura Blum. *The May 1983 Agreement over Lebanon*. Case Study Number 7, Foreign Policy Institute, School of Advanced International Studies, The Johns Hopkins University, Washington, D.C., July 1987.

Rubinstein, Amnon. *The Zionist Dream Revisited: From Herzl to Gush Emunim and Back*. New York: Schocken Books, 1984.

Sachedina, Abdulaziz. "Ali Shariati: Ideologue of the Iranian Revolution." In *Voices of Resurgent Islam*, edited by John L. Esposito. New York: Oxford University Press, 1983.

Sadat, Anwar el. *In Search of Identity*. New York: Harper and Row, 1977.

Sadowski, Yahya. "Egypt's Islamist Movement: A New Political and Economic Force." *Middle East Insight* 5, no. 4 (1987).

―――――. "The Sphinx's New Riddle: Why Does Egypt Delay Economic Reform." *American-Arab Affairs* 22 (Fall 1987).

Sahliyeh, Emile. *In Search of Leadership: West Bank Politics Since 1967*. Washington, D.C.: Brookings Institution, 1988.

―――――. *Middle East Consultation*. Presented at The Carter Center of Emory University, Atlanta, Georgia, November 18, 1987.

―――――. "Political Trends Among the West Bank Urban Elite." Colloquium Paper, International Security Studies Program, Woodrow Wilson International Center for Scholars, April 7, 1986.

―――――. "Understanding the Uprising." Paper presented at the Soref Symposium, Israel and the Palestinians: Imperatives for the Future, Washington Institute for Near East Policy, April 17–18, 1988.

Sammakia, Nejla. "Jublant Egyptians Take Control of Taba Resort from Israel." *The Washington Post*, March 16, 1989.

Satloff, Robert. *Army and Politics in Mubarak's Egypt*, Policy Paper Number 10. Washington, D.C.: Washington Institute for Near East Policy, May 1988.

―――――. *Islam in the Palestinian Uprising*, Research Memorandum Number 7. Washington, D.C.: Washington Institute for Near East Policy, October 1988.

―――――. "Islam in the Palestinian Uprising." *Orbis* 33, no. 3 (Summer 1989).

―――――. "Jordan and Reverberations of the Uprising." *Current History* 88, no. 535 (February 1989).

―――――. *"They Cannot Stop Our Tongues": Islamic Activism in Jordan*, Policy Paper Number 5. Washington, D.C.: Washington Institute for Near East Policy, 1986.

Saunders, Harold H. *The Other Walls: The Politics of the Arab-Israeli Peace Process*. Washington, D.C.: American Enterprise Institute for Public Policy Research, 1985.

―――――. "We Need a Larger Theory of Negotiation: The Importance of Pre-Negotiating Phases." *Negotiation Journal* 1, no. 3 (July 1985).

Schiff, Ze'ev. "Green Light Lebanon," *Foreign Policy* 50 (Spring 1983).

―――――. "Security vs. Democracy in Israel: The Clash of Conflicting Needs." Paper presented at the Harris Symposium on Middle East Communication, Covering War and Peace, Washington Institute for Near East Policy, Washington, D.C., December 6, 1988.

Schiff, Ze'ev, and Ehud Ya'ari. *Israel's Lebanon War*. New York: Simon and Schuster, 1984.

Schlessinger, Arthur M., Jr. *The Cycles of American History*. Boston: Houghton Mifflin, 1986.

Sciolino, Elaine. "Khomeini Purifies, and Confuses, Iran's Future." *The New York Times*, April 2, 1989, Section 4, p. 2.

Seabury, Paul. "The Moral Purposes and Philosophical Bases of American Foreign Policy." *Orbis* (Spring 1976).

Seale, Patrick. "Assad: Holding the Hardest Line." *The Washington Post*, May 7, 1989, p. B2.

————. *Asad: The Struggle for the Middle East.* Berkeley: University of California Press, 1988.

Seelye, Talcott. "Syria's Role in Lebanon." *American-Arab Affairs* 21 (Summer 1987).

Segal, David. "The Iran-Iraq War: A Military Analysis." *Foreign Affairs* 66, no. 5 (Summer 1988).

Seliktar, Ofira. "Israel: The New Zionism." *Foreign Policy* 51 (Summer 1983).

————. "Ethnic Stratification and Foreign Policy in Israel: The Attitudes of Oriental Jews Toward the Arabs and the Arab-Israeli Conflict." *Middle East Journal* 38, no. 1 (Winter 1984).

————. *New Ziomism and the Foreign Policy System of Israel.* Carbondale and Edwardsville: Southern Illinois University Press, 1986.

Semmel, Bernard. "Democracy, Virtue and Religion: A Historical Perspective." In *Virtue—Public and Private*, edited by Richard John Neuhaus. Grand Rapids, Mich.: William B. Eerdmans Publishing, 1986.

Shadid, Mohhamed, and Rick Seltzer. "Political Attitudes of Palestinians in the West Bank and Gaza." *The Middle East Journal* 42, no. 1 (Winter 1988).

Shamir, Shimon. "Israeli Views of Egypt and the Peace Process: The Duality of Vision." In *The Middle East: Ten Years After Camp David*, edited by William B. Quandt. Washington, D.C.: Brookings Institute, 1988.

Shamir, Yitzhak. "Israel at 40." *Foreign Affairs, America and the World, 1987/88* 66, no. 3 (1988).

Shapiro, Yonathan. "Generational Units and Inter-Generational Relations in Israeli Politics." In *Israel: A Developing Society*, edited by Asher Arian. Tel Aviv: Pinhas Sapir Center for Development, Tel Aviv University, 1979.

Sharif, Abu. Document and Final Communiqué. *American-Arab Affairs* 25 (Summer 1988).

Sharon, Ariel. *Warrior: The Autobiography Ariel Sharon.* New York: Simon and Schuster, 1989.

Shi, David E. *The Simple Life: Plain Living and High Thinking in American Culture.* New York: Oxford University Press, 1985.

Shimshoni, Daniel. *Israel Democracy: The Middle of the Journey.* New York: Free Press, 1982.

Shipler, David. *Arab and Jew: Wounded Spirits in a Promised Land.* New York: Times Books, 1986.

Shullman, Marshall D. "The Superpowers: Dance of the Dinosaurs." *Foreign Affairs, America and the World, 1987/88* 66, no. 3 (1988).

Shultz, George. "The Reagan Administration's Approach to Middle East Peacemaking." In *U.S. Policy in the Middle East: Toward the Next Administration*, edited by Jonathan Stern. Third Annual Policy Conference, September 16–18, 1988, The Aspen Institute at Wye Plantation. Washington, D.C.: Washington Institute for Near East Policy, 1988.

Sicherman, Harvey. *Changing the Balance of Risks: U.S. Policy Toward the Arab-Israeli Conflict*, Policy Paper Number 11. Washington, D.C.: Washington Institute for Near East Policy, 1988.

Sick, Gary. "Military Options and Constraints." In *American Hostages in Iran:*

The Conduct of a Crisis, edited by Warren Christopher et al. New Haven, Conn.: Yale University Press, 1985.
———. "Trial by Error: Reflections on the Iran-Iraq War." *Middle East Journal* 43, No. 2 (Spring 1989).
———. "What Do We Think We're Doing in the Gulf War." *The Washington Post*, Outlook Section, April 24, 1988, pp. D1, D2.
Sid-Ahmed, Mohamed. "Egypt: The Islamic Issue." *Foreign Policy* 69 (Winter 1987–88).
Silk, Mark. *Spiritual Politics: Religion and America Since World War II*. New York: Simon and Schuster, 1988.
Sivan, Emmanuel. "Islamic Radicalism: Sunni and Shiite." In *Religious Extremism and Politics in the Middle East*, edited by Emmanuel Sivan and Menachem Friedman. Albany: State University of New York Press, 1990.
Smith, Jeffrey. "Bush Advised to Hold Steady on Nation's Foreign Policy." *The Washington Post*, April 9, 1989.
Smith, Michael Joseph. *Realist Thought from Weber to Kissinger*. Baton Rouge: Louisiana University Press, 1986.
Sofer, Sasson. *Begin: An Anatomy of Leadership*. Oxford: Basil Blackwell, 1988.
Spiegel, Steven. "America and Israel—How Bad Is It?" *National Interest* 22 (Winter 1990–91).
———. "Does the United States Have Options in the Middle East?" *Orbis* 24, no. 2 (Summer 1980): 395–412.
———. *The Other Arab-Israeli Conflict: Making America's Middle East Policy, from Truman to Reagan*. Chicago: University of Chicago Press, 1985.
———. "The Philosophy Behind Recent American Policy in the Middle East." *Middle East Review* 13, no. 2 (Winter 1980–81).
———. "U.S. Relations with Israel: The Military Benefits." *Orbis* 30, no. 3 (Fall 1986).
Springborg, Robert. "Egypt: Successes and Uncertainties." *American-Arab Affairs* 33 (Summer 1990).
———. *Family, Power, and Politics in Egypt: Sayed Bey Marei—His Clan, Clients and Cohorts*. Philadelphia: University of Pennsylvania Press, 1982.
———. *Mubarak's Egypt: Fragmentation of the Political Order*. Boulder, Colo.: Westview Press, 1989.
———. "Patrimonialism and Policy-Making in Egypt: Nasser and Sadat and the Tenure Policy for Reclaimed Lands." *Middle East Studies* 15, no. 1 (January 1979).
———. "The President and the Field Marshall: Civil-Military Relations in Egypt Today." *Middle East Report* 17, no. 4 (July–August 1987).
Sprinzak, Ehud. "Fundamentalism, Terrorism and Democracy: The Case of Gush Emunim Underground." Wilson Center, History, Culture and Society, Occasional Paper 4, Smithsonian Institution, Washington, D.C., September 16, 1986.
———. "The Politics of Zionist Fundamentalism in Israel." Paper presented to The American Jewish Committee, New York, October 17, 1985.
Stauffer, Thomas. "Economic Warfare in the Gulf." *American-Arab Affairs* 14 (Fall 1985).
Stein, Janice Gross. "Extended Deterrence in the Middle East: American Strategy Reconsidered." *World Politics* 33, no. 3 (April 1987).
———. "Structures, Strategies, and Tactics of Mediation: Kissinger and Carter in the Middle East." *Negotiation Journal* 1, no. 4 (1985): 331–347.
———. "The Wrong Strategy in the Right Place: The United States in the Gulf." *International Security* 13, no. 3 (Winter 1988/89).

Stein, Kenneth W. "The Arab-Israeli Conflict: Making Progress Toward Peace." *Middle East Insight* 6, no. 5 (Spring 1989).

Stern, Jonathan, and Andrew Petricoff. "Between Two Administrations: An American Israeli Dialogue." In *Strategy and Defense in the Eastern Mediterranean: An American-Israeli Dialogue, Proceedings of a Conference* (Jerusalem, Israel, June 1988), edited by Robert Satloff. Washington, D.C.: Washington Institute for Near East Policy, 1988.

Sterner, Michael. "Navigating the Gulf." *Foreign Policy* 81 (Winter 1990–91).

Susser, Asher. *Double Jeopardy: PLO Strategy Toward Israel and Jordan*, Policy Paper Number 8. Washington, D.C.: Washington Institute for Near East Policy, 1988.

Swirski, Shlomo. "The Oriental Jews in Israel: Why Many Tilted Toward Begin." *Dissent* (Winter 1984).

Syrkin, Marie. "The Kahane Phenomenon." *Middle East Review* 19, no. 1 (Fall 1986).

Talal, Hassan Bin. "Return to Geneva." *Foreign Policy* 57 (Winter 1984–1985).

Tamir, Avrham. "Israel, The Intifada and the Peace Process." In *Proceedings of the Washington Institute Policy Forum, 1988*. Washington D.C.: Wahington Institute for Near East Policy, 1988.

———. *A Soldier in Search of Peace*. New York: Harper and Row, 1988.

Tanter, Raymond. *Who's at the Helm? Lessons of Lebanon*. Boulder, Colo.: Westview Press, 1990.

Taylor, Charles. "The Nature and Scope of Distributive Justice." In *Justice and Equality Here and Now*, edited by Frank S. Lucash. Ithaca, N.Y.: Cornell University Press, 1986.

Theobald, Robin. "Patrimonialism." *World Politics* 34, no. 4 (July 1982).

Tocqueville, Alexis de. *Democracy in America*, edited by J. P. Mayer from a translation by George Lawrence. New York: Harper and Row, 1966.

Tucker, Robert C. *Political Culture and Leadership in Soviet Russia*. New York: W. W. Norton, 1987.

Turner, Bryan S. *Weber and Islam: A Critical Study*. London: Routledge and Kegan Paul, 1974.

Twinam, Joseph Wright. "U.S. Interests in the Arabian Gulf." *American-Arab Affairs* 21 (Summer 1987).

Tyler, Patrick E. "Clerics Ordered to Obey New Iranian Leader." *The Washington Post*, June 10, 1989.

———. "Crisis Seen Looming in Jordan over Politics, PLO, Economy." *The Washington Post*, November 7, 1988.

———. "Iran Elects Rafsanjani President." *The Washington Post*, July 30, 1989, pp. A1, A32.

———. "Iran Has New Revolutionary Goal: Cash." *The Washington Post*, February 4, 1989, p. A16.

———. "Iran Offers, Bush Welcomes Help on Hostages." *The Washington Post*, August 5, 1989, pp. A1, A12.

———. "Iran Retracts Urging Death of Westerners." *The Washington Post*, May 11, 1989, p. A39.

———. "Iranian (Rafsanjani) Says Khamenei Appointment May Not Be Permanent." *The Washington Post*, June 9, 1989, pp. A29, A32.

———. "Iraq Nuclear Program Stirs Debate." *The Washington Post*, June 4, 1989, p. A35.

———. "Iraq Pursues Politics of Pragmatism." *The Washington Post*, May 13, 1989, p. A13.

――――. "Khamenei Succeeds Khomeini." *The Washington Post*, June 5, 1989, pp. A1, A27.

――――. "Khomeini Buried in Chaotic Scene." *The Washington Post*, June 17, 1989,, pp. A1, A15.

――――. "Kin Says Khomeini Had Cancer." *The Washington Post*, June 12, 1989, pp. A1, A24.

――――. "Mubarak Reassigns Key Deputy." *The Washington Post*, April 15, 1989, pp. A29, A30.

――――. "Pragmatists Emerging in Iran." *The Washington Post*, July 11, 1989, pp. A17, A20.

――――. "Rafsanjani Sweeps Out Hard-Liners." *The Washington Post*, August 20, 1989, pp. A1, A24.

――――. "Rafsanjani Takes Oath to Lead Iran." *The Washington Post*, August 18, 1989, pp. A25, A29.

――――. "Rafsanjani Touted as Khomeini's Successor." *The Washington Post*, April 27, 1989.

――――. "Rebuilding Plan to Cost 15 Billion, Tehran Says." *The Washington Post*, July 3, 1989, pp. A1, A27.

――――. "Syria Reported Prepared to Join Peace Discussion." *The Washington Post*, February 28, 1989.

――――. "Thousands Mourn Khomeini." *The Washington Post*, June 6, 1989, pp. A9, A20.

――――. "U.S. to End 'Convoy' Role in the Gulf." *The Washington Post*, September 26, 1988, pp. A1, A12.

Tyler, Patrick E., and Nora Boustany. "Assad: Diplomacy by Obstruction." *The Washington Post*, March 22, 1989, p. A22.

――――. "Solution in Lebanon Eludes Arab Summit." *The Washington Post*, May 27, 1989, pp. A15, A18.

US Congress, House of Representatives. "Crisis in the Persian Gulf: Sanctions, Diplomacy and War." Hearings Before the Committee on Armed Services, December 1990, 101st Cong., 2d sess.

US Congress, House of Representatives. "National Security Implications of United States Operations in the Persian Gulf." Committee on Armed Services, Report of Defense Policy Panel, July 27, 1987, 100th Cong., 1st sess. Washington, D.C.: US Government Printing Office.

US Government. *Report of the President's Special Review Board* (The Tower Report). Washington, D.C.: US Government Printing Office, February 26, 1987.

US Department of State. "U.S. Policy in the Persian Gulf." Special Report Number 166, July 1987.

Vance, Cyrus. *Hard Choices: Critical Years in America's Foreign Policy*. New York: Simon and Schuster, 1983.

Vatikiotis, P. J. *Nasser and His Generation*. New York: St. Martin's Press, 1978.

Vetterli, Richard, and Gary Bryner. *In Search of the Republic: Public Virtue and the Roots of American Government*. Towata, N.J.: Rowman and Littlefield, 1987.

Vuono, Carl E. "Desert Storm and Conventional Forces." *Foreign Affairs* 70, No. 2 (Spring 1991).

Walzer, Michael. *Exodus and Revolution*. New York: Basic Books, 1985.

――――. "What Kind of a Jewish State?" *Tikkun* 4, no. 4 (July/August 1989).

Waterbury, John. *The Egypt of Nasser and Sadat: The Political Economy of Two Regimes*. Princeton, N.J.: Princeton University Press, 1983.

Watt, W. Montgomery. *Muhammad: Prophet and Statesman*. London: Oxford University Press, 1961.

Weber, Max. *The Theory of Social and Economic Organization*. New York: Oxford University Press, 1947.

Weinberger, Caspar W. "Arms Reductions and Deterrence." *Foreign Affairs* 66, no. 4 (Spring 1988).

Wildavsky, Aaron. *The Nursing Father: Moses as a Political Leader*. Tuscaloosa: University of Alabama Press, 1984.

Wills, Garry. *Reagan's America: Innocents at Home*. Garden City, N.Y.: Doubleday and Company, 1987.

Wilson, John F. "The Status of 'Civil Religion' in America." In *The Religion of the Republic*, edited by Elwyn A. Smith. Philadelphia: Fortress Press, 1971.

Woocher, Jonathan. "Civil Religion and the Modern Jewish Challenge." In *Social Foundations of Judaism*, edited by Calvin Goldschneider and Jacob Neusner. Englewood Cliffs, N.J.: Prentice-Hall, 1990.

Wood, Gordon S. *The Creation of the American Republic, 1776–1787*. New York: W. W. Norton, 1969.

Woodward, Bob. *The Commanders*. New York: Simon and Schuster, 1991.

Woodward, Bob, and Walter Pincus. "U.S.-Israeli Accord Said to Authorize North-Nir Operations." *The Washington Post*, December 4, 1988, pp. A1, A16, A17.

Wright, Claudia. "Iraq: New Power in the Middle East." *Foreign Affairs* 58, no. 2 (Winter, 1979–80).

Wright, Robin. "Three New Dimensions of Palestinian Politics." *Middle East Insight* 5, no. 6 (March/April 1988).

Wuthnow, Robert. *The Restructuring of American Religion: Society and Faith Since World War II*. Princeton, N.J.: Princeton University Press, 1988.

Yaari, Ehud. *Peace By Piece: A Decade of Egyptian Policy Toward Israel*, Policy Paper Number 7. Washington, D.C.: Washington Institute for Near East Policy, 1987.

Yack, Bernard. *The Longing for Total Revolution: Philosophic Sources of Social Discontent from Rousseau to Marx and Nietzsche*. Princeton, N.J.: Princeton University Press, 1986.

Yanai, Nathan. *Party Leadership in Israel: Maintenance and Change*. Ramat Gan, Israel: Turtledove Publishing, 1981.

Yaniv, Avner. "Are Syria and Israel on the Verge of Peace?" *The Washington Post*, Outlook Section, January 11, 1987, p. C7.

———. "Israel Comes of Age." *Current History* 88, no. 535 (February 1989).

———. "A Syrian-Israeli Detente?" *Middle East Insight* 5, no. 5 (January–February 1988).

Yishai, Yael. "Israeli Annexation of East Jerusalem and Golan Heights: Factors and Processes." *Middle Eastern Studies* 21 (1985).

———. "Dissent in Israel: Opinions on the Lebanon War." *Middle East Review* 16, no. 2 (Winter 1983/1984).

———. *Land or Peace: Whither Israel?* Stanford, Calif.: Hoover Institution Press, 1987.

Zonis, Marvin, and Daniel Brumberg. *Khomeini, The Islamic Republic of Iran and the Arab World*. Harvard Middle East Papers, Modern Series, Number 5. Cambridge, Mass.: Center for Middle Eastern Studies, Harvard University, 1987.

———. "Shi'ism as Interpreted by Khomeini: An Ideology of Revolutionary Violence." In *Shi'ism, Resistance, and Revolution*, edited by Martin Kramer. Boulder, Colo.: Westview Press, 1987.

Index

Adams, John, 9
Al-e-Ahamad, 36
Amal, 64–65, 117–118, 120
Aoun, Michel, 65, 118
Arab Cooperation Council, 82
Arab League, 80, 97, 114
Arafat, Yassir, 44–45, 47, 49–50, 68–70, 85–86, 91–92; mentioned, 6, 98. *See also* Palestine Liberation Organization (PLO)
Assad, Hafiz, 61–62, 70, 101–103, 119–120; mentioned, 3, 97
Aswan formula, 5, 56

Baker, James, 90–93, 98
Begin, Menachem, 41, 43, 54, 58, 67; mentioned, 5, 30, 93. *See also* Camp David Accords
Berri, Nabih, 64–65, 117–118, 120
Brzezinski, Zbigniew, 55
Bush, George, 31–32, 89, 112, 117, 119, 121; Arab-Israeli peace process and, 90–93; Egypt, Israel, and, 110–111; Gulf region and, 82–87, 107–110. *See also* Negotiation strategies

Camp David Accords, 55–57; mentioned, 43, 60, 65–67, 90, 96, 102. *See also* Carter, Jimmy
Carter, Jimmy, 4–5, 71; Camp David and, 53–60; pragmatism and, 20–23; on US peace efforts, 28–30. *See also* Negotiation strategies
Civil religion: defined, 8–9, 11, 128 n. 47; role of, in Middle East policy, 71–73
Confessionalism, 63, 117

Dayan, Moshe, 29, 54
Democracy and leadership in the Middle East, 12–15, 130 n. 80
ad-Din, Jamal, 36

Egypt: economic integration of into West Bank–Gaza peace plans, 114–117; George Bush, Israel, and, 110–111; relations of, with Israel, 94–97; ties of, with United States, 98. *See also* Camp David Accords; Carter, Jimmy
Equality. *See* US creed
Erfan, 36
European Community, 103
Evangelicalism. *See* Fundamentalism

Faqih. See Velayat-e faqih
Fatah, 47, 61
Fez plan, 68
Franklin, Benjamin, 9–10
Fundamentalism: civil religion and, 71–73; in Egypt, 98; in Iran, 35–39; in Israel, 39–46; Middle Eastern and US policy, 50–51; role of in US Middle East policy, 120–122; in the United States, 32–34; in West Bank and Gaza, 46–50. *See also* Iran; West Bank and Gaza

Gemayel, Amin, 61–62, 65; mentioned, 64
Gemayel, Bashir (brother of Amin), 60–61
Gorbachev, Mikhail, 76, 102, 106–107, 119, 123; mentioned, 82–83
Gulf Cooperation Council (GCC), 76,

About the Book
and the Author

The recent Gulf War may be over, but the issues that made the Middle East so volatile a region still remain. Melvin Friedlander addresses many of these crucial issues by looking at how US administrations from Nixon to Bush have tried with little success to attain the goal of peace in the Middle East, how values have operated in the search for solutions, and how failed US policies have depended too much on the conventional wisdom of power politics.

Any viable peace initiative, asserts Friedlander, must be informed by a "new wisdom," a populist approach now emerging in the region, that makes a concern for human rights foremost. It is in this way that the US value system, with its roots in the concepts of equality and liberty, can be the basis of effective US efforts toward negotiating peace in the Middle East.

MELVIN A. FRIEDLANDER is associate professor of government and politics in the Department of Public Affairs at George Mason University. He is author of *Sadat and Begin: The Politics of Peacemaking*.